The
Cumberland

BOOKS IN THE
RIVERS OF AMERICA SERIES

RIVERS OF AMERICA *Edited by Carl Carmer*

As planned and started by Constance Lindsay Skinner

Associate Editor Jean Crawford

The Cumberland

BY JAMES McCAGUE

Illustrated by Charles Walker

HOLT, RINEHART AND WINSTON

New York   Chicago   San Francisco

Library of Congress Cataloging in Publication Data
McCague, James.
    The Cumberland.
    (Rivers of America)
    Bibliography: p.
    1. Cumberland Valley, Ky. & Tenn.—History.
2. Cumberland River. I. Title. II. Series.
F442.2.M3   917.68′5′03   72-91579
ISBN 0-03-085764-3

First Edition
Designer: Ernst Reichl
Printed in the United States of America

Contents

Introduction

Cumberland Country

M. Lou and I had driven up from Florida by way of the Virginia Tidewater, making a long and roundabout route of it to the Cumberland River. But it seemed logical to begin where the first men to see the Cumberland probably began, and about the best today's explorer can do along that line would be the restored colonial capital of Old Williamsburg. It is not possible to walk the streets there without establishing some sort of rapport with history, a virtual necessity for anyone who proposes to write of Cumberland country with any understanding.

It was a good beginning. The rapport stayed with us as we headed westward out of Williamsburg and the miles rolled away behind.

We passed through Charlottesville. Near there, on an estate named Castle Hill, once lived Dr. Thomas Walker: distinguished graduate of William and Mary College, physician, gentleman planter, patron of the sciences, surveyor, speculator in western lands, explorer of the same, and for some years legal guardian of young Thomas Jefferson. It was his footsteps, among others, that we followed through the Blue Ridge Mountains into the great valley of Virginia. And there, having turned left onto Interstate 81, we embarked down the approximate modern version of the Great War Path, that "plain Indian road" of the early chroniclers, over

which uncounted generations of red warriors raided and hunted
and occasionally met in peaceable trading in ages far beyond the
memory of the white man in America.

Nothing much of the Great War Path survives today. Nor does
any interstate highway differ much from any other, on the face of
it. More than most, though, I-81 gives an impression of traversing
not space alone but time as well. Even hurtling down its concrete
speedway on the surge of multiple horsepower, cradled in vinyl
and foam rubber, seat-belted, air-conditioned, thoroughly encap-
suled in the Machine Age, one becomes aware of a deep sense of
the past along with the valley's present unspoiled beauty. It is not
altogether such tangible memorials as the old homes of Robert E.
Lee and Stonewall Jackson. There is more to it even than the calling card of a spry young surveyor by the name of G. Washington,
scratched into the rock below the awesome arch of the Natural
Bridge in 1750. There are intangibles that run much deeper, for this
great valley offered one of the earliest ways west to the forebears of
a people whose history has been, in large measure, a tale of westward farings.

The valley is a kind of natural funnel: a broad trough slanting
southwestward between the Blue Ridge Mountains on the east and
the distant, mist-hazed ridges of the Alleghenies to the west. Thus,
subtly but inexorably, the traveler is hemmed in. The land dictates
the way that he must go. It is nearly as true today as it was when
painted Iroquois braves traveled down the Great War Path after
scalps and plunder. Not till he has gone far down toward the Tennessee line is one seeking the Cumberland River permitted to turn
westward. Somewhere in the vicinity, a branch of the Great War
Path did likewise. The Indians, and before them the bison and elk
and deer that first laid out these trails, knew what they were about.
So, thanks to modern road maps, do we. But the long-dead settlers
who moved by slow stages down the valley, and the half-forgotten
first probers into the lands back of beyond were groping in a strange
and often hostile wilderness. One's admiration for them grows with
every mile.

U.S. 58 is a poor highway only by comparison with the Interstate's perfection. It is paved; it is two-lane; there is nothing really
wrong with it. But U.S. 58 is a mountain road. It twists and turns in
impossible convolutions, climbs steeply, abruptly dips at peculiar
angles. No doubt much of this appears worse than it actually is to

folk, like ourselves, accustomed to driving the flat lands of Florida. Nevertheless, the country is a jumble of mountain ranges. One after another, fold on fold—the Clinch Mountains, the Powells, the first dim ramparts of the Cumberlands—they march off to the horizon. The land is cut into rugged, steep-sided valleys in which all the streams—the Clinch River, the north fork of the Holston, the Powell River, Copper Creek—flow swiftly down the universal slant southwestward.

M. Lou and I went through on a day in late September. What summertime tourists there might have been had gone their ways, and local traffic was so sparse it needed hardly any effort of the imagination to conjure up an illusion of virgin territory unchanged since America's earliest youth.

We were romancing, of course, for it is not all that remote. There is U.S. 58 itself to keep one's perspective based firmly in the twentieth century. And we skirted one valley where a long Clinchfield Railroad coal train labored upgrade with three big diesel locomotives on the head end and two more coupled into the middle, wheel flanges squealing as they clawed through a tight curve. Somehow the black monsters of a bygone age in railroading, steam-wreathed, blasting their exhausts sky-high, would have seemed more appropriate to the setting. But even they would have smacked of anachronism, as the diesels did; as we did, come to that. It was no great way farther on that we noticed smoke staining the sky ahead, and presently passed by its source and found a funeral pyre of junked automobiles burning fiercely. So this deep southwestern corner of old Virginia is not totally deprived of civilization's blessings after all.

Yet it still is backwoods country. An aura of the past hangs over it. Densely wooded mountain slopes crowd in on both sides of the road. There is never a sign of farmhouse or plowed field, and only an occasional clearing of ragged pasture glimpsed through the trees. Gas stations are so few and far between that the state of our tank became a matter of some concern. And when we did stop at a rundown country store with a single pump in front, the aged, broad-gallused, sleeve-gartered proprietor warned us forthrightly, in advance, that he wanted nothing to do with any credit cards. It turned out he felt no call to provide restroom facilities for the weary tourist, either. . . .

Well along in the afternoon we paused briefly at a roadside

marker informing us that we were not far from the spot where
Daniel Boone's son James and four companions were killed by
Indians in the fall of 1773. We knew about that. Young Boone was
only fifteen, but already playing a man's part as growing boys did
in those frontier days. Survivors told later how the party heard
wolves howling about their camp in the night, and how badly
scared were two brothers from the eastern settlements, arrant
greenhorns both. But other young fellows in the party, more seasoned, had heard wolves howl before and never suspected that
these might actually be signals by red warriors reconnoitering the
camp. The nervous brothers, they jeered, would hear worse noises
—bull buffalo roaring from the treetops, no less—once they reached
Kaintucke. That was where they were all bound, Kaintucke. The
brothers never learned the truth about tree-climbing buffalo, but in
a sense they were lucky; at least they went down in the first rush
when the attack came. A black slave who escaped the slaughter told
of lying out in the brush and listening while young Boone and another lad took a long time dying under torture. One ponders the
tale, in that place, and the mood it engenders and realizes suddenly, all over again, how sinister was the unknown those early
westward-farers faced. Again one feels a sense of awe at the un-
quenchable force, whether foolhardiness or courage, that drove
them on. And again, too, comes a shivery illusion that this country
is very little altered. . . .

Somewhat chastened by such thoughts, we came in the waning
hours of the day to Cumberland Gap.

Two hundred and some-odd years ago, Dr. Thomas Walker
noted in his journal that "this Gap may be seen at a considerable
distance." It still may be: a broad notch cut deep into the flank
of Cumberland Mountain, unmistakably visible even to the most
land-ignorant eye. Dr. Walker, accepted by most historians as
Cumberland Gap's discoverer—though other white men almost
certainly were there before him—also remarked on the "small en-
trance to a large Cave" in the north wall of the pass. It is really a
whole series of caves known today as Cudjo's Caverns and touted
as a tourist attraction by large and garish billboards as one approaches. A local tradition claims early settlers in the vicinity used
to hold dances in the largest cavern: an intriguing notion which
may even be true, for pioneer life in the wilderness was not always
as grim as hostile Indians and other varied hardships might have

made it. In 1797, long after Dr. Walker's exploration, another traveler through the Gap was vastly impressed with the jolly landlady of the inn he found there:

> We took our leave of Mrs Davis, who . . . may be Justly call Capn Molly of Cumberland Mountain, for she Fully Commands this passage to the New World. She soon took the freedom to tell me she was a Come by chance, her mother she knew little of and her Father less, as to herself she said pleasure was the onely thing she had in View; and that She had her Ideas of life and its injoyments. . . .

These days, Cap'n Molly's hostel has been succeeded by a Holiday Inn.

We had our first sight of the Cumberland River next morning, from high on Pinnacle Overlook in Cumberland Gap National Park. It was a promising introduction: the river a scimitar curve of shining silver away northward and far below, half-hidden in the early mist draping the shaggy shoulders of the mountains all about. The Cumberland begins—she cannot truly be said to rise—only some twenty miles to the north and east of the Gap, at Harlan, Kentucky. She is born of the union of three tributaries: Poor Fork, Clover Fork, and Martins Fork. All three are considerable streams in their own right, rising far back on the western slopes of the Cumberland Mountain watershed and taking their varied, devious ways to the meeting place. Thus the Cumberland springs to life full-blown, as it were, and boasts a quite respectable size from the outset. Dr. Walker described it as "60 or 70 yards wide" where he first saw it, and considering that he was there in the early spring, with the river running bank-full and perhaps a bit more, his estimate would not be too great an exaggeration today.

M. Lou and I had planned to shun the main highways as soon as we hit the river and instead keep to those back roads and byways that would enable us to follow its course most closely. And so we did. That is to say, we tried, though it shortly became apparent that no back road, nor any byway, could possibly match this river's meanderings. Surely no other in all Christendom is as crooked as the Cumberland. Her general course is westward, with occasional digressions to north or south in these upper reaches. But one finds few very lengthy stretches in which the river does not appear on the verge of wandering off into some new quadrant of the compass altogether. She never does, quite. But she twists, squirms, doubles back upon herself, sidles aimlessly in long sprawling loops, and generally seems in no great hurry to get anywhere.

We were not the first to notice that, either. The matter-of-fact entries in Dr. Walker's journal tell their own story, betraying a certain slight vexation only between the lines, thus: "After riding 5 miles from our Camp we left the River, it being very crooked. In riding three miles we came on it again. . . . We left the River but in four miles . . . came on it again and the Mouth of Licking Creek, which we went up and down another. . . ."

The creeks are still there. Some are good-sized streams and some are no more than gullies cut by the runoff of heavy rains. So numerous are they, however, and so rough and stony their banks, it is easy to see how irksome they must have been to horsemen trying to make their way without benefit of roads or bridges. Even today all the upper Cumberland is subject to sudden destructive spates of high water called *tides* in river parlance. Local folk long ago grew wise to the treachery of tides and so shun the bottomlands along creek or river, good though it may be, to build their homes and till their fields on the higher slopes.

First of the notable tributaries coming in to swell the mainstream is Yellow Creek, which flows down off the northward slope of Cumberland Gap. Next, also from the south, comes Clear Fork. The river has taken a northerly tack at this point, in order to break through the minor barrier of the Pine Mountains. Still holding more or less to the same course, she receives Straight Creek from the north, then Greasy Creek from the south, Stinking Creek from the north, and Brush Creek from the south again. Till now this southeastern corner of Kentucky has all been mountain country. But as we approach the town of Barbourville the land begins to flatten out somewhat. The Cumberland herself gives an early clue, as she did in the past also, which Dr. Walker was quick to notice: "The bottom of the river is sandy, ye banks very high and the current very slow. . . ."

It began to feel a trifle eerie, this unerring agreement between our observations and those so carefully set down by a man gone to his reward two centuries and more ago.

About here, though, the doctor reached his turning-back place. "We kept on westerly 18 miles," he wrote, "got clear of the Mountains and found the Land poor . . . Laurel & Ivy in and near the

Branches. Our horses suffered very much . . . for want of food."
That has not changed a great deal, either. This is the western
fringe of Appalachia: hardscrabble country that affords no easy
living, and looks it. The occasional small towns have that inde-
finable atmosphere of gray discouragement that seems always to
hover about depressed areas. The houses run heavily to frame bun-
galows with weathered paint, or to a type of excessively stodgy
cement-block construction obsolete since the 1920s, or to that newer
but still more hideous composition siding designed in shoddy imi-
tation of honest brick. Yet unprepossessing as all this is, to the river
aficionado it has its brighter side. Man, the great despoiler, has
wrought far less mischief here on the upper Cumberland than he
would have, in his multitudes, had this been a richer, more inviting
land.

The point takes on added emphasis when the river, after a brief
southerly jog just below Barbourville, turns right about and heads
northward through the Daniel Boone National Forest. It is singularly fitting that this immense tract of unspoiled native woodland
should be preserved as a monument to the old trailblazer. If he
knows, wherever he hunts now, Boone must be pleased; he was a
man soured on civilization's creeping blight. It seems quite as
fitting, too, that the Cumberland's last miles as a free river untrammeled by the works of man should wind through so lovely
a setting.

The traveler comes on Cumberland Falls almost as a surprise.
M. Lou and I did, anyway, in spite of the various appurtenances of
a well-kept state park, including signs. There is a rambling lodge
with log cabins for vacationing families, a campground that provides facilities for trailers as well as tents, and a couple of small
commercial attractions to snare the tourist's dollar—but not nearly
so blatantly advertised, praise Heaven, as is the common go-getting
custom. Everything, in fact, is somehow tucked away among the
trees so unobtrusively there is scarcely a false note anywhere. In
time we arrived at a modest sign advising us that we had reached
the Falls and pointing the way to a parking lot. We pulled in,
alighted, walked a few steps past the inevitable rustic souvenir
shop, and all at once emerged onto a broad shelf of rock with the
river there at our feet. Her recent spell of sluggishness was past.
The current rippled swiftly over a shallow, rocky bed. The pace
quickened as it glided smoothly to the lip of the falls and plunged

sixty-eight feet straight down in a cascade of spray and a muted river-beast roar.

The day was one of low-hanging clouds and a steady drizzle of rain: no kind of day at all for sightseeing. Yet maybe that was our good fortune. At least, it was no garden-variety tourist's eye view we got. Standing there on wet rock with dripping trees massed darkly against the sky all round, nothing fencing off the watery abyss below but a single thin steel cable strung in lieu of a railing, one feels . . . well, the awe one feels is not because these falls are so magnificently huge, precisely. The celebrated falls of Niagara are both higher and incomparably wider. But Niagara is a *citified* spectacle. It is surrounded in its undeniable grandeur by the humdrum works of man. Like some captive behemoth in a zoo, it seems there solely to be gawked at: a marvelous work of nature, of course, but . . . No "but"s, though, about these Falls of the Cumberland; nothing captive about this spectacle. So far as we know, daredevils have not made a practice of going over Cumberland Falls in a barrel or walking across on a slack wire. There are no legends to tell how a beauteous Indian princess threw herself into the cataract for unrequited love, or any other reason. "Remote" is the word for this place. Press agentry has not found it yet. Compulsively, almost, one is moved to wonder who did chance upon it first. We do not know. Some unsung Long Hunter or French *coureur de bois*, most likely . . .

Below the Falls the river has carved out a deep gorge with precipitous rock walls; between them the current swirls and tosses like an angry riptide. Stand looking downstream through the rain, as we did, and one sees a vista stark and wild and gloomy. The river might have looked so at the dawn of creation itself. Incredible: the thought that in another twenty miles or so this Cumberland meets her match and surrenders meekly to the U.S. Army Corps of Engineers.

That is what happens, all the same. Those twenty-odd miles are still rough ones, but it makes little difference anymore. It did once, though.

A short way downstream from the Falls the river makes an abrupt hairpin turn which brings her back into her general westward course. Still pent within the walls of her narrow gorge, she presently is joined by the Rockcastle River from the north. Almost at once, strengthened and spurred on by the new ally, she charges headlong into the turbulent eight-mile gauntlet of rocks and bars known as Smith's Shoals. There was a time when none but the best and gutsiest of rivermen were good enough to take a pirogue or flatboat through here. The breed was numerous enough, though, so that plenty tried. From the mid-1850s nearly to the turn of the century, in fact, a small but regular traffic went on in coal barged down to Nashville from mines in the vicinity. It was a primitive sort of commerce, one surmises. The wooden barges, differing very little from the more ancient flatboats, were usually small, the biggest of them carrying no more than a thousand bushels or so of coal, and a crew of three or four. As in all riverwork, it was necessary to wait for nature's cooperation: in this case a tide high enough to float the clumsy craft through the Shoals' worst stretches. Then it took brawn, alertness, and skillful handling of poles, oars, and steering sweep. Still, every season had its quota of those who failed to make it. Down the years Smith's Shoals collected a sizable toll in shattered boats, lost cargoes, and now and then a drowned riverman as well. But all that is long past now. There are easier ways to make a living.

The next morning the rain had stopped and we drove on to Burnside, just beyond the western edge of Daniel Boone's big woods. The name of the town derives from its occupation by Union troops under General Ambrose Burnside during the War Between the States. Up till then it was called Point Isabel, and one cannot help wondering who—besides the general's own self, perhaps—ever thought the change would be an improvement. But never mind. In its day, by whatever name, this town was a flourishing river port, the head of steamboat navigation because of the impassable Shoals. Today part of the area is a Kentucky state park; the Wolf Creek Dam has turned the river for some thirty miles downstream into sprawling, many-inleted Lake Cumberland; and Burnside takes a new lease on life, in season, as an outdoor recreation center.

We roamed for a while over the hills of General Burnside Island, located between the town on its jutting point of land and the mouth of the Big South Fork of the Cumberland, which zigzags up from below the Tennessee line and empties into the mainstream here. Such a meeting of the waters might be expected to result in some notable swirling, eddying, or similar disturbance. Not so, however. Look where we would, we saw not a ripple anywhere, so complete is the Cumberland's subjugation even these few miles below Smith's Shoals. The water in all directions lay as still and placid as green glass, dotted to the west with a moored armada of houseboats, cabin cruisers, outboards, inboards, big boats, small boats, sailboats, and other pleasure craft—so many they were past counting.

Well, no wonder. This is where the modern river begins. The dam at Wolf Creek is but the first of several federal works by which the Cumberland has been harnessed and broken to the uses of civil progress.

We settled one thing to our own satisfaction while pausing here between old river and new. It had puzzled us that so many writers of the past wrote so lyrically of "the clear green Cumberland," "the winding green ribbon of the Cumberland," and so on. It puzzled us because green is not usually a river's natural hue, we thought. Outside of some songwriter's cliché, of course. But no—the Cumberland *is* green! We scrambled down a steep pathway to the river's edge and took a closer look, and green she is. The green is somewhat tinged with muddy brown, to be sure. The river is no doubt more turgid than she used to be. Yet in the face of so many cherished myths disproved, we felt in some vague way gladdened.

Our route out of Burnside took us to the south of Lake Cumberland. Sometimes we were in sight of it. More often we were not, for the land still lies in rolling hills and hollows and still is studded with patches of timber. It still is sparse, rough-looking country, too, broken frequently by rocky outcrops. Though farms grew more numerous as we proceeded, houses and fields alike gave an impression of struggling with hostile nature and coming out with little better than a standoff. But we were startled to see an occasional billboard advertising choice lakefront properties for sale. The people are coming. Real estate developers have discovered the Cumberland—and after them, the deluge. . . .

Eventually the lake narrows to become a river again, and the river picks her way down a long leisurely slant southwestward into Tennessee. Soon after crossing the line she is met by the Obey River which winds in from the east and south. The Obey is, or once was, the only tributary of the upper Cumberland deemed navigable by steamboats. Just barely though, it appears, for many are the tales told of daring packet captains who would go churning in on a high tide some fourteen miles to Byrdstown Landing, hustle the available cargo aboard, and ride the tide back out before it could subside and leave them high and dry. In those days all this upper Cumberland country was prime hardwood timberland and bred a race of loggers and raftsmen who . . . but more about them in due course. Nowadays the lower Obey River is mostly Dale Hollow Lake, another extensive reservoir created by another dam. This one, though, afflicts the Obey alone. The Cumberland continues on her way relatively unmolested and after a few more miles curves gently westward into the beginning of her Big Bend through central Tennessee. Compared with her back-and-forth meanderings now, the river's earlier crookedness was nothing. This is the great Middle Basin of the Cumberland: in effect, a broad alluvial plain lying between the rugged hills of the Highland Rim to north, south, and southwest. The country still is rolling rather than flat, however, the riverbanks alternating between high wooded bluffs and stretches of deep, rich bottomland. The current flows with an easy-going serenity, save where it quickens through the narrow channel around an occasional small island or breaks, chattering, in a riffle over some hidden gravel bar.

Even to our inexpert eyes, and in the fall of the year to boot, the land seemed to grow steadily more fertile as we drove west. Cornstalks stood tall and sere in the fields beside the highway. The tobacco-drying barns were larger and more frequent, each with the leaves of rich brown burley hanging in clusters, row on row. Now, too, the towns came a little more frequently. We passed Gainesboro, at the Cumberland's junction with Roaring River from the south. Around the turn of the century Gainesboro was famous up and down the river for the quality of the table set by its one and only hotel and presided over with genial tyranny by Aunt Polly Williams, surely a legend in her own time if ever a lady was. When Aunt Polly rang the dinner bell, so folk said, it was like a royal command. All business in town came to a stop, and woe unto the diner, prominent man or not, who reached his place at table late.

We passed Granville. Next came Carthage, north of the river and a short way downstream from the mouth of the broad but shallow Caney Fork, another large southern tributary. We passed Hartsville, Lebanon, Gallatin. . . . They are all small towns. Somehow or other, this country keeps its small-town feel even as one approaches Nashville. We crossed Stone's River, yet another in the Cumberland's succession of tributaries from the south. And here, in the middle of more than six hundred acres of lush bluegrass, stands Andrew Jackson's Hermitage, a gracious antebellum mansion awash in historic memorabilia and stately as a jewel in a royal crown.

Andrew Jackson might have a little trouble recognizing the river he knew, though. Just above Nashville another dam conceived and erected by the U.S. Army Corps of Engineers, in their infinite wisdom, has transformed this section of the Cumberland into a long serpentine lake, christened Old Hickory in his honor. Dams have become frequent subjects of controversy in these times of awakening concern over man's proper relationship with the environment in which he lives. That is as it should be; sometimes one suspects the engineering mind of a near-obsession with damming for its own sake. Yet the matter is not often so simple as to be resolved by a thoughtless yea or nay. A river in its natural state is a lovely thing, and the Cumberland more so than most. Dams, though, are not without their legitimate reasons for being, either. This Cumberland, for example, never was quite the rambunctious bad actor her big sister to the south, the Tennessee, used to be before she was tamed by TVA. Still, the little sister had her tantrums too. Nashville was only one of the many river towns once plagued, but no longer, by all-too-frequent floods. Besides which, modern urban areas have vast appetites for hydroelectric power. So times change. One feels nostalgia for the old days on a lovely river that never again will be as she once was. But then, what will?

Whole books could be written about Nashville, and have been. Nashville is not only the oldest community on the river—though much too spry to look it—but the largest by far in all the Cumberland Basin. Nashville bears the proud nickname "Athens of the South": an accolade earned in part by her many and distinguished institutions of higher learning and in part by the prevailing Grecian-styled architecture of her public buildings—though nowadays that latter has all but yielded to the functional glass and steel and concrete of a more modern style. Nashville is the site of the Grand Ol' Opry House, the country music capital of the United States. Which seems appropriate, considering the city's location on this river whose headwaters spring from country that has nurtured mountain balladeers since 'way back when. But, plainly, Nashville also thrives on more prosaic industry. From the bluffs on which the city stands one can look down and count the big steel barges moored along the riverfront, practical proof that the diesel towboat has taken over where the old twin-stacked river steamboat left off. Transportation on the Cumberland is still very much alive and kicking. Some of those barges may have brought bulk cargo from points as distant as Houston, New Orleans, Pittsburgh, St. Louis, or anywhere in between—or for that matter, possibly beyond. And just about here the thought occurs, a little wryly, that the river's fabled greenness is no longer open to speculation. Her color now is the murky, oily gray common to all rivers that flow through big cities.

Once out of the Athens of the South, the Cumberland undergoes some other notable changes. For one, she abandons most of the sinuous twistings that marked her upper and middle courses. The lower river at once begins a long slow turn, first to the northwest but bearing steadily more northerly. Barring a few minor digressions, that is the direction she will hold till she reaches the Ohio.

Into this first stretch below Nashville comes the last of her southern tributaries. It is the Harpeth River, and right downstream from their junction a large island used to funnel the combined currents into a narrow channel rendered exceedingly treacherous by Harpeth Shoals. At its worst—and that was a condition much more frequent than its best—the five-mile passage was so ugly a piece of business that old-timers claimed every foot stood for a heartfelt blasphemy uttered by some sorely tried steamboat pilot. Perhaps it was no great exaggeration, for many a fine packet tore her bottom out there or burst a boiler trying to buck through. But neither shoals nor island survive today, even as objects of nostalgia. For a good many years now a series of locks and dams has assured towboat men of a safe nine feet of water, from the Ohio River all the way to the present head of navigation at Carthage.

In fact, the lower Cumberland is very much man-made. A little way downstream she is joined by the Red River from north and east, and then embarks on one final westward slant before turning across the state line for a Kentucky homecoming. As she does so she begins to widen out into the long placid reach of Lake Barkley, a backwater of some thirty miles impounded behind the last in the system of dams by which this Cumberland has been converted relentlessly from old river to new. Nowhere in all her rambling length, however, has she ever quite become a *modern* river, nor does she here.

She might have, once. Who first discovered this whole region along the western Highland Rim to be rich in iron ore, we do not know, but before the end of the eighteenth century there were men at Cumberland Furnace smelting iron in crude stone blast furnaces fueled with charcoal. They kept at it, and the business grew. When Andrew Jackson whipped the British at New Orleans in 1815, his stout Tennessee artillerymen fired cannonballs manufactured by one Montgomery Bell, a Cumberland Furnace ironmaster, and shipped by flatboat down the Cumberland, the Ohio, and the Mississippi. For a half-century more the mines, blast furnaces, and rolling mills proliferated all along the lower river, till the area threatened to become a close competitor with Pittsburgh in the production of high-grade iron. Then came the War Between the States, and ruination. Mills and foundries might have been rebuilt when the shooting stopped, but when the mines began to play out, too, it was all over. The entrepreneurs either retired or moved south to the Alabama diggings around Birmingham, and the lower Cumberland's first and only bid for industrial importance went glimmering.

These days, spared the afflictions of smoke, smog, slag heaps, and similar by-products of the good life, the river makes her serene way through country given over largely to farmland, forest preserves, wildlife sanctuaries, and the Civil War monument of Fort Donelson National Park. There are also a few historic memories of somewhat less august character.

The small town of Adams, several miles up the Red River, was once the locale of a famous haunting at the home of a respected and inoffensive citizen named John Bell. A female poltergeist known far and wide as The Bell Witch carried on so outrageously there—snatching people's hats off, cackling eerily in the night, singing obscene barroom ballads, and so on—that no less a personage than General Andrew Jackson journeyed down from the Hermitage to see for himself what all the talk was about. Local folklore insists so, anyway, though it seems not unlikely that a good bit of the Jackson fame may have rubbed off on an otherwise garden-variety spook. The year was 1817, the general a national hero with the laurels won at New Orleans still green.

With uncharacteristic prudence, or possibly in a spirit of scientific investigation, Jackson took along a neighborhood character of some reputed skill as an exorciser of ghosts. He, in turn, took along

a pistol loaded with a silver bullet and other paraphernalia supposed to be of use in dealing with the supernatural. All to no avail.
The witch treated Andrew Jackson with due respect, so the story
goes, but for two days and two nights she taunted and harassed
the silver-bullet fellow unmercifully, yet never showed herself.
Finally Jackson admitted he had had enough. He went home to the
Hermitage and, it is said, never again spoke of the experience. The
witch went right on with her wicked ways. She broke up the wedding of John Bell's daughter, was eventually the death of Bell
himself—poisoned him, the neighbors always thought—and even
disrupted the funeral service with her bawdy comments about the
deceased. Her grudge must have been a powerful one, for she
continued to haunt the house all the years that Bell's heirs lived
there.

Old Hickory was not the only man who never fathomed who or
what she was. No one else ever did either.

Much more down-to-earth was the brief fame of Golden Pond,
Kentucky. This tiny community tucked into the backwoods between the Cumberland and Tennessee rivers enjoyed a unique advantage of location and worked it to the fullest throughout the
hectic 1920s, when the Volstead Act was the law of the land. Those
were thirsty times, and the corn liquor turned out by Kentucky
moonshiners was in demand as never before or since. The golden
corn of Golden Pond may have been no better for corn squeezings
than that grown elsewhere in the state; old-timers still can debate
that, and perhaps do. But the area around Golden Pond was mostly
dense forest in which stills could readily be hidden from prying
revenue men. And with two fine rivers at its front and back doors,
in a manner of speaking, Golden Pond had superb water transportation with excellent connections all the way to the best market in
the world: the Chicago of Al Capone, Dion O'Bannion, and others
who ruled a whole commercial empire built on bootleg hooch.

It didn't last long: thirteen years was all. But they were years
of high old adventure on the river. Then legal liquor came back
and the Golden Age of Golden Pond was over. Today it is all but
forgotten, which is probably just as well.

As for the Cumberland . . .

Long before the lower river became Lake Barkley and the lower
Tennessee was changed to Kentucky Lake, the two streams par-
alleled one another so closely that in places they seemed on the

point of meeting, though they never did. U.S. Army engineers have now remedied this oversight by the Almighty. In erecting Barkley Dam they have created not only the lake of the same name, but a canal that connects its northern end with Kentucky Lake. The practical result is that traffic on the Tennessee and the Cumberland can be interchanged without the former necessity of a long down-stream-upstream haul by way of the Ohio River. Presumably, it is a development entailing worthwhile dollars-and-cents benefits to shippers. But the Cumberland has only about thirty miles left to her. It is too few in which to recover from this ultimate piece of meddling.

Reduced by the diversion of a goodly share of her waters to the Tennessee, she describes a last long loop westward, southward, and then westward again and, cutting through the high bluffs of the Ohio, loses herself in that river's mighty sweep to the Mississippi. At the junction stands Smithland, once a bustling river town but now sun-bleached and sleepy, the sole observer of the end of a journey that began some 687 miles to the east. In the course of it the Cumberland and her maze of tributaries have drained a land basin approximating 17,750 square miles in area. As America's historic rivers go, one would call that probably somewhere in the medium range. But the Cumberland, like all rivers, flows through time as well as space. And her time-journey has been incalculably longer, and frequently more devious, than any tracing on a map can show.

Some of it we know. A great deal of it is no more than fascinating speculation.

The CUMBERLAND

Louisville

IND.

WABASH R.

OHIO R.

ILL.

N

OHIO R.

K E N T

Smithland

BARKLEY CANAL

L. BARKLEY

LITTLE R.

RED R.

Martinsburg

Golden Pond

Celina

Ft. Henry

Ft. Donelson

Adams

OLD HICKORY L.

Gainesboro

Hartsville

Granville

KENTUCKY L.

CUMBERLAND R.

Gallatin

Palmyra

Cumberland R. Ashville

Carthage

Cumberland Furnace

HARPETH R.

Lebanon

The Hermitage

Nashville (French Lick)

STONES R.

Donelson

DUCK R.

Franklin

Spring Hill

T   E   N   N   E

TENNESSEE R.

NATCHEZ TRACE (CHICKASAW ROAD)

Pulaski

i
The
Wilderness

1

After Adam

THE first inhabitant looms out of time past as vaguely as a figure only half-glimpsed through the blur of a Cumberland River fog. So vaguely, indeed, that it is tempting to see him as the conventional burly, beetle-browed caveman: a sort of New World Neanderthal. Probably, though, he more nearly resembled the American Indian of historic times, whose ancestor in some sort he was. No doubt he clothed himself and his family in the skins of animals, for the climate in those years at the tag end of the last Ice Age was likely to have been considerably chillier than today's. And he would know how to come by animal skins, for he was a hunter. The most tangible thing of his that we have, in fact, is the hunting spear he carried. It was a good one. Its flint head was slender, skillfully chipped to keenness, and grooved up the middle for lashing into the split end of a wooden shaft. A few such spearheads have been found, mostly along the Highland Rim west and north of Nashville. The best scientific estimates make them some eight to ten thousand years old.

Thus we surmise man first came to Cumberland country about that long ago.

By that point in prehistory, the geography of the region had developed to substantially its present form. Aeons earlier the warm, shallow seas that once covered all the area had receded for the last of many times, leaving their primitive corals and shellfish and crawling trilobites to the long slow transformation from primal ooze to fossil rock. Similarly, the lush vegetation of one-time Carboniferous marshlands already had become the coal seams of southeastern Kentucky, though several millennia still would have to pass before there would *be* a Kentucky, or anyone there who would know or care. Meantime, the mountain chains that eventually would bear the name of Appalachian had reared up out of the shifting strata of folded and squeezed and tormented rock and been eroded flat and then reared up again, not once but many times.

One of these gigantic convulsions may have cut off a tributary of the ancient Tennessee River and turned it westward instead of southward, and so midwifed the birth of the Cumberland. That is only a theory; but however it happened, the river's tortuous course shows that she once had to pick her way over a flat, low-lying land newly risen from the sea and still so slightly above sea level the current barely flowed. In time the land rose higher and the river ran more briskly, but she already had carved her serpentine channel in the rocky earth and by and large she stayed there. The Cumberland was a very old river long before the first man set eyes on her.

It is generally agreed now that he arrived in the far northwest corner of North America from Asia, how many thousands of years ago no one can say—but *many*. We can only guess how numerous and how varied were the peoples who followed in each other's footsteps over the land bridge that once spanned the Bering Sea. But dimly and imperfectly we can trace the routes they took when the ceaseless need to hunt, or the pressure of tribal wars, or their own restless seekings drove them southward and eastward, ultimately to cover both Americas. Their slow migrations must have taken centuries and still more centuries on top of those. Yet such monsters as giant sloths and mastodons—the last of their kind, it may be, already heading downhill toward extinction—still walked the Cumberland earth when our first man finally got there. We know in the same way we know him for a hunter and weaponmaker of more than passing excellence, for some of his finely worked flints have turned up among the massive ribs of the beasts that died by them.

Our hunter's accomplishments seem to have stopped there, however. If he had others he has left no trace of them. The meager evidence suggests he led a nomadic life, following the herds he preyed on and taking shelter where he found it: usually some cave or the lee of a rock outcrop. Both occur frequently along many stretches of the Cumberland. He made no pottery, practiced only the crudest of decorative arts. To slay so formidable an adversary as a mastodon or a giant prehistoric bison, he must have devised some workable system of cooperation in the hunt. It is doubtful, though, that his grasp of tribal government went much further than simple rule by the strongest. Still, this ancient man lived long in Cumberland country and perhaps he developed a few social advances before his time was up. Bones found in caves on the upper river amid the vestiges of crude funeral wrappings of bark or bark cloth may indicate some slight efforts toward more-than-casual burials; in other words, possibly, a dawning concept of soul and a life after death. The bones sometimes bore the marks of violent death, too. Maybe it came in battle with others of his kind, maybe with the warriors of some upcoming, more aggressive culture. It may have been retreat before such invaders that took him farther and farther up the river—to his own extermination, finally, or clear off the Cumberland.

Our first hunter clearly had contemporaries, and some at least were considerably less advanced than he. Traces of a people who made no flint implements at all, but simply used stones as natural clubs or hammers, have been found on the Green River in western Kentucky, for example. No doubt, man's nature being what it is, everyone has always had someone he looked down on.

Another early people, most numerous on the Tennessee River but no strangers to the Cumberland either, were avid eaters of the mussels that teemed in many streams of the region. Possibly these folk had climbed a notch or so higher up the human ladder than the hunters. At least they contrived to live with somewhat less effort, if that is the criterion. Digging mussels out of the riverbed was not nearly so demanding a business, after all, as chasing down and dispatching some animal that often was quite capable of turning to hunt the hunters. Too, the great abundance of shellfish made it unnecessary to roam far afield in an endless quest for game. Consequently the mussel eaters were able to settle down in permanent communities of considerable size, suffering no greater inconvenience thereby than a mighty stink from the middens of shell and other refuse that gradually piled up around them. (And lest modern man be inclined to smugness about that, it probably was little worse than a bad smog over Los Angeles, say, or a New York City temperature inversion, or any of the corrosive stenches so commonly attending twentieth-century industry.)

Despite their advantages, the mussel eaters were not notably superior to the hunting folk. While they had mastered the making of a rather crude sort of pottery, their skill at working flint was far inferior. In any case, they were not destined to be the torchbearers of an emerging civilization. A good while before the beginning of recorded history's Christian era, both hunters and mussel eaters vanished from the Cumberland forever, and people of a wholly different stripe appeared there.

Archaeologists theorize that the newcomers were an offshoot of the same stock that went on to build the impressive Mayan civilization of Central America. Some of the largest of the earthen mounds they left as their chief monuments do, undeniably, resemble the truncated pyramids erected by Mayan engineers, though they are not nearly so sophisticated in either concept or construction. But whatever their background, the new folk were mound builders of tireless energy. They reared the earthen piles as burial places for their dead, as fortresses enclosed by walls of earth or rock, and as temple sites. Periodically they burned the temples—perhaps a sort of ritual cleansing by fire—and then heaped fresh earth over the ashes and built new temples there, and so the mounds grew. Apparently these compulsive builders reached the Cumberland in successive waves over a considerable length of time, for we find traces of differing cultures in various localities. The firstcomers naturally settled most thickly along the lower and middle river. But in time they were putting up their mounds and their fortified villages everywhere along the upper Cumberland and far up most of her larger tributaries as well. Harlan, Kentucky, was first called Mount Pleasant because of a large mound located about where Poor, Clover, and Martins forks meet. Nothing remains of it today, nor of the "round Hill made by Art about 20 feet high and 60 feet over the top" which Dr. Thomas Walker saw on the upper river in 1750. Many of the ancient man-made hills noted by early travelers in Cumberland country have not survived. Archaeology was a science not well understood by the rank and file in pioneer days. Besides, a settler with a family to feed was interested far less in "Injun relics" than he was in clearing the land, plowing it, and getting a crop in. And continued cultivation would eventually spread the earth enough to level even a good-sized mound.

But some were too huge to be so easily destroyed. It was a little difficult, too, for even the most practical farmer to disregard human remains when he found them sown in such immense profusion as they were in several places along the middle and lower river. These obviously were cemeteries, filled with the bones of folk who had been interred with reverence and loving care. In some places the bodies had been doubled up and laid in circular or hexagonal graves. In others they were stretched full length. Always, though, the graves were carefully lined and covered over with flat stones, and they often held pottery bowls and spoons of horn or mussel shell: mute proof that the departed had been provided with food for the long journey to another world.

In more recent times, fortunately, archaeologists have been able to get at several promising mound sites before the ignorant completely ruined them. As a result we have some evidence of other aspects of a mature and well-adjusted people.

Somewhere along the line they had mastered the art of wattle-and-daub construction: driving stout posts into the ground, interweaving pliant withes or lengths of split cane to make walls, then plastering the walls with clay and topping them off with a roof, probably of thatch. Like the longhouses of later Indian tribes, their temples or great halls quite likely doubled as community social centers, with plenty of room around the ceremonial fire and the chief's high seat for family groups to spread their deerskins or straw mats. Here, the weighty questions touching war or peace and other matters of tribal policy would be thrashed out. Here, too, folk probably found occasion for various festive entertainments, and no doubt in the proper season the sacred rites that ensured good corn crops were solemnized. For these were an agricultural people, and maize was their staple. With it they would almost certainly grow squash, beans, and other vegetables as well. We know nothing of their form of government, though obviously it was a stable one. It may have been very democratic too. There is nothing to indicate, anyway, that any man's house was larger than his neighbor's or better furnished with worldly goods.

A Stone Age people still, the mound builders chipped flint axes, knives, and other tools and weapons with great skill. But they had learned, too, to make pottery that was strong, beautifully designed, and often decorated in many colors. They knew how to work copper as well, not smelting it but beating the pure, raw metal into sheets which they then fashioned into ritual masks, ornamental breastplates, and the like. The copper they used was not native to the Cumberland. It appears to have come instead from the far northern peninsula of what is now the state of Michigan, a region where Indians are known to have carried on a rudimentary kind of copper mining in very early times. Many mounds have yielded up a wide range of other artifacts made of materials —species of marine shells, for example—never found naturally in Cumberland country.

There were other mound builders, of course—many different cultures of them over many centuries—throughout the Ohio River Valley and along the Mississippi. One can speculate, then, on a distant age when trade may have been a factor more potent than war in beating out such "plain Indian roads" as the Great War Path; the Warriors Path of Kentucky; the Great Lakes Trail that ran still farther west; the Chickasaw Trace that later was to grow famous, or infamous, as the Natchez Trace. And these are only the names white men gave to a few of the main trails. All of eastern North American was crisscrossed by a maze of others, never as well known to the white man but trodden deep and hard before Europeans ever began to think seriously of a New World. So the Cumberland mound builders surely took part in the growth of a native American commerce and exchange of ideas. Indeed, everything we know of them seems to show an intelligent, well-rounded people happily in tune with their time and their environment.

All of which only makes the puzzle of their final disappearance more baffling. They flourished a long time on the Cumberland, until well into Europe's medieval period, perhaps. Then, abruptly, they were there no longer.

None of the pat explanations as to where they may have gone, or why, or what became of them, would appear to fit. There is no archaeological evidence to suggest an outbreak of some deadly pestilence, say, or such other natural catastrophe as might have wiped out an entire population. If they had any reason for embarking on a mass migration, no signs of it survive. Several of the village sites excavated have turned up quantities of perfect, unbroken artifacts. The inference is that they were neither lost nor discarded, but probably were left behind when their owners fled, apparently in some haste. But fled from what? From whom? No conquering hordes moved in, either to loot or to take over. The abandoned villages were not destroyed. Homes and temples simply crumbled away before the slow onslaught of time, weather, and natural decay.

There is a still greater mystery, in that no successors to the mound builders appeared. Years passed: a century, two, three, perhaps more. Folk in the region all about the basin of the Cumberland went their ways, lived, died, left descendants who would eventually become the American Indians of recorded history. And still Cumberland country itself remained a lonely, forsaken land peopled only by ghosts.

Whose ghosts? Well, it makes an intriguing question.

Much later, the Cherokee had a legend that told how their forefathers waged war against a tribe of white men and defeated them at last in a bloody battle on the bank of the Tennessee River. The Cherokee lived on the upper Tennessee and laid claim to all the country far to the west and to the north all the way to the Ohio. Pleasant, fertile, and game-rich though most of the Cumberland basin was, however, the Cherokee never wanted to live there. It should be significant, but of precisely what we do not know. One version of their legend had the white enemy slaughtered to a man. But another had a small band of survivors fleeing down the Tennessee to the Ohio, and so westward. Now the Tennessee is not the Cumberland. But geographically the two are not very far apart, either. And the Shawnees, who did try at one time to settle on the Cumberland, had a legend of their own quite similar to that of the Cherokee. According to it, *their* ancestors were the ones who massacred a band of whites—and thereafter the land lay under a curse, so that Shawnees might hunt over it, having made the proper medicine beforehand, but could nevermore find homes there.

John Sevier, early Tennessee's premier frontiersman, Indian fighter, and several-time governor, was among those who vouched for the substance of the Cherokee story. The Shawnee tradition is hazier, not nearly so well authenticated. And of course no Indian legend is quite the same as proven fact. We know, for instance, that the Shawnees were hounded off the Cumberland by very real

warlike enemies: not only the Cherokee, but Creeks and Chickasaws who also claimed that land. So who needs white ghost stories?

Yet tantalizing hints persist, of white voyagers to America ages
earlier than any we know of now. There were the Norsemen who
reached the North American coast, or came very close to it, in the
eleventh century—and may have gone much farther than anyone
thinks. There was Quetzalcoatl, the white god who visited ancient
Mexico once and promised to return. Whoever he may have been,
the Aztecs believed in him so firmly they fell easy victims to Cortez
and his Spanish adventurers. There was Madoc, the Welsh prince
who sailed across the Sea of Darkness with ten ships full of stout-
hearted followers sometime in the thirteenth century. . . . Or did
he? Reputable historians have debunked Prince Madoc pretty
thoroughly, along with the various tribes of pale-skinned, blue-
eyed, Welsh-speaking Indians he is supposed to have left in his
wake as he wandered through the wilderness. And yet, and yet . . .
Bold seafarers *could* have sailed across the Atlantic from the
British Isles in the thirteenth century, or even a great deal earlier.
The Norsemen already had proved it could be done.

There is another piece of evidence, its possible significance unknown. Sixty-odd miles south and a little east of Nashville, very
nearly equidistant from both the Cumberland and Tennessee
rivers, stand the ruins known as the Old Stone Fort. The name is
not quite accurate, since the fort's walls actually are of earth
heaped over cores of rock. Apparently they once enclosed a village
of some size. But the fort is not a mound and probably was not the
work of any known mound-building people. An obvious guess is
that it was built by Spaniards with Hernando de Soto, whose line
of march in 1540 almost certainly followed a long stretch of the
Tennessee River. But de Soto's ill-fated expedition was very well
chronicled, by the nameless Gentleman of Elvas and by others who
took part in it, and none of them told of any fort-building in the
region. Nor does anything about the ruins suggest a Spanish touch.
De Soto was seeking golden cities, anyway; he scarcely would
have paused long enough to erect so large and permanent a fortress
in country that plainly had little to offer a conquistador.

Experts in such matters say the long-dead engineer who picked
the site for the place and laid out its ramparts was highly skilled
in the science of military fortification. As skilled, maybe, as the
men who were building English castles on earthen mounds from the

time of William the Conqueror, and even earlier. No one has yet come forward with any very conclusive estimate of the Old Stone Fort's age. So, inevitably, the notion refuses to lie down and die: *could* Madoc and his stout Welsh carls . . . ?

No, of course not. Preposterous! And yet . . .

For a fact, no one can say for certain what white man *did* first look upon the Cumberland.

2
The
Shawnees

IT was an unknown world, vast, dark, strange, full of promise, full of threat. When they met for the first time at Michilimackinac in the spring of 1673, neither Louis Jolliet nor the Jesuit Father Jacques Marquette ever had seen the river they were ordered to explore. All they knew of the Mitchisipi, or Meshasabi, were some tales told by Illinois braves with whom Father Marquette had talked. But he took at least a little encouragement from what they had said. "This great river can hardly empty in Virginia," he wrote shortly before he and Jolliet set off, "and we rather believe its mouth is in California."

If the mistake stemmed partly from wishful thinking, it was no more than natural. The concept of a short route across America to the "South Sea" and the riches of the Indies, sought by virtually every westward-faring explorer for a century after Columbus, still was a powerful spur to men's imaginations. Nor was it confined to the men of New France alone. Two years before Jolliet and Marquette got their commission, a prominent Virginia landowner and Indian trader by the name of Abraham Wood sent a pair of his men into the wilderness beyond the Blue Ridge Mountains with instructions to search for "the ebbing and flowing of the Waters on the other side of the Mountains, in order to the discovery of the South Sea."

12

Wood's men, Thomas Batts and Robert Fallam, returned with no very conclusive findings to report and have long since been forgotten. But the two Frenchmen were successful and won lasting fame. Their voyage by canoe far down the Mississippi and back enabled them to correct a whole hatful of earlier misconceptions so thoroughly that there never again would be any serious doubts about the great river's course. They also passed along a wealth of valuable information gleaned from friendly Indians they met. Not all of it was strictly accurate; nevertheless, in substance, it was knowledge no European ever had had before.

A map drawn by Jolliet from memory after his return to Quebec in the summer of 1674 located the Ohio River properly in relation to the Mississippi, for example, but showed it merely as a stub jutting eastward into limbo. He labeled it the Ouabouskigou, and thus laid the groundwork for a new error destined to remain current for years to come: that the Ohio was a comparatively minor stream emptying into the much larger Wabash—the French Ouabouskigou or, more commonly, Oubache. The truth, of course, was exactly the other way around, but Jolliet had only hearsay to go by. He drew a lone tributary for his Ouabouskigou, far down toward its junction with the Mississippi. It was a quite inconsequential tributary and what there was of it dangled almost straight southward, rather like the appendix on one's intestine. If his Indian informants gave him any name for this stream, Jolliet did not record it. He did, however, show a large village of "Challounons" close to its headwaters.

Save for that, he might have been drawing an early clue to the Tennessee. But his Challounons—more correctly rendered *Chauouanons*—indicate it was the Cumberland instead, or the river that one day would be known as Cumberland.

Such details, though, were of no more than passing interest to Louis Jolliet. A Frenchman of broad strategic vision, he saw the Mississippi as a watery road to empire: a vital link between the Great Lakes and the Gulf of Mexico, and his report to the governor of New France stressed that. It was the gentler missionary, Father Marquette, who was concerned much more with the Indians. His account of the expedition described the Chauouanons as a very numerous people, but so meek and timorous a lot that they offered no more resistance "than flocks of sheep" when the savage Iroquois raided them. "And innocent though they are," he added, "they . . .

sometimes experience the barbarity of the Iroquois, who cruelly burn them."

The Jesuits already disapproved emphatically of this Iroquois penchant for torturing captives—including an occasional captive missionary. Hence Father Marquette may have let his feelings get the better of him here, for the Chauouanons were by no means as docile as he made them out to be. The English who knew them by various spellings as Shawnees, Shawanons, or Shawanoes, never found them so, at any rate. Nevertheless, they were without doubt a badly put-upon people. An Algonquian tribe akin to the Delawares, the Shawnees had lived in the region north of the Ohio River at a very early date. But in Marquette's time the dreaded Five Nations of the Iroquois were indeed forcing them out of that ancient homeland and scattering fugitive bands of them far into the south and southeast.

Most Frenchmen were only vaguely aware of that as yet, and few besides Marquette would have cared. The important thing was that colonial authorities at Quebec readily accepted the reports of their two Mississippi explorers. It was a time when men mapping North America had to work from uncertain sources that were scant at best, and sometimes had to use their imaginations too, and did, and so before long other French maps began to show a river flowing into the Oubache from the south or east, with Chauouanon towns along its banks. Probably they all owed something to Jolliet and Marquette. But some, at least, of the mapmakers must themselves have met and talked with Indians of the Mississippi Valley. Many were missionary priests like Father Marquette. French missionaries were active during these years, eternally striving farther and farther into the unknown, always bent first on harvesting heathen souls for salvation but ever alert, too, to advance their nation's territorial claims in the New World. For all their activity, though, there is no solid evidence that any missionary ever reached the *Rivière des Chauouanons* in person. Nor can anyone say surely what Frenchman first gave it that name, or when.

The first man actually to look upon the river may well have been English. Within a year or two of the time Jolliet and Marquette paddled past the mouth of their Ouabouskigou, in fact, this fellow was wading across their other river with the Chauouanon towns on it. He was a long way to the east, but it was the same river. As for the man, we know little except that he was young, illiterate, and a bond servant probably indentured to the Virginian Abraham Wood. Beyond that, he was either stupendously resourceful and blessed with great good luck, or a truly gifted teller of tall tales— or a combination of both. His name was Gabriel Arthur.

Abraham Wood's interest in the Virginia back country was of long standing. Apparently the unimpressive report of the party he sent out in 1671 failed to discourage him, for he soon followed up with another. That one left his trading post at Fort Henry on the Appomattox River, about where Petersburg now stands, in the spring of 1673. An experienced Carolina trader named James Needham was in charge, with young Arthur as a sort of first assistant and man of all work. A number of Appomattoc Indian hunters also went along to supply meat and serve as guides. Traveling southwest, then west, the party struggled through the Blue Ridge and the Great Smoky Mountains and eventually—far into unfamiliar country by this time—reached a large town of the Cherokee on the Little Tennessee River. These Cherokee clearly had had some contact with other white traders, probably Spaniards from the Floridas, for several of the braves carried good flintlock muskets. The two Englishmen were greeted with signs of friendship, well fed, and made comfortable. But the party's stock of provisions had now been used up and they had but one horse left of the large string with which they had started. After a few days' rest, therefore, Needham decided to return to Fort Henry for remounts and fresh supplies. He ordered Gabriel Arthur to stay with the Cherokee, making use of the wait by learning their language and gathering what information he could about the country westward. Then, with the Appomattocs and a party of Cherokee braves who elected to go along, he left on the long backward trek.

With what misgivings young Arthur watched them out of sight, we can only guess.

Needham never returned. Presently the Cherokee who had accompanied him did, though, and with dire news. The party had reached Fort Henry safely, they said, and started back. But a quarrel developed between Needham and one of the Appomattocs. It ended with the Indian murdering Needham, helping himself to the best of the horses, and riding off into the forest with a word of advice to the Cherokee in parting. They had better go home and dispose of the other Englishman, he told them, lest great trouble come upon them. Worse, they had about convinced themselves he was right. Worst of all, the chief happened to be away on a hunt when they arrived and none of the other Cherokee were disposed to argue the point. Poor Arthur was at the stake, bound fast and with dry wood piled around his feet, when the old chief suddenly appeared. Plainly, he was a no-nonsense sort of chief. *Who was it wanted to burn this white man?* he thundered. One of the braves answered that *he* did, and snatched up a brand to set the pyre blazing. Whereupon the chief shot him, announced ringingly that the young Englishman would be under his aegis thereafter, and that put an end to the matter.

So went the story Arthur told later, anyway. It sounds a little trite today, considering the long succession of heroes from Captain John Smith on who escaped gruesome Indian executions only in the proverbial nick. But in all fairness, too, we must remember that Gabriel Arthur was among the first; in his day the tale had not yet grown hackneyed.

The young man's status in the tribe was now that of adopted son, and he seems to have slipped into it with remarkable ease. He traveled with a hunting party far down the Tennessee River, very probably the first white man to do that since de Soto. He went along on forays by war parties against other tribes in Carolina and the Spanish Floridas—and finally against the Shawnees to the north. Just how far north they had to go to find Shawnees is not altogether clear from Arthur's later account, for of course the country was all strange to him. But they reached the Ohio River, certainly, and may even have crossed it. They would obviously have had to cross the Cumberland too, at some point, though Arthur made no mention of it.

The raid went badly for the Cherokee. They were beaten off, Arthur wounded by an arrow and left in the Shawnees' hands. But still his luck proved indestructible. Puzzled because he was clearly some different kind of human being, his captors tried scrubbing him and were amazed to discover white skin under the dirt and war paint. Apparently he was the first white man they had ever seen, for this must have been a very primitive band of Indians indeed; Arthur noticed that they were immensely impressed by his musket and steel hatchet also. The upshot was, they decided not to kill him for a while.

This lease on life provided time for his wound to heal, and in the

interim he kept his eyes open and his wits about him. Beaver seemed plentiful in the region, he observed, for hunters frequently brought them in. When he was put to work one day helping squaws prepare several for the pot, it occurred to him to let these Shawnees know that the people where he came from would be only too happy to trade muskets and steel hatchets for all the beaver skins they could get. He contrived to put the idea across to the tribal elders by means of a blend of sign language and Cherokee, and it worked. After some dickering the Shawnees not only set him free, but furnished guides to lead him to the best trail southward and gave him a buckskin pouch full of parched corn to sustain him on his journey, all this in return for his promise to send back other Englishmen with trade goods.

Arthur's story leaves no doubt that the Shawnees sent him down the famous Warriors Path of Kentucky, the Indians' *Athawominee,* or Path of the Armed Ones. It was blazed and well trodden and, trail-wise now, he had little difficulty with it. The way led through narrow, laurel-choked valleys and up over the shoulders of wooded hills that rose in steepening wave on wave toward the western ramparts of a mountain range the Shawnees called *Wasioto,* and Englishmen eventually would know as the Cumberlands. A far piece south and close up under those ramparts the trail descended to a river—the someday Cumberland once more; whether he recognized her from his earlier crossing we do not know—and forded her, and climbed again to pass through the broad gap that also would be called Cumberland in days to come.

So at last, in time's own fullness, Gabriel Arthur walked into Fort Henry like a ghost risen from the dead. And a shaggier, more darkly tanned, more Indian-looking ghost the folk there doubtless never had set eyes on and never would again.

It is a great pity that Arthur had not the learning to set his own story down on paper. The tale's dramatic climaxes probably lost nothing in his telling, but the only version to survive for posterity is the one Abraham Wood, his master, passed on in reports to Virginia's governor, Sir William Berkeley, and the British Lords Proprietors of the Carolinas. After that, history has no more to say of Gabriel Arthur. Presumably he worked off his indenture in time and became a free man. A trifle sadly, one imagines him: the nine-days' wonder with the bloom slowly rubbing off . . . settling back into the humdrum, hard-working routine of a poor man in a

Virginia frontier settlement . . . marrying, perhaps, and siring a
covey of brats to keep his nose to the grindstone . . . and perhaps
in his tedious old age still afflicting skeptics with the threadbare
saga of his escapades among the savages.

In the end, anyway, the great adventure went for naught.
Abraham Wood was already well along in years. He died without
sending another exploring party into the west, and it appears no one
else was very interested. Virginia Englishmen of the landowner
class were more and more preoccupied, in these years, with the
fat tobacco profits from Tidewater plantations. Nor were there as
yet any marked population pressures to push land seekers out into
the wilderness. Not even the Great Valley of Virginia had thus far
felt a plow or a settler's axe. The fact that young Gabriel Arthur
had found a gateway through the still more distant Appalachian
barrier into a vast virgin land beyond was generally overlooked,
his exploits soon forgotten. For nearly fifty years more that trans-
montane land and its river flowing westward would be forgotten
too.

Over the long haul, that was going to make less difference than
it might have. In any case, it would have taken a regiment of
Gabriel Arthurs, complete with his good luck, to match the breed
of men already ranging the western country for New France. They
called themselves *coureurs de bois,* woods runners, and they wore
the name with a very special kind of swagger and élan.

Frenchmen of many backgrounds had begun to adapt to the
wilderness, to Indian life and the harsh mores it imposed, almost
as soon as France founded her first colony in Canada. They did it
with a thorough-going gusto unequaled by any of France's New
World rivals. Why this should have been so—what obscure ethnic
strain persisted more sturdily in the Gallic bloodstream than in
other Europeans'—is a question for anthropologists to ponder. But
because it *was* so, France got off to a long start in North America.
Not that *coureurs de bois* were men of the caliber of, for example,
Louis Jolliet. They were not discoverers at all, per se. Most of them
were, rather, the rough common sort with no pretensions to fame
or greatness. But they carried the burden of danger and hard work
out in the dim back country where France slowly stitched together
the fabric of a wilderness empire. It was the *coureurs de bois* who
rowed the bateaux and paddled the pirogues, sweated over the
portages, toted the packs, built the far-flung, lonely forts and

trading posts of more ambitious men who hired them. They commonly took Indian wives or mistresses and begat half-breed sons to carry on, more woodswise even than their sires. And among so lusty a lot of woods runners, inevitably, would be many of the restless, questing kind to strike out into the wilderness on their own, trapping furs, or setting themselves up as independent traders, or simply living the wild, free lives of their Indian friends.

Such a man was Martin Chartier. His roving started in the winter of 1679/80, when he was one of several who deserted the Sieur de La Salle's Fort Crève Coeur, far out in the uncharted Illinois country. The men claimed they were justified in leaving, since the wages promised them were long in arrears. But La Salle accused them of making off with valuable furs and trade goods, and thus, the true rights and wrongs of it aside, they wound up afoul of French law.

Most were speedily run down and taken, but Martin Chartier spent nearly eight years dodging about the length and breadth of New France. Finally, back once more in the Illinois country, he fell in with a band of friendly Shawnees. But presently they headed southward for the shadowy land below the Ohio River and he left them. Then he thought better of it and set out to find them again. The sketchy accounts of his hegira, pieced together later from various contemporary sources, say that he traveled by canoe, guessing his way along the course of a river, and "found water in all places." It must have been a navigable river he followed, then, and all that is known of his subsequent roaming points most logically to the Rivière des Chauouanons—a stream still, at the time, little more than guessed at by his fellow Frenchmen. At some point on the river he overtook his Shawnee friends and stayed with them for the next two or three years. But they had found no very comfortable haven after all. The whole Cumberland basin, teeming with wild game but lacking permanent human residents since the time of the vanished mound builders, had gradually become an Indians' no-man's-land. It was claimed, hunted over, and eternally fought over, too, by the Cherokee from east and south, the Chickasaws from what is today western Tennessee, the Creeks from below the Big Bend of the Tennessee River, and several tribes, including the fierce Iroquois, from north of the Ohio. The Chickasaws and Cherokee, in particular, were implacably jealous of hunting grounds they considered their own, and both were accustomed to prey without mercy on Shawnee intruders.

This situation, incidentally, makes it all the more likely that early French mapmakers simply repeated hearsay from other tribes in locating their Chauouanon towns so freely along the river. Some villages there were, assuredly: over a long period of years, perhaps a great many. But it seems doubtful that they could have been more than semipermanent at best, and never very numerous at any given time. Most were probably the encampments of groups like Chartier's, who occasionally stopped long enough to grow and harvest a crop of maize, but otherwise found it healthier to keep on the move.

Two or three years of this kind of existence took Martin Chartier's people a good way up the river. They may have left it, finally, at Smith's Shoals. They could have portaged around the shoals and the falls above, however, and continued by canoe all the way to the ford where the Warriors Path crossed. Then, like Gabriel Arthur before them, they might have passed through Cumberland Gap and turned northward on the Great War Path. Or they might have used any of several other Indian trails to get through the mountains farther to the north. However they got there, they emerged into Maryland's Anne Arundel County in the summer of 1962: three hundred-odd braves, squaws, and children with Chartier now their acknowledged leader.

They had not yet done with wandering, but the happy ending was in sight. If Martin Chartier truly was the rascal the Sieur de La Salle had claimed, he was a rascal of many parts, not the least of them an engaging knack for landing on his feet. When suspicious Maryland folk clapped him into jail as a French spy, he promptly talked himself out again. Before long he had found the wherewithal somewhere to open his own trading post on the Susquehanna River. He prospered, with his Shawnees still around him. A few years later he led them out to the western Pennsylvania frontier and opened up another trading post. He prospered there, too —plainly a man, as one visitor remarked of him, "in great credit with the wild Indians."

During the following years other *coureurs de bois* from the Illinois country undoubtedly found Chartier's route to the Rivière des Chauouanons. Little is known of any of them. Some are vouched for by history, though hazily, and some only by tradition. None, so far as we know, ever penetrated beyond the general area of present-day Nashville. In 1714, one du Charleville is believed to have taken a bateau-load of furs down to the Ohio River, and thence via the Mississippi to the Gulf of Mexico. The story may be slightly suspect, however, because New Orleans had not been founded and would not be for another four years. Thus the mouth of the Mississippi would have offered no discernible market for a fur trader. Yet du Charleville *may* have made his epic river voyage, and, if so, he was not only the first in a long line of French hunters and traders, but the forerunner of a still longer, later line of Cumberland River flatboat and keelboat men.

Scattered bands of Shawnees continued to hold out on the river for several years into the eighteenth century. But the unrelenting hostility of Chickasaws and Cherokee made it a losing proposition. Outnumbered and chivied without letup, all were forced out sooner or later. Some found their various ways past the upper river into western Pennsylvania, like Chartier's people, while others fled northward to the Illinois.

In a year not definitely known, but soon after 1717, Guillaume Delisle, court geographer to King Louis XIV, drew a beautiful map embodying all that Frenchman knew or surmised about North America. He flattered the Cumberland exceedingly, making her a relatively straight river flowing east and west and a very large one besides; much larger, in fact, than either the Ohio or the Tennessee. Significantly, his name for her was Rivière des *Anciens* Chauouanons, for, as he explained, "the Chauouanons who lived here in other days."

The Shawnees were a tenacious people, however, and stubbornly proud of their tribal identity. A time was coming, no long way off, when the decline of the Iroquois enemy would permit most of their widely dispersed elements to come together again in the old homeland between Lake Erie and the Ohio River. There for a while they would flourish and grow strong, and one day produce their great warrior-statesman Tecumseh to lead a gallant but foredoomed fight against the encroachment of the white man. But in the early eighteenth century that still was years away, and it would be no part of the Cumberland's story anyway.

The river, like time, flowed on. Neither would be hurried. Change was coming at its own slow pace, but not yet, not yet. . . .

3

At Last:
The Cumberland

THE first entry in the journal Dr. Walker would keep set a style commendably brief and matter of fact. He wrote: "Having on the 12th day of December last, been employed for a certain consideration to go to the Westward in order to discover a proper Place for a Settlement, I left my house on the Sixth day of March at 10 o'clock, 1749–50. . . ."

It was actually a bit *too* matter of fact, and far too modest. The doctor was considerably more than a hireling. He was one of the prime movers in Virginia's Loyal Land Company, holding a grant of eight hundred thousand acres of good western land from His Majesty King George II. Hopefully, such land could be disposed of to prospective settlers at an excellent profit—if and when found, of course. In short, the company was in land speculation, among the earliest in that new and fabulously promising field of American enterprise. Dr. Walker and his associates proposed to find their acres in the unknown country beyond the Allegheny Mountains. Somewhere out there, Walker believed, was a region known as Kentakee: a Cherokee name he understood to mean a place of fertile, well-watered plains, assuring good farmland.

Vague as that might be, it still was about as much as any Virginian could claim to know of that wilderness west of the mountains. And Thomas Walker, a wiry, blue-eyed little man of thirty-five, possessed of physical strength that belied his small stature, was about as good a leader for the projected undertaking as Virginia could have produced. No mere plantation aristocrat, he had made several previous journeys into frontier parts, including one that took him far down the Holston River to Cherokee country. There, with Indianwise Carolina traders, he had sat in on endless conclaves in smoky council houses; had even come to be well acquainted with the famous Little Carpenter, Chief Attakullakulla, England's oldest and staunchest friend among the Cherokee. It may have been the Carpenter himself who first told Walker of Kentakee.

For this present exploration the doctor had enlisted five companions from his own neighborhood, all men seasoned to woods living. They would travel light: a single saddle horse for each man, with two packhorses to carry gear and provisions. In addition every man would take with him at least one good hunting dog, as was customary when traveling in the wilderness for any length of time.

(The doctor dated his journal 1749/50 quite properly, by the way. England still used the Old Style calendar with its new year beginning on March 25. It would not adopt the modern Gregorian calendar for another two years.)

Times had changed since the days of Abraham Wood and Gabriel Arthur. A rising tide of westward emigration had been spilling through the Blue Ridge Mountains ever since the early 1700s. Traveling down Virginia's Great Valley between the Blue Ridge and the Alleghenies, Walker's men were able to find lodgings at some settler's cabin nearly every night and had no difficulty in buying the corn, bacon, and hominy they needed to fill out their slender store of provisions. Eighty years earlier, Wood's men, Batts and Fallam, had gone no farther to the southwest than New River and had found no trace of human habitation there except a few abandoned Indian cornfields. But now a man named William English operated a gristmill on the river, and a group of German Dunkards—"an odd set of people," Walker thought them, but "very hospitable"—had recently built another. Not all the aspects of civilization's rapid advance were so salutary, however. Of a large salt lick near the present site of Roanoke, the doctor commented in terms that sound curiously modern: "This lick has been one of the best places for Game in these parts and would have been of much greater advantage to the inhabitants than it has been if the hunters had not killed the Buffaloes for diversion, and the Elks and Deer for their skins. . . ."

Two weeks after leaving home the six horsemen rode into the headwater valley of the Holston's North Fork. Somewhere in the vicinity they found an old acquaintance of Walker's putting up a cabin. Samuel Stalnaker was his name; he was an old frontier hand and his little farm would be the farthest outpost of settlement in Virginia for some years to come. The doctor had sought him out deliberately and now tarried a day to help with the cabin, hoping that Stalnaker might consent to guide the party through the wild country ahead.

He didn't, pleading that he was too busy to go. But he must have supplied some very good directions, for eighteen days later Walker led his men up a branch of a river he called the Beargrass, "and from thence six miles to Cave Gap, the land being levil. . . ." In spite of rain, snow, and some rough going through the Clinch and Powell mountains they seldom had been in any real danger of losing their way, and suffered no worse mishap than an encounter described by the doctor with his customary economy of words: ". . . our dogs caught a large He Bear, which before we could come up to shoot him had wounded a dog of mine, so that he could not Travel and we carried him on Horseback, till he recovered." As for the gap itself, Cave Gap seems to have been the name by which Stalnaker knew it, which suggests that he and perhaps others had already been there. If Dr. Walker knew about Gabriel Arthur, and so much as guessed that this was the same way Arthur had passed through these mountains more than seventy-five years before, he said nothing of it in his journal. But he too found the Warriors Path plainly blazed. He also commented on some laurel trees marked with crosses, "and several figures on them." Indulging in no idle speculation as to who might have done that, he cut his own name into a large beech tree and went on. The party camped that night on Yellow Creek—Flat Creek, Walker named it—and spent the next two days following its course down the gap's northward slope. Rain forced them to hole up on the third day, a welcome interlude the doctor used to advantage by cobbling up a pair of "Indian shoes" to replace his worn-out boots. The next day, April 17, he wrote: "Still rain. I went down the Creek a hunting and found that it went into a River about a mile below our Camp. This, which is Flat Creek and some others join'd, I called Cumberland River."

Thus, without fuss or fanfare, the river was christened with the name she would bear permanently. During a trip to England some years earlier, Walker had had the privilege of an introduction to the Duke of Cumberland, second son of King George II and Queen Caroline. No doubt so signal an honor made its impression on the little doctor from America, there being a streak of snobbery in most men. Besides, Cumberland's rout of the Jacobite pretender Bonnie Prince Charlie Stuart at Culloden in 1746 still was recent enough to make a loyal Englishman deem his name eminently worth commemorating. Nevertheless, there is not a word in the journal to suggest that Walker also gave the name to Cave Gap or the mountain range it penetrated. Both were named sometime later, probably because they were associated with the river but by whom we do not know. There is no indication, either, that the doctor suspected his newfound river might be the same one France long had known as Rivière des Chauouanons, or that he would have cared.

Such considerations were beside the point anyway. Dr. Walker had come looking for eight hundred thousand acres of likely land for settlement, and he failed to find them. The fertile bluegrass country of Kentakee was just a little farther than he managed to go, though he pushed on westward for another eight days.

Unable to wade the flooded Cumberland at the Warriors Path ford, he and his companions made a canoe of elm bark and tough hickory withes and crossed in that. They built a tiny log house, broke a plot of ground around it, planted corn and peach stones there—and so in effect, "settled" on the land against the off chance that some future rivals might come along to claim it. For the same reason they carefully blazed several trees in the vicinity and carved their initials on others. At one place near the river they found the ruins of Indian huts. At another they came upon the fresh trail of a party of Indian hunters and tried hard to overtake them in order to find out what they might know about the elusive Kentakee, but could not. Various misadventures occurred, more than once testing Dr. Walker's medical skill. "This day Colby Chew and his horse fell down a bank," he wrote. "I bled and gave him Volatile Drops & he soon recovered." On another afternoon, "Ambrose Powell was bit by a bear in his knee. . . ." We are not told how the doctor

handled that emergency, nor what he did when his dog had another run-in with a bear and came out of it with a broken foreleg.
But he saved three snakebitten horses by judicious applications of
bear oil and "rattlesnake root." The unfortunate Ambrose Powell,
however, had *his* dog killed by a bull elk cornered on a creek bank
". . . and we named the run Tumbler's Creek, the dog being of that
name." On several occasions the party had to lie up long enough
to cure the hide of an elk or a deer and make new moccasins for
themselves. They found salt licks where as many as a hundred
buffalo at a time milled and bellowed and lapped the briny mud.
They remarked on any number of outcrops of excellent coal; at one
place they all wrote their names with coal on the face of a huge
overhanging rock under which they camped. And once they
cowered through a nightlong storm of rain and hail, with a furious
wind "which blew down our tent and a great many trees about it.
. . . We all left the place in confusion and ran different ways for
shelter. . . ."

For the return trip Walker elected to head north and east instead
of going back through Cave Gap. By that route the little party
presently stumbled onto the headwaters of Station Camp Creek,
which they followed down to its junction with the Kentucky River.
Dr. Walker did not know either stream by name. Indeed, they had
no English names as yet, since this still was undiscovered country.
Ironically, though, the lower Kentucky flowed through the very
bluegrass lands he sought. All unknowing, the six men tried to
head downstream along the river but found the going so difficult,
through almost impenetrable brush, that they had to give up. "We
then . . . attempted to go up the River, but could not," wrote the
doctor. "It being very deep, we began a bark conoe. . . ." So, having
crossed over, the party wandered for some two hundred miles more
through the rugged, cut-up hills and tangled forests of what is
today eastern Kentucky and West Virginia. At last they hit the
New River, followed its course upstream through the Allegheny
ridges, and emerged once more into familiar surroundings in the
Great Valley of Virginia.

"I got home about Noon," Dr. Walker wrote on July thirteenth,
exactly five months and one week after setting out. One is left with
the strong impression that he and his five had enjoyed the experience. For all their having fallen down banks, been bear-bitten,
rained on, snowed on, and all the rest—and found no promised

land of Kentakee either—it had been an adventure, a welcome change from humdrum routine. It had been more, too. The simple fact of six Englishmen surviving for nearly half a year in a remote and unknown wilderness, with no help from other human beings, either white or red, was a plain portent of things to come.

Walker closed his journal with a methodical listing of all game killed during the exploration, and a mighty bag it was. The six men had shot no fewer than fifty-three bears, possibly because bears were so plentiful or possibly because their meat was preferred to any other. But the list also included large numbers of buffalo, deer, elk, and "about 150 Turkeys, besides small game." And, added the doctor, "We might have killed three times as much meat if we had wanted it." Yet survival entailed more than the mere lucky circumstance of finding themselves in a hunter's paradise. Their return journey took the party through a region where game was scarce, but they had prudently salted or jerked quantities of meat when they had it, and so never went hungry. Seventy-nine years earlier, in comparable country and with Indians along to do their hunting, Thomas Batts and Robert Fallam had nearly starved. Apparently Walker and his people had the very great advantage of hunting with rifles instead of the old-fashioned smoothbore muskets. Yet that was not the whole story either. Skill with the rifled gun could be of only limited use to a man until he mastered a wide range of woods lore along with it.

Obviously, England's westward-looking colonies were beginning to breed a new kind of knowledgeable, self-reliant frontiersman capable of vying with France's *coureurs de bois* on something like even terms.

High time, too, for England and France were rapidly drawing toward collision. The war that finally broke out between them in 1754 was a far-flung conflict variously known in England as the Maritime War, the Great War for the Empire, and by other names as well, but its North American phase came to be called simply the French and Indian War. It was aptly titled, for the colonial authorities of both nations ardently courted Indian allies to help do their fighting. They did it in cold-blooded awareness that, once aroused and painted for war, the red warriors were not going to be denied the wholesale, wanton destruction, the slaughtering of innocents and the torturing of prisoners they considered their just rewards. So it frequently became a very nasty little war, regardless of which side one was on. But Frenchmen, with their natural affinity for the Indians, were generally better at the game than Englishmen—and the frontier paid in blood.

The once-feeble Shawnees, grown bold and powerful in their new homeland north of the Ohio River, swept down the Warriors Path to kill and pillage and burn. Caught between them and the Cherokee, peacefully inclined to begin with, but turned hostile by some incredibly stupid British blundering, the westward push of English settlement was blunted and turned back for nine years of raids and counterraids all through the back country. They were years of tragic learning for folk who had at stake everything they owned in the Great Valley, and out in the fledgling New River settlements, and still farther out in Holston country. Young wives learned sudden widowhood, and husbands came to know how it was when cabins were laid in smoldering ruin, fields wasted, families tomahawked and scalped, or carried off into distant captivity; some to be rescued eventually and some lost forever. But out of the learning and the testing arose a hard-bitten elite who would never again be daunted by anything the wilderness could do to them.

No part of the French and Indian War was fought in Cumberland country, or within many miles of it. Nor, even when it all ended, was there as yet any other speculator in western lands looking to follow Dr. Thomas Walker through Cave Gap. The little doctor had been a few years ahead of his time. The next to go his route would be men of simpler ambition, but in a sense cut from the same cloth as Ambrose Powell and Colby Chew and the rest of Walker's five—men bent on the good hunting alone, ready to leave homes and wives and young sprats and stay out there on the far side of the mountains for as long as the spirit moved them.

This was the long hunt and they were Long Hunters, not settlers. Well, at least not yet. Hard to say what drove them; mostly, perhaps, just the restless discontent with the status quo that awakens in some men when wars are over. They were a varied lot, though, with scarcely anything in common save that they all were fiddle-footed. They were scarcely a band of heroes, either. Some simply found hunting a deal more congenial than following a plow under a hot sun all day, or grubbing weeds in a corn patch. And there were those, no doubt, in whom it was pure cussedness: solitary roamers asking nothing more of life than freedom and space to stomp about in, and plenty of both. Such men would find even the loose restraints of frontier civilization irksome.

But among all Long Hunters, surely, ran an aggressive curiosity as to what lay out there beyond the farthest settlements, a very real and hardy itch to go and see, to find, to know . . . and maybe one day, if things fell out that way, to take hold and possess.

And so they would, one day.

4

Some Others Besides Boone

DANIEL BOONE's fame came a little late to be of much benefit save to the legend. His contemporaries accepted him as a man among men, and he was that, which should be sufficient praise. There were many Long Hunters, and most of them were good at their trade. The ones who were not did not usually live long enough to be remembered.

There was Elisha Walden; if it is possible to call anyone the founder of the fraternity, he would be it. A big swarthy Virginian of uncertain antecedents, Walden came from a settlement safely to the east of the Blue Ridge Mountains and hence, unlike many Long Hunters, had had no experience as an Indian fighter in the war. But hostilities were not yet over in 1761 when he led a band of kindred spirits down into the same country around the Holston and Clinch rivers that Dr. Walker had traversed eleven years earlier. They found no Samuel Stalnaker there to furnish traveling directions, though, for Indians had captured Stalnaker and wiped out his little family early in the war. But Walden's men needed no directions and saw no Indians. They roamed at will through the high, forested valleys and the mist-shrouded mountain meadows for a year and a half, and went home with so bountiful a take in deerskins and furs that they lost no time in planning a return trip.

The men of this party, first of the true Long Hunters, probably looked not a whit different from hunters who had been going into the woods closer to home for years before them. Their gear and weapons represented no radical new departures, but were simply the tools experience had shown to be best for the work at hand. Undoubtedly, the men all carried some version of the long Pennsylvania rifle that was already, with its patch box in the stock and its accessories of powder horn, bullet pouch, and bullet mold, an indispensible hunter's friend. Each man would have the essential butcher knife, hatchet—seldom called a tomahawk unless one was speaking of Indians—and awl for mending leather. Television and other popular fiction to the contrary, there probably was no such thing as a coonskin cap among the lot of them. What is there about the hide of a raccoon, after all, to make it suitable as a piece of headgear? No, the hat favored by these hunters would be the one commonly worn in the settlements: of felt, with a low, flat crown and a broad brim to shade the eyes. Few Long Hunters ever liked the buckskin hunting shirt of the Indian, either, for it tended to grow clammy in cold weather and to stiffen uncomfortably as it dried out after a wetting. Much preferred was the smocklike garment of linsey—linen cloth—or the mixture of linen and wool known as linsey-woolsey. It was long and loose, reaching about halfway down the thighs and cut with a generous overlap in front. The shirt had neither buttons nor laces to fasten it, but was belted or tied with a sash around the middle. The overlap thus became a handy place to stow a snack of jerked meat of a pone of cornbread, or such other small items as a man might wish to have with him on the trail.

Beneath the hunting shirt would be leggings reaching well up a man's thighs, for protection in going through brushy country. Rough cloth generally was preferred for these, too, though they were sometimes of buckskin. In hot weather, men often made do with no other undergarment than a breechclout; otherwise the knee breeches that were normal wear in the settlements served in the woods also. Pantaloons, however, grew more common as time went on. Their great advantage was the saving in stockings. Moccasins, reaching above the ankle and snugly tied there, were by now the universal woods footgear.

Like Dr. Walker and his companions, most Long Hunters had their dogs along. Little was written about them; Ambrose Powell's Tumbler, killed by the big bull elk on Tumbler's Creek was one of the very few dogs ever mentioned by name in frontier writings. Folk were not given to sentimentalizing the dog as man's best friend or to making a pet of him. He was simply another domestic animal, of account only when he pulled his own weight, and was expected to. No thoroughbred, the common frontier dog ran to good size, ruggedness, and truculent disposition. He could stand up to most animals that prowled the woods—and sometimes, if necessary, to most Indians, too. All in all, a good creature to have around.

On their second trip, Walden's party crossed the Clinch River and hunted along the farther stream Dr. Walker had named the Beargrass. But some of Walden's men changed that to the Powell. The reason, so it is said, was the great number of trees they found on the bank with "A. Powell" carved into them. Some also give Elisha Walden himself credit for changing the name of Cave Gap to Cumberland. The party went through there, at any rate, and far enough down the Cumberland River to set up a station camp on Stinking Creek. The country still was as rich in game as Dr. Walker had found it; so much so that reports of the Walden party's success, later circulated by word of mouth among the settlements, may have had much to do with sending other men out to try their luck during the years that followed.

Others went anyway, whole hosts of them. Men like Uriah Stone, one of Walden's original companions, whose name survives in Stone's River where Andrew Jackson's Hermitage now stands. Men like Obediah Terril, described as a silent little loner with neither wife nor family, and maybe that was what first sent him out into the wilderness. No one knows what finally became of Terril, but he gave *his* name to Obey's River. Many Long Hunters left such memories over Cumberland country. There was Stoner's Lick, for big, slow-spoken Michael Stoner, Daniel Boone's friend, and Skaggs Creek up in Kentucky, named for a whole clan of Skaggses; one of them left his bones there. Some men are remembered for things other than names. Thomas Sharpe Spencer was a genial giant whose friends called him a very Hercules for strength. Big as he was, Spencer lived for some weeks in a hollow sycamore tree a little way north of present-day Nashville. Indians in the neighborhood kept him holed up there, but he outlasted them and stayed on the Cumberland for years, none the worse for the experience.

Not all Long Hunters were that nervy. The fear of Indians sent

more than one faint heart home for good. Then too there were discouragements like the one suffered by Abraham and Isaac Bledsoe, a pair of brothers hunting somewhere about the Cumberland's Big South Fork. They returned to their station camp one day and found that Indians had been there and made off with the proceeds of a whole season's hunt. Either furiously or philosophically, we cannot tell which, the brothers recorded their frustration in an eloquent carving on a tree trunk: LOST 2300 DEERSKINS RUINATION BY GOD.

Always, and with justice, Indians made the long hunt a hazardous proposition. Cumberland country still remained a hunting ground jealously defended by any number of tribes from neighboring regions. Defeat in the French and Indian War had only tended to bury the hatchets of ancient enmities—as between Shawnees and the Cherokee, for example—and bring the tribes together against the common foe. Thus the Long Hunter was fair game. He ran a calculated risk, and knew it. It was a big country, so that even a large party might range over it for months, finally pack their skins out, and never see Indian sign or be molested. Yet losses like the Bledsoes' were not uncommon and there was, too, the ever-present possibility of a hunt suddenly transformed into a running skirmish with some chance band of braves.

Such men as Kaspar Mansker, in fact, ended up with reputations as Indian fighters rather than as Long Hunters, good hunters though they were. As an old man full of years and wisdom, this German immigrant who had been born on a ship in mid-Atlantic often looked back and recalled incidents in a storybook life for early Tennessee historians. One thus handed down to posterity concerned his encounter with a brave who tried to lure him into an ambush by imitating a wild turkey's gobbling. It was a common Indian trick that fooled many a poor greenhorn, but never Kaspar Mansker:

. . . He thought two could play at that game, but that his was the most dangerous part, being the "moving object." . . . He approached so cautiously that he designated the tree behind which was his adversary. The human gobbler was there, certain. Art was now to make him "uncover." So, keeping his left eye upon that tree, and the muzzle of "Nancy" in the same direction, he moved along. . . . The distance was greater than an Indian would be likely to fire, but just right for "Nancy." And she "wished to speak to him." He was sure the Indian had seen him, therefore, he feigned to pass to the right. . . . The Indian began to "slip slyly along" to another tree. . . . Though moving slow and low, that left eye was on him through the bushes and wild grass. "Nancy" spoke to him, "bang!" The fellow fell on his face with a "yah!" "I took his old gun, and there she is. . . ."

Fighting Indians or hunting, there were none better than Mansker and very few as good. But he was also a great deal more: farmer, frontier militia officer, and, eventually, permanent settler on the middle Cumberland. In none of this was he unique, however. Most of his fellows were farmers and settlers essentially, going out on the long hunt only when they had growing sons to get the crop in and see to things back home. Being farmers, they knew good land when they saw it, and kept an eye out for it in all their wanderings. A good many even picked out choice tracts in the fertile creek bottoms or around the big salt licks and filed claims to them for future settlement, if and when.

As a class, for all that, Long Hunters were spoilers. In the heedless questing after profits to be gained with trap and long rifle, they launched a brutal ravaging of the land that was to set a pattern for all westward expansion. It has not stopped to this day, and is only now beginning to appall man with the tardy awareness of his own rapacity.

The long hunt was not sport but business, and the hunters went about it in that spirit. They went out in parties of as many as forty or fifty, partly for protection against the Indians but mainly because large parties could cover more country more efficiently and kill more animals. Since each man customarily had at least two packhorses to carry out the skins he took, plenty of provisions for a long stay could be packed in, and were. Otherwise the men traveled with the bare necessities: ample powder and lead, of course; bullet molds; axes and a few other tools; spare parts for rifles that might need repairing—and that was about it. The station camp set up in some selected location became a more or less permanent base. Shelter was provided by a rude, open-faced hut of poles covered with peeled bark, buffalo hides, or whatever else was at hand. In many places along the Cumberland, a cave or the lee of a shelving rock, still called a rock house in regional parlance, served more admirably than any hut.

From the station camp, hunters spread out into the surrounding country, usually in pairs for safety's sake, and to it they returned at intervals to replenish supplies and leave the pelts and deerskins they had taken. These were roughly cured, then stored on pole scaffolds high enough to be out of reach of scavenging animals, and covered against the weather with buffalo hides or sheets of bark. For packing out, the skins would be tied up in bales of a hundred or so, depending on their size and weight. Two bales, one slung on each side, were considered a normal packhorse load.

Most hunters did some trapping, chiefly of beaver. But the major take was in deerskins, always in demand by trading houses on the Atlantic seaboard, from where huge quantities were shipped overseas. Totally unconsciously, the Bledsoe brothers' lament for two thousand three hundred lost deerskins says a great deal about the rich bounty of this trans-Allegheny hunting ground—and about the unbridled slaughter that went on as well. No animal was safe from the booming long rifles. New Orleans and Spanish Natchez afforded good markets for bear oil and salted bear meat for any hunter willing to build boats and undertake the long downriver voyage. Much of this oil and meat, it was said, ended up as food for slaves on West Indian plantations. Buffalo hides appear to have had little or no commercial value, probably because their weight and their unwieldy bulk made it impracticable to pack them out. Yet as time went by the buffalo disappeared from the Cumberland more rapidly and completely than either the deer or the bear. Hunters shot a comparative few for the pot—tongues and marrow-bones, in particular, being favorite delicacies—but much of the butchery seems to have had no better reason than the habit of wanton killing. Stinking Creek, a common locale for station camps in the early years, was named for the stench of rotting carcasses left there in such profusion.

But the hunters who crossed the mountains from Virginia and the Carolinas took a while to work their way westward to the river's middle and lower stretches. Meantime, *coureurs de bois* had been hunting there a long time, and those tough woods runners were not the men to be driven out simply because British redcoats and British traders had arrived to take over France's old settlements in the Illinois. They stayed on, bothered hardly at all by the Englishmen's resentment of them. One George Morgan, a trader out from Philadelphia in 1766, complained in a letter to his partners back home that there were "twenty large Perrigous up from New Orleans, killing buffaloe chiefly for tallow." He knew because he had already begun to bring crews of hired hunters out from the Pennsylvania frontier and send them up the Cumberland; it was not the decimation of the herds that bothered him, but the French competition. At least, however, Morgan did better than waste good meat. Before long he was boasting of his salted buffalo beef: "All ours is now as good as the day it was killed, & will keep so for seven years . . . with the same kind of Coarse Salt & the same Cooper we now have."

Perhaps it would. In passing, though, one cannot help wondering. It was said that much of the miserable salt beef doled out to the poor seamen of His Majesty's Navy about this time was really ancient London drafthorses gone to their reward. Could some of it also have been, by any chance, Morgan's salted buffalo from the Cumberland?

Inexorably, so much undisciplined slaughtering had its effect. The supply of game was not inexhaustible, though the animals' last stand was a stubborn one. For years to come, a knowing man would be able to find a reasonable plenty of deer, bear, and even buffalo in the thick canebrakes and brushy coves of the river and her maze of tributaries. When in time the cabin builders and plowmen followed the Long Hunters into Cumberland country, many a man's family was kept from starvation because there was wild meat to eke out the first meager harvests. But the day of the long hunt as a truly profitable enterprise was soon over. By the early 1770s it was no longer possible for the large parties of other years to take skins enough to make a hunt pay. Thereafter, for a spell, the Long Hunter carried on as an individual on his own, and a little past his time. If he stayed anywhere about the Cumberland, and many still did, it was more and more with the thought of settling there some day, the hunting only a temporary thing now. The true Long Hunter, scornful of plow and cabin, wanting no other kind of life but the one he knew, had to go seeking farther and farther west—and there were some who did that.

Elisha Walden, who started the whole business, would die an old man in Missouri, away across the Mississippi River. So would Daniel Boone, though *he* would go as a disenchanted land seeker soured on the speculators, the sharp lawyers, and all the various frontier opportunists whose ways he never understood.

Boone was something of a latecomer among Long Hunters, actually. The message he carved on a tree near his home in North Carolina's Yadkin River country—D. BOONE CILLED A BAR IN TREE IN YEAR 1760—is remembered as a classic bit of historical folklore, but not until seven years later did he go out on his first long hunt, or try to. He was getting along in his thirties then, no longer a young man by frontier standards. He had a wife and a growing family to support, was beginning to feel a prodding need to get out and find some better prospects for the Boones somehow, somewhere. And the *somewhere*, as with others of his kind, lay always to the west. But he went astray in the tangle of mountainous country on the approaches to Cumberland Gap and had to turn back empty-handed.

His second chance came in the spring of 1769 when he happened to run across John Finley, an old acquaintance he had first met in 1755 while serving as a teamster in General Edward Braddock's disastrous march on Fort Duquesne. Finley had been an experienced Indian trader even in those days. And since the war's end he had been down the Ohio all the way to the Illinois and back, had traded and had fought Indians on both sides of the river, and was already building the reputation that would in years to come bring him a modest fame as one of the pathfinders of Kentucky. Plainly a man very much after Daniel Boone's own heart, and just the fellow to arouse Boone's restlessness anew. They were on their way for another try at Cumberland Gap by early May, with a party made up of John Stuart, a brother-in-law of Boone, and three other men from the Yadkin settlements. This time, with Finley as guide, there was no difficulty about locating the Gap. They passed through without incident, forded the Cumberland River at the ancient Warriors Path crossing, and followed the six-year-old trail blazed by Elisha Walden's party to Flat Lick on Stinking Creek. From there Finley led them northward through the brushy, broken hills and rocky outcrops of the Kentucky River country and so, at last, out into the rolling bluegrass of Dr. Thomas Walker's futile questing.

Game was abundant beyond the Yadkin men's dreams, and "fearless because ignorant of the violence of man," as Boone put it, revealing a dash of the philosopher in his nature. He is supposed to have said it, that is, though same abler speller than he must have been the one who later got it down on paper.

The hunt turned out to be two years long. They were years of discovery and deep gratification, of hardship and peril, too: all in all, the kind of experience that makes or breaks a man. It made Boone. Early on, the party had Indian trouble. Boone and Stuart, hunting by themselves along the Kentucky River, were captured by a band of Shawnees. They escaped and made their way back to the station camp, only to find it plundered and the rest of the party gone. They stuck, nevertheless, and went on hunting by themselves for several months till their people back home grew worried and sent Boone's brother Squire with another man to look for them. How they managed to find one another in that broad and unmapped wilderness must have made an epic of woods adventure in itself, and of some very good luck as well. They did it, anyway, and hunted together through the fall and winter. Then John Stuart was caught out alone and killed by another band of roving Shawnees. That was enough for the man who had come out with Squire Boone; he promptly said good-bye and headed for home. Still the two Boones stayed on, stubbornly refusing to panic, continuing to hunt till their provisions gave out and their powder and lead ran low. So Squire left to get more, packing out the baled deerskins and beaver pelts they had accumulated. But Daniel, his long absence from wife Rebecca and the youngsters notwithstanding, elected to stay behind for some further exploring. James, his eldest, was twelve: plenty old enough to keep the wolf off the Boones' doorsill a spell longer.

July was almost gone by the time Squire returned. In the meantime Daniel had done a good bit of roaming and grown steadily more enamored of the country. But he had seen so many Indian signs, also, that the brothers talked it over and decided to move south and set up a new station camp on the Cumberland River. There, probably somewhere among the wooded hills around what is now Lake Cumberland, they spent the winter of 1770/71. There too, according to the legend, Daniel was overcome by loneliness one day. He spread a deerskin on the ground, sprawled out on it, burst into sentimental song—and was surprised in the midst of it by Kaspar Mansker, possibly under the impression that a new version of the Indians' old turkey-gobbler trick was being tried on him. If any part of this tale is true, the hunters must have visited awhile and compared notes, and it would seem likely that Mansker told the Boones something about the good hunting on the middle

Cumberland. Had they chosen to try it, and had they liked the country as well as many others did, Daniel Boone's future might have turned out differently. But instead, come March, the brothers pulled out for the long trek back to the Yadkin.

A long hunt was never over till the hunter reached home, though. They were through Cumberland Gap and well down the Powell Valley when they fell in with a large party of Cherokee braves who relieved them of horses, skins, rifles, everything, and sent them on their way with a warning to stay out of the Cherokee hunting ground thereafter.

Thus ended Daniel Boone's first long hunt, and his last. It brought him virtually no profit: nothing but the small proceeds of the skins packed out by Squire the preceding spring. A pretty trifling return for two hard and dangerous years out of a man's life, had it been all. But it was not, for Daniel Boone had also seen the bluegrass of Kentucky and come to know it as few other white men did. He had fallen in love with its dim forests and its rich, rolling grasslands, what was more. And for Boone, now, there would be no contentment till he moved out there as a settler, to take land and make it his own.

The dream would disappoint him cruelly at last. It would make him famous, though.

5

Kentucky Fever

THE sturdy old Dutchman Stalnaker had escaped from captivity among the Indians long ago and come back to Holston River country to stay. But Stalnaker's place was no longer an outpost on the Virginia frontier. Other settlers were moving on past him these days, not only down the Holston but over into the once-remote valleys of the Clinch, and then the Powell as well. And in North Carolina the story was much the same: folk headed relentlessly westward, settlements now creeping down the Watauga River toward the headwaters of the Tennessee.

More men than Daniel Boone were looking in the direction of Kentucky, too, with something more than hunting on their minds. He was not the only Long Hunter to come home with glowing tales of the land out there beyond the mountains. Few were as vocal about it as Boone, though, or could match his great fervor. "I . . . Sepose I am no Statesman I am a Woodsman," he would confess ruefully in his old age. True enough, but Daniel Boone had a broad streak of the real estate promoter in him all the same, at least where the bluegrass of Kentucky was concerned.

The old homestead on the Yadkin failed to hold him long. He moved his family westward into the Holston Valley as so many others were doing, but for the Boones it would be no more than a stopover along their way. For two years Daniel farmed and hunted and roamed the country roundabout, and all the while he went on preaching the gospel of a promised land across the Cumberland to anyone who listened. Some did. By the fall of 1773 he had a group of friends and neighbors convinced, and a party organized to go out and found a permanent Kentucky settlement. There are indications it was plagued by some fatally bad judgment, however. The group was small: only five families, some forty people all told, and even they did not travel together. Boone, his family, and a few others led the way up the Powell Valley, with a somewhat larger party under a Captain William Russell following several miles behind. The reasoning behind such an arrangement is not clear, since both Boone and Captain Russell were supposedly experienced on the frontier. Nevertheless, Boone carried on almost to Cumberland Gap before he stopped to let those in the rear catch up. Then he sent his son James back to establish contact.

The boy did so, but instead of remaining to guide Russell's people in person, he simply gave them directions and started back to rejoin his father. Several young men from the Russell party went with him, taking two of their slaves along. It was another tragic blunder, for darkness caught them short of the advance camp. They were only three miles short, but they did not know that and perhaps young Boone was not sure of his bearings. They chose to stop and bed down for the night, anyway. And there, just before sunrise next morning, they were overrun by Indian attackers. Apparently it was a band of renegade Shawnees, though nobody ever was sure. A youth named Isaac Crabtree managed to cut and run. So did a slave named Adam. But they were the only survivors. Six men died, two of them under torture, slowly. One of those was James Boone.

When at last the two emigrant parties sorted out what had happened and met for the melancholy chore of burying their dead, little heart was left in them for the Kentucky project. Only Daniel Boone, clinging to his dream despite the grief and vain regrets that gnawed at him, still held out for going on. But the others would have none of it. And even Boone was shaken more severely than he knew, perhaps, for later that year he recorded an impression of the Cumberland Gap approaches that seems oddly contrary to his enthusiasm for the bluegrass paradise beyond. "The aspect of these cliffs," he wrote, "is so wild and horrid, that it is impossible to behold them without terror."

A softer man might have given up. Boone did not. But he was in debt now, still had no solid prospects, must have realized how slim were his chances of another try at founding a Kentucky settlement on his own. It was in something of a last-ditch mood, no doubt, that he made his deal with Judge Richard Henderson. Just how and when they first got together is not known. Some of their contemporaries suspected that Boone had acted as Henderson's secret agent as early as 1763 and that his job had been the scouting out of wilderness lands suitable for future settlement. Few modern scholars take any stock in that, but the two men may have been acquaintances of long standing.

History has all but overlooked Richard Henderson. A pity, too, for quite possibly America has never seen his like as an audacious mover and shaker in the sometimes parlous, often dubious, world of big-scale land speculation. A man with a shrewd legal mind for searching out every crack and cranny in the law, Judge Henderson undoubtedly had been looking westward, and thinking westward, for a long time before his term as a Superior Court justice of North Carolina expired in 1773. Mark the coincidence: it was the same year Daniel Boone's Kentucky plans collapsed so violently. At a guess, it would be about then that Boone went to work for Henderson.

The judge too had designs on Kentucky, far more ambitious ones than Daniel Boone's. The stumbling block for any would-be organizer of a land company, however, was the necessity of obtaining either a royal grant or a charter from one of the colonial governments. Neither was easily come by. But after much poring over old records and weighing of points of law, Henderson concluded that there might be a loophole in the case of Kentucky. Legal title to the lands west of the Alleghenies tended to be a complicated patchwork of claims and counterclaims. Usually, though, they all rested on territorial treaties between the British Crown and the various Indian tribes concerned. The treaties were set aside repeatedly at the Crown's convenience, to be sure, and the Indian always lost, but it was customary to make such maneuvers legal by drawing up new pacts to replace the old. The interesting point, to Henderson, was that two treaties still in force recognized the

Cherokee as sole owners of all the land from the Ohio River southward to their ancient holdings on the Tennessee. Therefore, he
reasoned, the Cherokee had a perfect right to sell as much of this
vast tract as they chose, to whomever they chose.

Anyone setting out to act on this sort of reasoning was going to
find himself treading pretty shaky legal ground, admittedly. There
were those in authority who would take a very dim view of it.
Henderson realized all that. But possession was nine points of the
law; by acting quickly, he thought, a bold man might bring it off.

Richard Henderson was a bold man. His plans sped so well that
March of 1775 saw more than a thousand members of the Cherokee
nation gathered in a great conclave at Sycamore Shoals on the
Watauga River. There and then, largely through the good offices
of Chief Attakullakulla, Henderson negotiated the deal he wanted.
It differed scarcely at all from the many treaties that already had
carved away much of the red man's American birthright, or from
others that would go on doing so for years into the future. The
Cherokee got trade goods to the value of some ten thousand
pounds. Henderson took title to most of the immense region lying
between the Cumberland and Kentucky rivers: roughly twenty
million acres in all, comprising a massive chunk of present-day
Kentucky and a generous slice of Tennessee. In addition, for another wagonload or so of trade muskets, rum, blankets, fancy shirts,
and whatnot, the Indians ceded a narrow strip of land running from
the Holston settlements to Cumberland Gap, thus providing an
access corridor to the purchase.

Yet the bargain was not wholly one-sided. The Cherokee were
selling only their claim to the land. Other tribes who claimed it
had not been consulted. The chiefs knew that, of course, but were
not worried; that was the white man's worry. No doubt Henderson
knew it, too; he had Daniel Boone to advise him, besides any
number of prominent frontier leaders who attended the proceedings. But the judge was not worried either. Future Indian troubles,
if any, could be dealt with. Already deep in his plans for a mammoth Transylvania Land Company, Richard Henderson was beginning to envision himself as rich as Croesus—maybe, one day,
even lord proprietor of a fourteenth colony. He was no small
thinker, Henderson.

Still, the negotiations did not go quite as smoothly as they might
have. The Cherokee had been at peace for a good while now, but

the settlements had been encroaching, crowding them for a good while, too, so there was latent edginess. A stocky young chief by the name of Dragging Canoe, possibly a son of Attakullakulla, spoke out passionately against Henderson's proposal. Giving up their tribal lands could mean nothing in the end but extinction for the Cherokee, he cried. And he warned: "As for me, I have my young warriors about me. We will have our lands!" But Henderson spoke soothingly to the elder chiefs. He repeated his assurances of friendship and good faith. He was an impressive figure of a man, by all accounts: tall, portly, with a bluff, square-chinned face and a manner of imposing dignity. The chiefs listened to him. Attakullakulla went among his people, counseling sober reflection. The Little Carpenter was an old man now. For most of his life he had watched the power of the white man burgeon like corn ripening under the summer sun, even as the power of the red man waned. Angry talk availed nothing. Was it not simple wisdom to make the best of the way things were?

Simple wisdom prevailed, after some days more of deliberation. Dragging Canoe was not resigned to the treaty, and would never be. But there was nothing he could do, finally, except utter his dour warning that the white men had bought themselves a land under a cloud, "a dark and bloody ground."

Tradition has him saying it to Daniel Boone. That is good drama, but unlikely, for the chances are that Boone was long gone from Sycamore Shoals by the time the treaty was signed. Judge Henderson had laid his plans in advance. As soon as there was reasonable assurance that things would turn out well, Boone was off for the Holston settlements to recruit a company of axmen and head for Kentucky. He got the men without difficulty: thirty of them, all seasoned woodsmen, well mounted, well armed—and all promised a bounty of good Transylvania land for their services. Boone himself was to get two thousand acres.

The projected route led up the now-familiar trail through Cumberland Gap, down Flat Creek, and across the Cumberland River, westward through the old hunting ground along Stinking Creek, then north to the bluegrass. There were men in the party who knew that way as well as Boone: his brother Squire for one, another old hunting companion named Benjamin Cutworth, the veteran Long Hunter Michael Stoner, and a number of others. They traveled rapidly, chopping their way where necessary, felling trees and clearing brush to make a trace suitable for large family parties of settlers. Their objective was the mouth of Otter Creek on the south bank of the Kentucky River, a spot Boone remembered from his long hunt six years before. It lay near the northern boundary of Henderson's purchase, and the plan was to build a forted station there, strong enough to stand off any forays by hostile Shawnees or other tribes from north of the Ohio River. The treaty, of course, would provide sufficiently against trouble from the Cherokee. Boone and Henderson assumed so, anyway—mistakenly, as they would see.

Before the end of March Henderson was on his way to Kentucky, too, with a company of thirty-odd prospective settlers and a long train of wagons and packhorses carrying tools, farm implements, seed, powder and lead—everything, in short, that a newly founded settlement in the wilderness would need. Spare horses and even beef cattle were driven along, the latter a precaution in case the supply of wild game in the promised land should fall short of . expectations. But the wagons were a typical mistake of the un-initiated. The trail through the Clinch and Powell mountains was far too rough for them, even after the passage of Boone and his axmen. So the wagons had to be abandoned, their loads shifted to additional packhorses. Still it was slow going. Livestock strayed, and men who went out to look for it got lost themselves and had to be searched out by others. The first week of April passed before the cavalcade toiled up into Cumberland Gap. By then, newcomers picked up along the way had brought its total strength to fifty or more. Some of these, sold on Henderson's grandiose program, signed for land on the spot. But there were others, like Captain Benjamin Logan from the Holston, who had no interest in Richard Henderson or his Transylvania Land Company, no intention of paying anyone for the privilege of settling anywhere, and joined the party only for protection in case of attacks by Indians.

No one was inclined to quarrel over this rather fundamental difference in points of view—at least not yet. Far to the rear, how-ever, Henderson's big deal already had begun to set off angry repercussions. A proclamation issued by Lord John Murray Dun-more, governor of Virginia, warned the public to have nothing to do with "the unwarrantable and illegal designs of . . . Henderson and his abettors." Colonel George Washington, a respected and influential Virginia landowner, wrote to a friend commenting on

". . . something in that affair which I neither understand nor like."
And North Carolina's Governor Josiah Martin bluntly labeled
Henderson and his associates "an infamous Company of land
Pyrates."

For the moment, though, Richard Henderson had some problems
much more pressing than governmental disapproval. A few miles
short of Cumberland Gap he was met by a messenger with the
first report from Daniel Boone. The advance party had reached
its destination at Otter Creek, Boone wrote, but only after a fight
with Shawnees that cost two men's lives and left a third gravely
wounded. The rampaging Shawnees, moreover, had slain two members of another band of settlers in the vicinity: one brought down
the Ohio River from Pennsylvania by a Captain James Harrod
several weeks earlier. Boone proposed to call the survivors of both
parties together, the better to withstand any other attacks. But, he
told Henderson in closing, "Your company is desired greatly, for
the people are very uneasy, but are willing to stay and venture their
lives. . . ."

Well, not quite all of them were, it appeared. The very day after
the arrival of Boone's messenger, William Calk, a member of a
group that had joined Henderson en route, noted in the journal he
kept that "we Met a grat maney people turned back for fear of the
Indians but our Company goes on Still with good courage. . . ."
But Calk too was a bit hasty. The party took four days to get down
Flat Creek to the Cumberland River. And there, by the fitful fire-
light of a camp at the Warriors Path ford, Henderson wrote glumly
in *his* journal: "The general panic that had seized the men we were
continually meeting, was contagious; it ran like wild fire; and, notwithstanding every effort . . . it was presently discovered in our own
camp; some hesitated and stole back, privately; others saw the
necessity of returning to convince their friends that they were still
alive. . . ."

In the four days the number of panicky fugitives had increased
to a hundred, and only one man of the whole lot could be persuaded
to stay with Henderson and go back. Next day, nevertheless, the
company pressed on. It was "a lowery morning & like for rain,"
wrote William Calk, but "We Cross Cumberland River & travel
Down it about 10 miles through Some turribel Cainbrakes. . . ."
Their troubles continued. A packhorse bolted, plunged into the
river, and swam across. It was finally caught only after a long and

arduous chase. Men who went out to hunt did nothing for the party's morale by coming back empty-handed with reports that they had seen Indian signs all about. A beef cow was slaughtered in lieu of game. Then to top off the trying day—and this seemed to upset Calk as much as all that had gone before—"Mr. Drake Bakes Bread with out Washing his hands."

The rainy weather held on, and their woes with it. But presently events relieved Mr. Calk of the necessity of eating any more bread baked by the unclean Drake. At Richland Creek, "We toat our packs over on a tree & swim our horses over & We meet another Company going back, they tell Such News Abram & Drake is afraid to go aney further. . . ."

Regardless of the setbacks, though, and as all the history books tell, the permanent settlement of Kentucky had begun. Both Boonesborough and Harrodsburg would hang on, somehow, through the bitter times ahead. So would the station soon to be built on Dick's River by Benjamin Logan and at first called St. Asaph. But little has ever been said about the fugitives Henderson and his folk met along the way. Who were they, and from where did they come? They were far too many to have been deserters from Daniel Boone's party alone, or even from Boone's and Harrod's together. Yet those two are generally accepted as the first parties of settlers in Kentucky, and the only ones there at that time. It seems likely that they were not. Individuals or smaller groups of three or four, perhaps, may have been venturing into the region for some years, finding land they liked and taking up so-called tomahawk claims they never got around to filing; of which, therefore, no records would have survived. It would be no very long step, after all, from the Long Hunters' half-faced station camp to a more permanent cabin of logs with a patch of corn nearby. And in the isolated coves and the deep, remote valleys around the upper Cumberland and the upper Kentucky, a lone man or a lone group could have lived indefinitely, unknown and self-sufficient, as descendants of the original pioneer stock still do in that country today. Not all such folk would be frightened away by Indians, either—anymore than those who stayed would have left any record of their staying. It was in the nature of things that not all the frontier story ever was formally recorded, or ever could be.

On April 20, 1775, an entry in Richard Henderson's journal describes his arrival "at Fort Boone on the mouth of Otter Creek,

Cantukey River where we were saluted by a running fire of about 25 guns. . . ." Writing that, the judge was blissfully unaware that some twenty-four hours earlier and somewhat more than seven hundred miles away, another "running fire" at the little Massachusetts town of Lexington had signaled the onset of rebellion against the government of King George III.

Throughout the back country the War for Independence was a virtual replay of the French and Indian War, with the difference that this time the Indians painted themselves and took up the tomahawk on the side of King George. To hard-pressed frontier folk that was no difference at all. They were the ones whose long intrusions had kept Indian resentment smoldering even in peacetime, kept the red man a touchy friend at best and quite as often an enemy, if undeclared. The old grudges ran deep, needing only redcoat officers promising to restore the Indians' ancestral lands, furnishing the guns and powder and lead to win them back, even paying bounties for the rebel scalps taken, so every settler and his wife believed—and Kentucky speedily became the dark and bloody ground of Dragging Canoe's prophecy.

Soon a growing spate of the fainthearted fled southeastward down the trail that was already coming to be called the Wilderness Road. It was met by a small trickle of militiamen hurrying to the northwest from the Holston and the Watauga. Among the early casualties of the war was Richard Henderson's Transylvania Land Company. The judge may have had some plan for setting himself right with Governor Lord Dunmore, but he had a new regime to deal with now. The House of Burgesses of a Virginia committed to liberty could afford scant time or sympathy for land speculators. The men fighting for their lives and their families' lives out in Kentucky could afford still less. Transylvania died with very little fuss, actually, and was regretted only by those trusting folk who had so eagerly staked their all on Henderson's big dream. It was but one among many complications destined to becloud land titles on the frontier for generations yet to come.

Most of Cumberland country remained untouched by war. Why should it not, since there was no reason for war where no men lived. The redbud and dogwood bloomed and faded along the creek banks as it had in ages before the white man's time. Oak and chestnut and hard maple, sycamore and hickory budded, greened, turned red and bronze and sere brown as the changing seasons passed and the river ran her ancient course in high tide and low. The Long Hunters and the persistent Frenchmen who still ventured there went warily, as always. But the Long Hunters were fewer now.

It was not only that the great hunting days were past. Many of the best of the hunters were caught up now in the Kentucky settlements' bitter struggle for survival, or were busy fighting redcoats back east. For the Cumberland it was a time of waiting.

6

The Land Takers

PEACE still was nearly four years away; there was no real promise of victory in sight. If the war in the north had bogged down in something like a standoff, the southern colonies had yet to feel its worst hardship in the fall of Charleston and the redcoats' brutal harrying of the Carolinas. But out in the Illinois that February, Colonel George Rogers Clark retook Vincennes, captured along with Kaskaskia the year before and then lost again to the British. With it he took another prize immensely uplifting for the border folk's morale: Lord Henry Hamilton, England's governor of the Northwest Territories—the man who paid for scalps, the hated hair buyer in person.

The year was 1779.

In the west, this recapture of Vincennes was the war's turning point. The frontier was quicker to grasp that than leaders back in Continental capitals, though the grasping was perhaps as much hope as sober reason. But militiamen from the Holston settlements had marched with Colonel Clark's ragtag little band of heroes, and news of their triumphal return got around, and it was bound to have a tonic effect on people whose zeal for emigration had been dampened by the Indian terror in Kentucky.

To Richard Henderson that may have smacked of poetic justice. George Rogers Clark was among the foremost of the opponents whose vigorous lobbying at Williamsburg had led Virginia to scuttle Henderson's Transylvania Company. It would be only fair, then, if Clark's victory out in the Illinois should contribute its bit to a partial recouping of the judge's fortunes. No man to give up easily, Henderson probably had begun to overhaul his ambitions even before he heard the news of Vincennes. Kentucky was lost to him; very well, forget it. But his treaty with the Cherokee gave him title to lands running all the 'way to the north bank of the Cumberland River, and it was probable—or at least possible—that a lengthy stretch of the Cumberland dipped southward into territory belonging not to Virginia, but to North Carolina. And North Carolina's revolutionary government had not thus far acted to outlaw Henderson's purchase. The hitch was that no survey of the Virginia–North Carolina boundary ever had been run west of the Alleghenies. Hence no one could say with any assurance just what lay on which side of the imaginary line. A little preliminary reconnaissance of the lay of the land might prove well worthwhile, however, from Henderson's point of view. He had nothing to lose, certainly.

Some such line of thought must have occurred to the judge, and been examined and found good. Good enough, at least, to send him out to the Watauga that winter for talks with some prominent citizens there.

The Watauga settlements had grown and prospered even in the midst of war. The people, mostly Scotch-Irish Covenanter stock, came of a breed that had known more than its share of persecution and hardship across the ocean, but had learned a stiff-necked self-reliance too. Isolated as they were, the settlements had elected to govern themselves and "share in the glorious cause of Liberty" under a code of laws that has come down in historic tradition as a remarkably enlightened document for its time, though no copy exists today. The people had raised "a company of fine riflemen" and solved their own particular Indian problem by soundly thrashing Chief Dragging Canoe and his Cherokee dissidents in two separate outbreaks. Two years after the second one the settlements had been organized formally as Washington County of North Carolina. The action had come at their own request when a survey revealed that the Watauga district was not a part of Virginia, as most people had believed till then. It was a development, one suspects, that gave Richard Henderson a deal of comfort and perhaps no little inspiration.

By and large, all this points up the fact that life on the Watauga was about as safe, pleasant, and well ordered as backwoods folk had any right to expect, considering the perilous times. Still, some Watauga men continued to think restlessly of better land farther west, as some on every frontier always did. This time, though—and it was partly Henderson's doing, no doubt—they were not all thinking of Kentucky.

Captain James Robertson was not when he appeared on the Cumberland early that spring of 1779, with a party that included seven other white men and one of his own black slaves. Shunning Cumberland Gap, they hit the river a short way below Smith's Shoals after traveling cross-country from somewhere around the Holston's mouth. Why they took that rather roundabout route, and on foot at that, we do not know. But they knew where they were going, plainly, and had a very clear notion as to what they would be looking for when they got there. They camped on the Cumberland no longer than it took to fell trees and chop out a pair of dugout canoes, then headed downstream.

How much Richard Henderson may have had to do with this party is only guesswork. It appears the judge had learned a degree of caution from his setback in Kentucky, and was calling no overt attention to himself this time around. But later developments would show clearly that Robertson was setting out with his blessing at least, if nothing more.

In his own right, needing no blessing from anyone, James Robertson already was well known as one of the stalwarts of the southwestern frontier. He would have been still better known had he been more of a self-seeker; as it was, his credentials were broadly based and solid. Robertson had led a contingent of Watauga men to Point Pleasant on the Ohio River and helped beat the Shawnees in the single battle—but a hard and bloody one— of Lord Dunmore's War in 1774. Elected captain of the Wataugans' "company of fine riflemen" in 1776, he had fought through all the settlements' campaigns against the Cherokee, and later followed up that service with nearly two years of striving to establish a lasting peace as North Carolina's agent to the defeated tribe. It was a job always difficult and often hazardous, but in it he had won a large measure of the Cherokee's trust and respect. He had also picked up a good understanding of their outlook and their ways— for whatever that might be worth out on the distant Cumberland. At thirty-seven he was a broad-shouldered, blue-eyed six-footer: a man of "fine appearance," so his friends described him. Before he died they would be calling him the "Father of Tennessee," for his best years still lay before him.

There was no very sound reason why the Cumberland should have been ignored so long by the land seekers. That good land was to be had in the river's great southward bend—land every bit the equal of Kentucky's bluegrass—was no secret. That had been known a long time, the word spread by any number of men like Kaspar Mansker, Uriah Stone, and others who had hunted there. Many years earlier one Jones, first name unknown, had even traveled up the Cumberland from the Illinois and tried to settle in a broad loop of the river not far above the present location of Nashville, then known as French Lick or Big Salt Lick. He had hung on long enough to give his name to the place, Jones Bend, before the fear of Indians drove him off. Then he had fled upstream instead of back to the Illinois, and finally wandered into the Watauga settlements. Many men there, James Robertson among them, had been acquainted with him and knew his story. In his time as Indian agent Robertson also had heard much about the middle Cumberland, no doubt, during long, solemn sessions before the sacred Cherokee council fires in their towns on the Tennessee—even as Dr. Walker had first learned of Kentakee so long before.

With spring's high tide making for a speedy passage downriver, the party reached Big Salt Lick with no difficulty. It may have been the objective from the start, for Robertson's own account says that he recognized the place from descriptions by Jones, and perhaps others as well. In any event, everyone in the party was pleased with the country. There was an abundance of fertile bottomland, well watered, with plenty of good timber for building. Apparently, too, the region's wild game was not yet badly depleted in spite of ten years' merciless working over by Morgan men, Frenchmen, and Long Hunters, for a cabin in the vicinity was found to be full of buffalo tallow.

It belonged to a colorful French-Canadian hunter and trader by the name of Jacques Thimote de Monbruen, who had come up the Cumberland for the first time in the early 1760s, well ahead of any

Long Hunter. He had been in and out of the country ever since and had probably brought his wife with him on at least one trip. There is a romantic tradition which holds that they once took refuge from hostile Indians in a cave somewhere on the river, and that Mme de Monbruen bore her first child while they lay in hiding there. If the story is true it must have been the first white baby ever born in Cumberland country, by a long margin. In any case, de Monbruen himself was destined to be a permanent resident; he would still be around at the founding of Nashville and would live to be one of the town's most popular citizens.

He was not present at this time, however, so that Robertson's party saw no more of him than his cabin and his buffalo tallow.

Their all-but-final decision was made on the spot. Four of the men would stay at Big Salt Lick to clear a patch of ground, plant corn, and put up a permanent or semipermanent station. Robertson led the others downstream on an extended reconnaissance that took them, ultimately, all the way down the Ohio River and up the Mississippi to Kaskaskia. From there—mounted now and driving a herd of Spanish horses Robertson had bought from a band of Osage Indians at a trading post on the Mississippi—the little party proceeded across the Illinois prairie to Vincennes.

Possibly this journey had another objective than a mere look at the Illinois, though that country too was reputed to be a good land for settlement. It was more than likely that Colonel George Rogers Clark would still be at either Kaskaskia or Vincennes, and Clark stood very tall just then as a leader in the west. His attitude—already known to be a touchy one as concerned schemes like Richard Henderson's—was not to be taken lightly by a prospective settler. Besides, Colonel Clark himself held Virginia land warrants to some three thousand acres around Big Salt Lick, bought up from French and Indian War veterans who had received them in lieu of pay. Whether or not James Robertson was aware of that we do not know, but it may have been a reason for the story that presently got about, and was perpetuated by some later historians, to the effect that he felt it necessary to come to some kind of terms with Clark. As against that, Robertson was a surveyor of some ability, in addition to his other frontier skills. Since some question already existed as to the location of the Virginia–North Carolina boundary line, he would almost certainly have taken observations on his way down the Cumberland—and if he did he must have come to the conclusion that Judge Henderson's suspicion was correct: the middle river basin was North Carolina country.

The chances are that Robertson did find Clark, if not at Vincennes then perhaps at Corn Island just above the Falls of the Ohio, at present-day Louisville, Kentucky, for that was the Robertson party's next stop. Nothing came of their meeting, assuming there was one. But the news that his Virginia land warrants might turn out to be worthless may have been one of the first in the dismal series of misfortunes and disappointments that would in time leave George Rogers Clark an embittered, whiskey-sodden wreck.

Robertson and his companions were back on the Watauga by August, having taken the four-year-old Wilderness Road past Benjamin Logan's station, down across the Warriors Path ford of the Cumberland and through Cumberland Gap. They had covered something over a thousand miles since early spring, a great part of it through regions where Indian tribes still warred on England's side against the colonies. A pretty strenuous half-year's work, one would think, for even the most hardened of frontiersmen. For them, though, it was but preparation for a more serious undertaking. An exodus to the Cumberland was organized and set in motion so swiftly that plans for it must have been laid out in advance, at least in broad outline, with action awaiting only Robertson's favorable report. In their final form, the plans called for him to lead the more experienced woodsmen and Indian fighters overland, driving everyone's livestock with them but carrying only such light gear as could be handled by packhorses. After a suitable interval to ensure the proper timing, Colonel John Donelson and the rest of the men were to push off by boat down the Holston and Tennessee rivers. With them would go the women and children as well as all the bulky supplies and household goods. Robertson then would be waiting for them with the packhorses at a rendezvous on the Tennessee somewhere south of Big Salt Lick.

This was not necessarily as chancy an arrangement as it may appear today. Flatboats—cumbersome, square-ended arks as long as thirty or forty feet or more, with the homely virtues of cheapness, ease of construction, shallow draft, and immense carrying capacity—had come into wide use as river transports on the frontier. They were thicker on the Ohio than anywhere else as yet. But there already was a boatyard at Fort Patrick Henry in the forks where the Watauga and the Holston met, and parties of hunters, traders, and occasional settlers had been venturing down the Tennessee for some years past, the settlers usually bound on the long, circuitous voyage to Natchez on the Mississippi. The traffic never had been precisely heavy, to be sure. In addition to Indians of doubtful goodwill, the Tennessee held such little-known but forbidding obstructions as Muscle Shoals and the great whirlpool called the Suck, to daunt all but the bravest or the foolhardy. But there was no way to travel westward *without* danger and discomfort, and a flatboat seemed to offer less of both, all things considered, than a march overland in the dead of winter. Too, the Donelson flotilla stood to avoid the worst of the hazards on the lower Tennessee if the rendezvous came off as planned.

It might be a very large and prickly *if*, however. There was no dependable map of the Tennessee available, or of the Cumberland either. Both rivers had been thoroughly charted some years earlier, but the job had been done for the British army by a Lieutenant Hutchins, and the outbreak of revolution had prevented the publication of Hutchins's charts in America. But Robertson had seen for himself that the two rivers flowed into the Ohio within twelve miles or so of one another, from which he reasoned that the Tennessee ought to lie no farther than some thirty miles south of Big Salt Lick. In fact, the distance was more than a hundred. But apparently no one foresaw that as a serious problem, Colonel Donelson least of all.

John Donelson remains a somewhat shadowy figure behind the recorded facts of his life. We know that he was a Virginian of good family and fairly influential connections. He had been a surveyor and land speculator for most of his life, with fortunes that appear to have been now up, now down. Perhaps it was one of the down periods that first sent him out to the western settlements. Practically all men of any substance on the frontier were prone to occasional fliers into land speculation. There was nothing wrong in that, per se, but it was easy for a serious speculator to step over the line and involve himself in shady practices, and Donelson had drawn complaints from North Carolina officials on that score. Apparently they grew out of some connection he had with Richard Henderson's Transylvania machinations. Whatever it was is not clear, though it may have been Henderson who first kindled his interest in Kentucky and then the Cumberland. His title of colonel to the contrary, Donelson never had been either soldier or Indian fighter.

His sole military experience, such as it was, had been the raising of a company of Holston militia to go out with George Rogers Clark on the Illinois campaign in 1778. But the company had somehow missed connections, never joined Clark, and never saw the Illinois.

Such a background did little enough to qualify him as a trail-blazer or a boatman capable of taming a treacherous serpent of a river like the Tennessee. At fifty-odd years, a big man described as "fleshy," he seems to have been neither success nor failure but something in between, still grasping—perhaps a little frantically now, as the years piled up—for the big prize life had so far denied him. He had in him the stuff of leadership, nevertheless, and a certain dogged tenacity to see him through the rough spots. He was the kind of man who could write sometime later, things gone all awry, his people starting to desert him: "Some intend to descend the Mississippi to Natchez; others are bound for the Illinois—among the rest my son-in-law and daughter. We now part, perhaps to meet no more, for I am determined to pursue my course, happen what will. . . ."

And so he would, but luck was never to meet John Donelson all the way, not to the very end. He had six more years to live, and would die violently. His seed would grow and flourish, though, and be long remembered as a proud Cumberland aristocracy.

By early October, far ahead of the Tennessee flotilla's pushing off, James Robertson was on the road to Cumberland Gap with the overland party. In the Powell Valley he fell in with an old friend named John Rains who had pulled up stakes and was on his way to Kentucky. But Robertson spoke so glowingly of the Cumberland that the Rains family changed their minds and decided to go there too. Strangely, after all the years of Kentucky fever, the Cumberland was at last growing popular. One John Buchanan already was on his way there with his three grown sons and their families. So was another group led by an Amos Eaton, leaving the Holston settlement where he had lived for seven years. Somewhere in the region, also, were two surveying parties, for both Virginia and North Carolina suddenly had awakened to an urgent concern with the westward extension of that doubtful boundary line. In charge of Virginia's party was that oldest Cumberland hand of them all, Dr. Thomas Walker. The little doctor was in his sixties now, but still wiry and spry. He had prospered greatly despite his old failure to find Kentakee, and was possessed of all the land one man would ever need; still, though, he was looking westward with pioneering vision. As for his opposite number—it was due to something more potent than coincidence, surely, that Richard Henderson had his own crew out to run the line for North Carolina.

Each of these parties seems to have known about the others, but no two traveled together. The surveyors, forced by the nature of their work to take a straight course through any and all obstacles, had the roughest going and soon lagged far behind. The settler parties took Daniel Boone's road across the ford of the Cumberland and westward to Flat Lick, the Long Hunters' old station campground. But instead of turning north from there, they all held on westward, each party by its own route. They went slowly, stopping to hunt when necessary and always picking ways that afforded suitable grazing for their livestock. Most of these people, like most early pioneers everywhere, were men of property. Many, probably the great majority, were slave owners. John Rains had several horses and more than a score of beeves. James Robertson had his herd of fine Spanish horses from the Illinois, and his party's procession of animals included sizable droves of sheep and hogs in addition to the cattle: all these besides their string of packhorses.

The Robertson party made the slowest time: three months to Big Salt Lick. Robertson apparently chose to bear somewhat to the north of the other groups, heading out across the treeless plains of northwest Kentucky, the so-called Barrens, before cutting southward for the Lick. No party's route is exactly known, however. Of difficulties met and overcome along the way there were remarkably few, or few worthy of mention, anyway, in any of the scattering of journals that were kept. Getting masses of reluctant, butt-headed livestock up and down an endless succession of stony, step-sided creeks was a perishing nuisance, for certain, but quite in the nature of everyday experience: something to be done, not cried over. So was the necessity of forcing one's passage through the all-but-impenetrable canebrakes that choked every watercourse. The cane grew as tall as twenty-five feet, varied "from the thickness of a quill to that of one's waist" and had a nasty trick of bending pliantly before a man or an animal only to spring back and slash the next in line like a whiplash. The British Lord Henry Hamilton, taken down the Wilderness Road a prisoner after his capture at Vincennes, commented bleakly that "the difficulty of marching through such a country as this is not readily imagined. . . ." But the present marchers were mostly veteran Long Hunters, or at least men seasoned to this country sufficiently to take the diffculties as they came. And if the womenfolk complained—surely there were *some* who wondered querulously what evil star ever possessed their men to come so miserable a journey—why, it was woman's lot to suffer, was it not, and her nature to complain? No one, after all, had thought it would be easy.

December brought a bitter cold snap. Modern weather records kept in Nashville show how rare have been years with temperatures low enough to freeze the Cumberland River, but 1779 was such a year. John Rains's people arrived on Christmas Day to find the river frozen so hard they crossed to the south bank on the ice, with all their packhorses and cattle. The Buchanans were there already, and one George Freeland had a station partly built a mile or so downstream. Freeland was one of the four men Robertson had left at the Lick in the spring. They had accomplished very little before the appearance of Indians in the neighborhood had sent them running for safety to the nearest Kentucky settlement, more than a hundred miles away. To their credit, though, they had come back, and all four would stick it out as first settlers on the Cumberland. Amos Eaton was there ahead of Rains also, but his party remained north of the river, living in tents and half-faced camps.

Early as these folk were, however, Kaspar Mansker had beaten them all. The old Long Hunter, ready to put down roots at last, was already settled in a station of his own on the creek to which he gave his name, some twelve miles north and a little east of Big Salt Lick.

James Robertson led his party in about the end of December. No rest for him, though; almost at once he was on his way again, southward this time to meet John Donelson on the Tennessee as promised. But his ignorance of the country caught up with him now, and he never saw the Tennessee. The thirty miles he had figured on grew to four or five times that, through winter weather that stayed bitter. He hit the Duck River and wasted days and miles scouting along its bank, never realizing it was not the Tennessee. When at last he did it was too late; he had lost his way, and knew it. So there was nothing to do but go back to Big Salt Lick and tell the Wataugans who had come out with him that their wives and youngsters, like his own, were . . . Well, it was a good question: *where* were they?

How they took it we do not know. No doubt they were shaken. No doubt Robertson was, for he loved his Charlotte, the gentle girl who had married him at eighteen. Till then he never had found the time to learn reading and writing, but she had taught him, and borne him five children too. . . . There still was hope, of course. Donelson's people were capable of taking care of themselves in a pinch. But these men were realists, already grown as used to endings wrought by tomahawk and scalping knife as to the happier kind. Meantime, there was work: Freeland's station to be finished, ground to clear, livestock to tend. It is not their courage that strikes one, nor the toughness of their fiber when worst came to worst, so much as the matter-of-fact quality of both. If these were heroic people they never knew it, would have deemed the notion silly had anybody tried to tell them.

January passed, and February, March too, and most of April. Then, finally, the Donelson party—or what was left of it—came struggling up the Cumberland. "It was a source of satisfaction to us to . . . restore to [Robertson] and others their families and friends, who . . . sometime since, perhaps, despaired of ever meeting again." So John Donelson wrote in his log of their odyssey on the day of arrival.

The little flotilla had survived pestilence and death, wreck and frostbite; had run a brutal Indian gauntlet that went on for days on end; had come through the tossing chutes of Muscle Shoals; had floated down to the Tennessee's mouth at last. Still the people had faced a long, grueling haul upstream: first the Ohio and then the Cumberland, both swollen and swift running in spring freshet. It was a passage virtually impossible—except that they had done it. Flatboats, large and unwieldy as they were, never were made for anything but downstream work. Donelson's own *Adventure*, we are told, was big enough to accommodate fifteen whites and thirty slaves, in addition to all her cargo: a crushing mass of dead weight to be powered into the teeth of a relentless flood tide by nothing but the muscles of men straining their hearts out at poles or clumsy gouge oars, or floundering over banks and through icy shallows with the thick towropes called cordelles. Not all the flotilla were flatboats, presumably. Some would be big pirogues, deep-laden too but built to make easier work of it. But all the crews were near exhaustion to begin with, worn down by exposure, short rations, and little rest. The upstream haul had started on March twenty-first. Wrote Colonel Donelson: "Set out and on this day labored very hard and got but little way. . . ." And later: "Passed the two following days as the former, suffering much from hunger and fatigue. . . ."

Still, they had made it. Or most of them had. There was a family named Stuart who had smallpox break out in their boat early in the voyage, back on the Tennessee. They lagged behind the main flotilla so as not to spread the contagion, and were cut off by Indians. "Their cries were distinctly heard . . ." wrote Donelson. Others were lost to Indians, too. A slave died when gangrene developed in his frozen feet. And there was a Mrs. Peyton who bore her first child somewhere above Muscle Shoals; next day the infant was lost overboard, somehow, in the confusion of a desperate effort to jettison cargo and lighten a boat that ran aground in a hail of Indian bullets.

Helping to balance bad news with good, though, was the presence of Judge Richard Henderson himself, picked up some way down the Cumberland. Henderson too had had his troubles. He had fallen out with Dr. Walker over the proper location of the boundary, set out to run his own line some way north of the little Virginian's, then discovered the middle Cumberland was safely in North Carolina by either reckoning. So all was well that ended well, and the jubilant judge already had sent men up to the Kentucky settlements to try to buy corn for his hungry settlers.

Before that spring grew much older the Cumberland Compact was drawn up and signed, no doubt after some ceremony of appropriate solemnity. Scarcely the milestone document it has often been called, the compact was chiefly a compendium of rules and conditions governing land sales. It did, however, include a provision for the election of a board of commissioners by the men of all the stations, and another for the recall of any commissioner who failed to carry out his duties in a manner satisfactory to the electorate. Some have said this latter was the first provision for an official's recall in any American code of laws. It was, at least, a reaffirmation of the Watauga men's sturdy bent for self-government. It was the compact's only lasting significance as well, for North Carolina presently followed Virginia's lead and annulled

Richard Henderson's Sycamore Shoals treaty, lock, stock, and barrel, leaving the settlers wholly on their own.

Eventually though, to look a little farther into the future, Virginia recognized the value of Henderson's efforts in behalf of
western settlement and rewarded him with a generous grant of
land along Kentucky's Green River. In that, too, North Carolina
followed suit, with a grant of good East Tennessee acres: two
hundred thousand of them. So the speculating judge came off
very handsomely after all.

It was more than would ever be said of many a hopeful settler.

Two hundred and sixty-three men signed the Cumberland Compact. An unknown number abstained, for reasons of their own. Of
them all, the signers and the nonsigners alike, there probably was
not one who stopped to think that the land south of the river still
was claimed by the Cherokee. Not even Henderson's purchase
gave any white man the right to build his station there.

7

The Long Siege

Dragging Canoe had been overruled by the elder chiefs at Sycamore Shoals, but the spirit of Dragging Canoe was strong. Had this young Cherokee hotspur possessed the charisma and the genius for organization of a Tecumseh or a Pontiac, he might have drenched all the southwestern frontier in the blood and misery of a mighty Indian war. He fell no great way short of that as it was.

Old peacemakers like Attakullakulla died and young warriors still chafed at the arrogant crowding of the white man, and in time Dragging Canoe came into his own. "We will have our land!" he had warned, and he never stopped fighting for it. When the riflemen of the Holston and the Watauga proved unbeatable in open warfare, he gathered a hard core of irreconcilables about him and retreated down the Tennessee River, ultimately to make a stand deep in the fastnesses where the river winds through a jumble of Cumberland Mountain heights. The warlike, the discontented, and the outcast of many tribes rallied about him. In time a good few renegade whites found a haven there as well. Uniting with the original band of unreconstructed Cherokee they took the new tribal name of Chickamauga, and for more than fifteen years the Chickamauga waged an unrelenting guerrilla war on the takers of their land. They raided the length and breadth of the border settlements in the whole region soon to be called East Tennessee. Their war parties ranged still farther, to mark the Wilderness Road with the graves of the unwary and the ill-prepared from Cumberland Gap far up into Kentucky. And, inevitably, the full brunt of their fury fell on the enemy nearest at hand—which meant a long and grievous siege for the newcomers to the middle Cumberland.

The cold winter of 1779/80 may have been a blessing of sorts. At least it kept Dragging Canoe's warriors close to their fires down on the Tennessee while the new settlers got wives and families safely out of half-faced camps and into forted stations. It was a comparative safety at best, though. The station building went slowly. Even with slave labor there were all too few hands to do the work, and some had of necessity to spend much of the time hunting. A station, even a small one, would usually include the cabins of several families besides a number of stables, storehouses and so on, depending on the builders' notions of their needs. All would be joined into a single defensive unit by the stockade of upright pickets, their own rear walls comprising part of it. A station of some size like Freeland's or the Buchanans' would enclose an area of more than an acre, becoming a virtual walled village. But all this meant a vast amount of axwork and rough carpentry. Such little refinements as laying puncheon floors and chinking cabin walls simply had to wait. More often than not it would be a long wait. Yet the winter passed with no sign of Indians and no apparent concern over the likelihood of an attack. The Indian was an old familiar neighbor to most of these frontier folk. They knew him too well to be cocksure about whipping him, should it come to that, but they were not panicked by the thought of him either. They had spent a good share of their years on earth learning to take trouble as it came, Indian trouble with the rest.

Spring brought planting time. Ground needed to be cleared and broken and the precious seed corn put into it; cottonseed and flaxseed, too, and vegetables, if a man was to feed his family and survive. But spring brought the Indians, too.

William Neely had come out to the Cumberland with James Robertson on the previous year's reconnaissance, had been one of the four left there to put in a corn crop and start a station. When the Indian scare sent all four running for their lives, Neely had run all the way home to the Watauga. He didn't stay there, though. Instead he brought his family, his several slaves, and his other worldly goods back to the Cumberland, by flatboat this time with Colonel Donelson. Evidently he was a man of modest affluence, not that it was any help the day the Indians caught him out. There is no record to say he was the first victim that spring. It would be a pretty grisly distinction in any case: first man shot down and tomahawked and scalped—and maybe beheaded too, to have his head borne triumphantly back on a pole to the Chickamauga stronghold of Nickojack or Running Water. They did that sometimes, and sometimes set the pole up within eyeshot of a station stockade, to taunt and frighten the people inside.

Jonathan Jennings was another who had come out with Donelson. It was his boat, in fact, out of which poor Mrs. Peyton lost her firstborn, and Jennings had a son taken by the Indians in that same skirmish. He himself and the rest of his people had come through only by rare good luck. In his case it was good luck wasted, for the Indians got Jennings, too, that spring of 1780.

They got a great many, the toll rising fearfully as spring merged into summer and summer ran its course. Some were cut down as they cleared the land they had selected, or worked in their fields. Some never came back when they wandered too far into forest or canebrake after strayed livestock. Hunters were fair game, and terribly vulnerable. Every rifle shot was likely to bring Indians prowling, to turn hunter into hunted. Few men dared try to go it alone, installing their families in cabins of their own on the land they claimed. One who did was an old German borderer named Frederick Stump, in his place a mile north of the river. He was a rather terrible old man, by some accounts; it was said he had once slaughtered a whole Shawnee war party back in Pennsylvania, all by himself with no weapon but his ax. A surly loner who had lost everything he owned in the war back east, Stump was on the Cumberland to rebuild his fortunes, and apparently did. He stuck it out, anyway, thus vindicating his stubbornness. But the Indians killed his son.

Slaves could be sent into the fields only under guard, and white men worked with rifles handy. The work went more slowly that way, though, and still there was no assurance against the unheralded shot from cover or the swift, slinking onset if a tired man relaxed his vigilance. The Indians grew bolder, bent as implacably on keeping the intruders from this land as their ancestors had been in the time of the old Frenchmen's Rivière des Chauouanons. A family of Renfroes had elected to leave the Donelson party soon after starting up the Cumberland. They turned aside into the Red

River, where they found a piece of land to their liking and put up a station. Before the summer ended they were all dead: sixteen of them, men, women, and children butchered without mercy, their station burned to the ground. Chickasaws did that, it was thought, for they too claimed this lower Cumberland country. There was, in truth, no lack of enemies anywhere.

The second winter set in. It was a bleak season, of doubtful promise. Corn crops had been meager, what with so many men killed at the plowing and the hoeing, or driven from the fields at harvesttime. But the great need, even with hunger a looming threat, was for *people*: more families with more riflemen to build the settlements to a strength sufficient to hold the land. James Robertson set out to bring them. The mission took him a long, lonely ride all the way to the Falls of the Ohio, nearly two hundred miles away. Then it proved a wild-goose chase. If there had been any prospective settlers at the falls, they had gone elsewhere. The rumor there, in fact, was that every station on the middle Cumberland already lay in ruins, the people all dead or fled away. Robertson scotched that in a hurry, but had to ride home with nothing more to pay him for his journey than a supply of salt. In spite of its name, Big Salt Lick was a poor source of salt, apparently, and so was Sulphur Spring near Freeland's. And salt was always a necessity, the more so if Cumberland folk were going to have to preserve the meat the hunters brought in to see them through.

This was only the beginning of James Robertson's long service to his fellow settlers. The quest for new people would take him to Kentucky again, and back to the Holston and Watauga country more than once. After that there would be a need for still more journeys, and always it would be James Robertson who made them: longer, more tiresome journeys still, to the North Carolina legislature at Hillsborough to petition for such tokens of official recognition as his people's own land office on the middle Cumberland; the creation of a new county of their own there; above all, for a settler's right under law to keep the land he cleared and held at so heavy a cost in sweat and blood. None of that would come easily. But much of it still was far distant, hidden in time yet to come. It is a safe guess there were more immediate cares on Robertson's mind as he rode home from that first trip to the Falls, early in the year of 1781.

Seven weeks he had been away. He found Charlotte waiting to

greet him with their sixth child, a son they would name Felix, born just two days before his return. He had little time to spend with the boy, though. The second night he was home the Indians made their first all-out attack and picked Freeland's station for the target.

They came silently, by moonlight. Strangely, there was no one standing sentry go. Or perhaps it was not so strange; the station dogs would be counted on to give the alarm. And so they did, but it appears the folk slept soundly that night. Robertson was the one finally aroused by the frenzied barking. It was very nearly too late by then. Warriors already were over the stockade, darting like shadows across the station yard, opening the gate for others. What followed was all confusion: a deadly, groping melee in the dark, the night made hideous by the flash and crash of point-blank gunfire, the choking reek of powder smoke, the high and eerie quaver of battle yells voiced as savagely by white men as by red. Up at Buchanans', more often called French Lick station lately, other men tumbled from their beds, caught up ready-loaded rifles and muskets—and then could only crouch at their loopholes, listening. Freeland's was a mile downstream. The road was narrow and hemmed in by canebrakes and dense scrub-cedar thickets: cover altogether likely to mask an ambush. They were too few to risk a sortie in any case.

All night they waited and listened. The wildest of the yelling died away after a while, except for an occasional scalp-prickling burst of Indian wolf howls, but a continued scattering of gunfire told that the station still held out. Then as the eastern sky began to lighten the firing slacked off. Impossible to guess whether that was good or bad, till presently a small party of volunteers ventured down the bluff to see what was going on.

Freeland's still stood, but barely. Powder-blackened, hollow-eyed defenders told of beating the first sneak onset back through the station gate and holding off succeeding ones. They had their wounded, though, among them two men dying. The Indians had tried repeatedly to set the station afire. Each time the flames were doused somehow, but all night long it had been touch and go. The horses, kept in the station yard, were safe. But the cattle had been penned outside the stockade, and most of them the Indians killed or stampeded. Most of the stored fodder for the livestock had been burned, as well. The prospect of starvation, grim enough before, suddenly looked grimmer still. In a hurried council of war it was decided that Freeland's had best be abandoned, and the station's defenses concentrated at French Lick. Possibly the decision was not unanimous, however, for George Freeland and a few others went back after some days and stubbornly remained there, while the Robertsons and most others never did. But for the present, anyway, the women, the badly wounded, and the small children were bundled onto horses, men formed a mounted guard around them, and the forlorn little cavalcade headed through the gate and up the bluff. The Indians were still about, but made no serious effort to interfere. They too had put in a grueling night.

This year of 1781 would be remembered in local history as the Cumberland settlements' worst, a long ordeal that discouraged all but the very steadfast. John Donelson was only one of many who called it quits as spring came on. He had taken his *Adventure* up Stone's River and settled his family on a choice tract known as Clover Bottom, a few miles north and east of French Lick. The cotton he put in there along with his corn crop is said to have been the first ever planted in Tennessee. But an untimely flood washed out the young corn, and Indian raiders interfered continually with the cotton picking. Before long they drove the Donelsons off Clover Bottom altogether and into the shelter of Kaspar Mansker's station. One winter there was enough for Colonel John. Perhaps he had begun to realize that this winning of the wilderness was not for him. Donelson was a surveyor by calling; was more speculator than farmer under the best of circumstances; was not really an Indian fighter at all, save by necessity. He took his family and left for the somewhat safer country around Harrodsburg, Kentucky.

Soon after the Donelsons pulled out, it came Mansker's turn to stand off an Indian siege. The station did not fall, but it was a near enough thing to make the old Long Hunter decide to follow the example of the folk at Freeland's. He and his people moved into French Lick station too.

Of the three settler strongholds now left on the middle Cumberland, French Lick probably was the strongest. Well sited for defense on its limestone bluff above the river, and with its garrison reinforced by many of the men from Freeland's, it was also the only station to boast a blockhouse at one corner of the stockade. The blockhouse still was not quite finished after more than a year, but in it was mounted a four-pound swivel cannon that originally had armed Colonel Donelson's *Adventure.* For all that, French Lick suffered the next Indian attack.

The several contemporary accounts vary so widely that sorting out what actually happened needs a touch of guesswork. All agree, however, that the attack came in broad daylight on an April morning. Possibly some sight or sound of Indian activity had been reported in the night, for it seems the station was not caught wholly by surprise. Nevertheless, the marauders struck swiftly and cut out a number of horses picketed outside the stockade. There was a savage little skirmish as the defenders rallied, then the yelling warriors vanished with their stolen horses down the landward slope of the bluff. Something about the way it went must have flicked egos on the raw, or perhaps it was simply that many of these one-time Virginians and North Carolinians had an innate feeling for good horseflesh, a pride of possession bred into their very bones. An instant hue and cry went up, a rage for pursuit and vengeance. Most accounts lay that to one James Leeper, a popular young man, newly married, a shade too eager to show off before his bride, maybe. Some other versions have James Robertson urging restraint. Still others say he backed Leeper, and he may have; Robertson was a great horse fancier too. A majority of the men were hot for the chase, at all events, and when two of the Indians rode back up the bluff and deliberately stopped just out of rifle range to jeer and gesture obscenely, there was no holding them. Horses in the station yard were saddled. The men mounted, all but one who was mortally wounded already. The gate swung open and they poured through at a gallop—but it was straight into an ambush they galloped.

The women watching from the stockade had not quite lost sight of them down the bluff when a ragged volley of rifle fire signaled the trap's closing.

Seasoned Indian fighters like Robertson and Kaspar Mansker slid out of their saddles and took cover in the thick cedar growth, shouting for the less experienced to follow them, else the whole party might have been annihilated in short order. It was close-in, no-quarter fighting, hot and brutal. Afterward, no man could recall more than disjointed snatches of it. There was John Cotton who had a sword, the only man who did, and with it he hewed off two Indians' heads one after the other. Edward Swanson, who had gone out to the Illinois and back with Robertson in 1779, had the muzzle of a warrior's musket rammed right up against his chest. He seized the barrel so desperately the priming was shaken out of the pan; the gun misfired, but the warrior wrenched it free, clubbed it, and knocked Swanson down, then was cut down himself by John Buchanan. James Robertson shot another Indian in the act of scalping one Samuel Barton . . . At some point in the hurly-burly the horses stampeded, creating a diversion that helped the hard-pressed settlers to close ranks. They were vastly outnumbered, though, and still surrounded. It was a losing fight until, abruptly, unexpectedly, the dogs got in among the Indians.

Charlotte Robertson was the one who turned them loose, according to popular tradition. But it was no radical departure for a frontier woman. The Robertsons' little daughter, Lavinia, was watching with her mother that day. As a grown woman, years later, she recalled how the dogs went for the sounds of combat the moment they were released, "being trained to fight Indians." We are not told how large a pack they made. Obviously it was large enough.

The doughty swordsman Cotton wrote of the dogs' attack in a journal he kept, and a grisly, nightmarish spectacle he made it, a bedlam of yelling men and snarling animals: the Indians beset from all sides, harassed, pulled down, bleeding from torn arms, legs, throats. Still it was hardly a band of conquering heroes who fought their way back inside the stockade at last. They had paid a fearful price for their rashness. At least seven men never got back at all, and were not even brought in for decent burial till several days later when it was certain the Indians had gone. Many of the survivors were wounded, four so badly they could not live. One was the firebrand James Leeper. He died in his pretty Susan's arms, leaving her widowed within a year of being wed. John Cotton told of a young friend of the couple, so affected by the sight of her tears that he ran out to the battleground, cut the scalp from a fallen Indian who still lay there, and nailed it to the station gate. In that place, at that time, perhaps it was a fitting gesture. There was no minister in any of the stations. James Robertson, a man of many parts, preached a brief funeral service for the dead.

This Battle of the Bluff, as it would be called forever after, was fought about where Third and Church streets intersect in modern Nashville. The victory, if so bare a staving off of catastrophe could be called a victory, undoubtedly was the turning point on the middle Cumberland. Few could grasp that, however, in the dismal weeks and months that followed. Had the Indians tried one more all-out attack it is unlikely they would have been repulsed again, for French Lick and Freeland's probably mustered no more than a score of able-bodied men between them. And had they gone under, the people across the river at Eaton's might well have lost their stomach for holding on. As things stood, morale in all three stations sank to its lowest ebb. The Indians' old hit-and-run harassment continued till no woman dared leave the stockade to milk her cow, no boy or slave to gather wood, without a rifleman standing over them. As the summer wore on, the war parties took to scorching the earth, laying waste whole fields in their savage determination to make the land untenable. They very nearly succeeded. More and more families pulled up stakes and left for Kentucky, "despairing," as James Robertson wrote, "of being able to accomplish the enterprise of settling the country. . . ."

One wonders why anyone stayed. Today's man has no true answer, anymore than he can explain with any real logic what spur it was that drove them out into Cumberland country at all. The hunger for land, of course; there was always that. And to the eighteenth century's way of thinking, this rolling, fertile wilderness watered by its clear green river must have seemed illimitable, a place where even the greediest man could have his fill of land. Yet that could not have been the whole story. Not that nor any of the whiskered clichés, like a frontiersman's inborn urge for untrammeled elbowroom; or the sturdy American instinct for independence; or the equally celebrated, natural-born cussedness that just plain had to break out into new country or bust. No; most men on the middle Cumberland had *had* elbowroom, a high degree of independence, plenty of outlets for high spirits, back there on the other side of the mountains. They had been reasonably prosperous to boot, and still they had come west.

One wonders: did anyone—James Robertson, say, or Kaspar Mansker, or tough old John Buchanan, sire of the Buchanan clan, or any of that kind—ever stop to ask himself why? We do not know. They never said.

But they stayed; a hard core of them stayed, and after a while, against all reason, a trickle of new settlers began. On Christmas night, that winter of 1781, a Virginian named William Ramsey led his party into Eaton's station and found "frolicking and dancing . . . in the different cabins."

ii

The

Frontier

8

The Public
Prosecutor

ANDREW JACKSON arrived on the Cumberland late in October 1788,
riding in the first emigrant train over the new Avery Trace from
East Tennessee. Tradition says that on the way the train was saved
from a Chickamauga war party one night only by the keenness
of his frontier-trained ear. Recognizing the hooting of owls around
the camp as made by no owls at all, but actually by Indians preparing to attack, the young man alerted his fellow travelers so
promptly the warriors retired without a fight. Or so the story
claims. On another night, Jackson is said to have shot a big she-
panther and tomahawked her half-grown cub when they attacked
the horses of the train.

One doubts that. There was very bad Indian trouble throughout
the whole region, for a fact; so bad the train was guarded by a
sixteen-man escort provided by the state of North Carolina. But
another quarter of a century would have to pass before Jackson
could be called any kind of Indian fighter. A town boy in the Carolina Waxhaws for most of his short life, he was no kind of woodsman either, and never would be.

No matter. The important fact about Andrew Jackson was that
he came to the Cumberland in the role of aspiring public prosecutor of the Western District of North Carolina. He was described
as riding a blooded horse and leading another; as owning a good

77

rifle, a brace of pistols, a half-dozen lawbooks, and a black slave girl for whom he had recently paid two hundred dollars. A pack of dogs followed at his horses' heels. He was a sapling-thin six-footer with eyes the color of blued steel and a mane of sandy hair that a girl he had once courted back in the Waxhaws suspected was "made to lay down with bear's oil." With him was his friend John McNairy, newly appointed judge of the Superior Court of the Western District. McNairy was twenty-six, a young man of excellent family and important political connections in the state. Jackson was twenty-one, an orphan of acceptable family background but no legal reputation nor any important connections save McNairy's friendship. It was only by a stroke of luck, in fact, that the North Carolina legislature had neglected to name a public prosecutor when it named McNairy and so left the way open for the new judge to select his own appointee. Between them, the two were expected to establish the rule of North Carolina law in a district of a thousand square miles or so, sprawled for some fifty miles along both sides of the river.

The country still was backwoods, still frontier. The day of the forted station was not yet over, though it was passing. The land was not yet won, but was being won. All the middle Cumberland was North Carolina's Davidson County now, with settlements spreading: Gallatin and Hartsville up the river from the bluff where French Lick had stood; Ashville a few miles downstream; Lebanon to the southeast; Franklin over on the Harpeth River. Many of the stalwarts who had seen the dark days through were still around. Kaspar Mansker had built another station on the site of the abandoned one the Indians had burned. James Robertson was out on Richland Creek now, not far from his old friend John Rains. The Indians had finally done in old John Buchanan, but the rest of the clan had a place on Mill Creek. Amos Eaton's old station was deserted, as were French Lick and Freeland's; the Eatons now lived on White's Creek. All these holdings lay within a snug little radius of ten miles or so of Nashville, the seat of government—such as it was—of the Western District.

Earlier the town had been called Nashborough, and before that simply the Bluff. It was no more than a straggle of log buildings clustered in a rough square around a courthouse of hewn logs. Cedar trees still stood among the buildings, and the stumps of others dotted the dusty square. The courthouse itself measured

less than twenty feet by twenty. It had a rough porch across the front, but no other appurtenance either of beauty or of comfort. In addition, besides the cabins and half-faced camps of its inhabitants, the town consisted of a pair of taverns, a busy whiskey distillery, and Mr. Lardner Clark's general mercantile establishment stocked with wares brought by packtrain all the way from Philadelphia. The meanest of these buildings probably was more impressive than the residence of law and order.

There is no reason to assume this meant that Cumberland people, by and large, were overly tolerant of crime. Any frontier was tough, however. It had to be; and the same toughness that helped fight off Indians, starvation, and other hardships led naturally to a certain impatience with the workings of due legal process. Inevitably, too, the first settlers had been followed by others of less staunch character. Already the middle Cumberland was becoming something of a crossroads for travelers overland from East Tennessee, upriver from the Illinois, and even from the lower Mississippi by way of the old Chickasaw Trace, soon to be better known as the Natchez Trace of ominous repute. On average alone, some who traveled these routes would be misfits and ne'er-do-wells seeking the easy pickings a new settlement always seemed to promise. Back there in East Tennessee, besides, the abortive "lost state" of Franklin had recently died its untimely death in a flurry of bitterness and strife. None of this was conducive to any great respect for the law. Clearly, the new judge and his lean young public prosecutor had their work cut out for them.

They wasted no time in getting at it. McNairy called the Superior Court's opening session to order in November. One of the first cases of which there is any record concerned the alleged theft of a beaver skin. Whether Andrew Jackson got a conviction, the record does not say. Inside of a month, though, he had won judgments in a total of seventy cases, most of them for the collection of debts long overdue.

Bad debts, it turned out, were the Western District's besetting sin. In the past, lacking any court of law, honest creditors had had no recourse against a large and arrogant body of debtors who simply refused to settle up. The situation was a flagrant scandal, and correcting it became the new prosecutor's most urgent business. Very shortly it also became his golden opportunity. Creditors, as a class, included a majority of the most substantial citizens of the district: men it would pay an up-and-coming young attorney to cultivate. If they found Andrew Jackson a willing and able champion, Jackson found them a very profitable clientele. Soon they were giving him all the private law practice his official duties allowed time for. And since cash money was scarce, and much of it still the proverbial, worthless Continentals, he took most of his fees in the two media of exchange most common locally: slaves and land.

Contemporary documents indicate that slaves were already numerous in the Cumberland settlements. And in a pioneer region constantly in need of labor, a prime slave was readily negotiable. Thus, early in his career and quite in the natural order of things, Andrew Jackson took on the trade in black flesh as a sideline. Even in those days, in the well-ordered plantation society back east, there was a certain stigma attached to the slave *trader* as against the mere slave *owner*. Apparently, though, such nice distinctions did not hold on the frontier. Abolition, in any case, was not yet a force to be reckoned with. As for land, it was so plentiful that almost any well-to-do citizen was likely to own more of it than he knew what to do with. Not necessarily the best land, of course; a great deal of it was remote, neither cleared nor fenced, only sketchily surveyed. But a man had merely to hold onto it and sooner or later the steady growth of settlement would push the value up and yield him a tidy profit. It required no special foresight to perceive that, just a healthy ambition and a normal amount of faith.

Young Jackson had both. In no long time he began to lay the foundations of future affluence.

He found the middle Cumberland very much to his liking. Jackson had squandered a modest inheritance in Charleston, so was no stranger to city high life. But due perhaps to its crossroads location, Nashville was a livelier town than many on the frontier. Its taverns might, as a traveler complained some years later, keep sleeping quarters that were "open at all hours of the night for the reception of any rude rabble that had a mind to put up at the house." Too, linsey-woolsey and homespun cotton might be seen a deal more commonly than silk or broadcloth. Nevertheless, an amazing number of women, even among the first settlers, had managed to bring out their fine dresses and fancy bonnets, and many a man appeared in public in the buckled knee breeches, waistcoats, ruffled shirts, and snowy stocks worn by gentlemen back east. The town had two distinguished preachers: Dr. John Craighead officiating for the Presbyterians and a Dr. Ogden for good Methodists. It also had its premier physician. Today Dr. John Sappington is best remembered for the pills he made up and dispensed, their formula described as "equal parts of mystery and sugar coating." It was the doctor's custom to step outside his office and ring a bell at a stated time each morning. Every patient in town then knew it was time to take a pill. If Andrew Jackson ever needed Dr. Sappington's services, however, no one bothered to make a note of it.

With a thousand square miles to cover, the Superior Court actually functioned as a Circuit Court, for all practical purposes, and its judge and public prosecutor spent a good part of their time riding that circuit. Occasionally they went by boat, no doubt. River traffic was developing on the Cumberland, so there would be boatmen with skiffs or pirogues for hire. It would be slow, though, the lazily winding river almost always the long way 'round to anywhere. More often they rode horseback and put up at some station or settler's cabin wherever night happened to catch them. Often enough they slept in the open, eating cold smoked pork and corn pone from their saddlebags and spreading their blankets on the ground.

In any small outlying settlement where visitors were rare and opportunities for amusement limited, the presence of the court tended to become a gala occasion, with folk gathering from the surrounding countryside in a spirit of robust fun. At such times other young men frequently made the most of their chance for "familiarities with females of unlaxed morals," but never Jackson. At least that was the story always told by his friend and fellow attorney John Overton. Yet Jackson had enjoyed a notable reputation as a gay blade back in the Waxhaws. It may be that official responsibilities brought an awareness of public opinion.

An attorney who spent much of his time and energy in seeking judgments against deadbeats could hardly avoid making enemies, though, and Andrew Jackson was not one to sidestep trouble. In his old age he himself used to tell of his encounter with the town bully at Gallatin. He stood in the street in conversation with an acquaintance, he said, when a great, hulking fellow jostled him in passing and trod heavily on his toes. He took no notice and went

on with his conversation, supposing it an accident. But back the big man came, jostled him, and stepped on his toes once more. It happened a third time, according to Jackson's story, though such patience on his part seems a bit much. It was enough, anyway. The young prosecutor turned, tore the top rail off a fence at hand and doubled his man up with a mighty jab in the belly. The big fellow collapsed, retching and gasping for breath, and "I stamped on him," Jackson recalled with satisfaction. "Soon he got up, savage . . . I stood ready with the rail pointed. He gave me one look, and turned away, a whipped man, sir, and feeling like one. . . ."

But the onset of law and order could do nothing to curb the Indians who continued to make life hazardous all over the Western District. War parties still roamed and raided virtually at will: not only Dragging Canoe and his Chickamaugas but the bellicose

Creeks from farther beyond the Tennessee River. The red warriors had learned their lesson well. There were no more Battles of the Bluff, no more long sieges of stations. It was pure guerrilla warfare now, stealthy and relentless. Corn- and cottonfields still had to be worked under guard, even on the outskirts of Nashville. Not too many years later, writing when local memories still were strong, the Tennessee historian Judge John Haywood reckoned the toll at a victim every ten days throughout 1789. He quoted a grim chapter and verse:

In the spring a man named Dunham was killed just outside his own station; a Joseph Norrington and another Dunham were killed later. Several others whose names no one remembered were killed that summer. Two emigrant families were slaughtered on Sulphur Fork of the Red River. The hunters Evan Shelby and Abednego Llewellen were killed. One John Blackburn was found scalped, a spear still sticking in him, near the Buchanans' station on Mill Creek.

The Indian depredations may have helped put point to an idea that must have been brewing on the middle Cumberland for a long time past. Cumberland men had been on their own from the day of James Robertson's first westward faring, with precious little help from anybody. Understandably, they were growing tired of it. The War for Independence had been won a good five years earlier, yet England still kept garrisons in her forts up in the Northwest Territory and showed no sign of giving them up. There was excellent reason to believe she expected to take over her former colonies again, or their western regions at any rate, in her own good time. Certainly no one on the Cumberland had a jot of confidence that the new federation of United States could or would do anything about it. The state of North Carolina had not even joined —not that North Carolina ever had been much protection for her Western District, come to that. It was high time that the lone and isolated settlements looked around for a strong-armed friend. And Spain appeared to be the best bet; indeed, the only one. Spain was the one power capable of matching British strength on the North American continent. What with the Spanish Floridas and Louisiana, the Spanish already had the Cumberland settlements encircled on the south and west. They were allies of the powerful Creeks and other southwestern tribes, besides. As the main suppliers of rifles, powder, and all sorts of trade goods needed by the tribes, they were in a position to stop much of the raiding on the middle Cumberland if they chose. Then too, Spain held the mouth of the Mississippi, and with it the power of life or death over all waterborne commerce with the world outside. As yet such commerce amounted to little, on the Cumberland. But presumably it would grow as the settlements prospered—with Spain's encouragement. It was significant that Kentuckians, whose own flatboat trade depended on the Ohio and the Mississippi, were also thinking in terms of a Spanish connection about this time.

The upshot of it all was some rather heavy-handed backwoods intrigue not completely unraveled to this day. And it was altogether in character for Andrew Jackson to involve himself before he had been six months in Nashville.

As early as mid-February of 1789 he sat down to write a letter to Daniel Smith, a one-time officer in the Continental Army who had come out to the Cumberland with Dr. Thomas Walker's survey party ten years before and stayed on to become brigadier general of militia for the Western District. The letter introduced a Captain Fargo who was on his way to New Orleans to seek a Spanish trading license. It was Jackson's notion that if Smith interceded in Fargo's behalf with Governor Esteban Miró of Louisiana, Fargo could in turn enlist the governor's help in "having peace with the Indians."

How Andrew Jackson and the ambitious trader happened to get together is a mystery. Some of the circumstances suggest the kind of casual tavern acquaintance that can ripen out of hand over a drink too many. The captain's name was not "Fargo," but André Fagot. He was a Frenchman who had indeed traded up in the Illinois at one time, but it appears his chief asset was a glib tongue. He got his letter from General Smith, but it introduced him somewhat obliquely as the bearer of a verbal message for Governor Miró's ears alone. The letter also included the fulsome reminder that, "We have honored our district with Your Excellency's name. . . ." In closing, Smith invited His Excellency's reply.

The Western District's rechristening was a fact. The middle Cumberland was now, without a by-your-leave from the North Carolina legislature, the District of Mero. It was a misspelling of Miró's name, to be sure, but frontier spelling was offhand by nature; the compliment was sincere enough for all that. There were designs afoot which a newcomer like Andrew Jackson only guessed at, probably. About the same time James Robertson was writing to

Governor Miró too, and dispatching his letter by a trusted son-in-law. Robertson was the one man who, more than any other, could speak for the whole middle Cumberland. His statement of his people's favorable sentiments toward Spanish authority was no light thing. "Nature," he added pointedly, "seems to have designed the whole Western Country to be one people. . . ."

Don Esteban Miró was a diplomat. He answered both letters with lofty courtesy, expressing his gratification at the great honor paid him and sending warm regards to his good friends on the Cumberland. As to General Smith's verbal message, he was noncommittal. He anxiously awaited the consequences of an "operation" Smith expected to carry out in September. Only to the Spanish colonial authorities in Madrid did His Excellency confide that, come September, one delegation from the District of Mero would petition the North Carolina legislature for an act of separation, while another would be in New Orleans "with the object of placing the territory under the dominion of His Majesty." In a gesture no doubt inspired by his own wholehearted approval of the object, Don Esteban presently proclaimed liberal Spanish land grants to all American settlers favorably disposed toward Spain.

Among the first takers was none other than Andrew Jackson, who acquired a valuable acreage at Bayou Pierre, some miles up the Chickasaw Trace from Natchez. There is no evidence he had delved any deeper into the mysterious affairs of his "Captain Fargo," or was pleased with the prospect of Spanish dominion if he had. Within a very few years, in fact, Andrew Jackson would be making no effort to conceal a dislike of Spain second only to that he felt toward England. But Jackson had an acquisitive feel for land and was very much a young man with a burning itch for wealth. Many who knew him remarked on that, not all of them in terms of admiration.

For good and sufficient reasons, nothing ever came of the Cumberland's flirtation with Don Esteban. This in spite of the fact that there were more than Cumberland men involved. A good many in East Tennessee leaned Spain's way for a while, or were suspected of it. The famous John Sevier was one. William Blount, a land speculator and politician with many irons in the fire, was another. So was Dr. James White from still farther east, a former delegate to the Continental Congress and a recent appointee as United

States Indian agent for the Southern Department. Nevertheless, Governor Miró had been much too sanguine in his report to Madrid. Many of his own Louisianans were less than happy with the prospect of welcoming a pack of rough and ready American frontiersmen as fellow citizens. Don Luis de Panaverte y Cardenas, the bishop of Louisiana, for one, declared that ". . . the toleration of our government has introduced into this colony a gang of adventurers who have no religion and acknowledge no God, and they have made much worse the morals of our people by coming in contact with them in their trading pursuits. . . ."

Undoubtedly, too, there were plenty of men on the middle Cumberland who felt less cordial toward Spain than Smith and Robertson had led His Excellency to believe. The Spaniards' strict control of trade down the Mississippi was a constant sore point among hard-bitten frontier rivermen. There were widespread suspicions, as well, that Spain was inciting many of the bloody Indian raids in a deliberate campaign to soften up the settlements for just the sort of take-over Don Esteban anticipated. Even Smith and Robertson, in making their cordial overtures to His Excellency, may simply have been endeavoring to maintain friendly relations with a potentially dangerous neighbor while keeping their options open as regarded the new and none-too-promising union back on the eastern seaboard. One way or another, in any case, there were two sides to the question of Spanish affinity.

September came and went and no more was heard about Smith's "operation," whatever it may have been. Then in November, North Carolina finally voted to become one of the United States, and come December the legislature deftly brought the whole Spanish conspiracy to nothing—if indeed there ever had been one.

Both the District of Mero and the defunct state of Franklin got their act of separation. It was only a device making it possible for North Carolina to offer her western territory to the federal government, however—and thus rid herself of a frontier that promised little but knotty problems and scant revenues for years to come. The offer had been made once before, and Congress had turned it down. But this time no hitch occurred; Congress accepted and before its people were quite sure what had happened the District of Mero had another change of name. It became part of the Territory of the United States South of the River Ohio, and it got a governor of its own. He was William Blount of East Tennessee, and if the appointment smelled of behind-the-scenes horse trading, what was one to make of Daniel Smith as the secretary of the territory, or James Robertson in Smith's old post as general of the Davidson County militia, or Dr. James White going to Philadelphia as the new territory's first representative in Congress? Andrew Jackson was not forgotten either. Not only did he keep his office as public prosecutor "during good behavior," but the office itself was dignified with the impressive new title of attorney general. The sudden turn of events brought something for everyone, it seemed, except Don Esteban Miró.

Very shortly, another outbreak of Indian raids fell on the middle Cumberland. Whether or not Spanish pique had anything to do with it could not be proved, of course. Again Judge Haywood recorded only the facts, in the homely terms of a country not yet grown large enough to settle for statistics instead of people:

> . . . They killed Alexander Neely at the fort where Anthony Bledsoe had lived; also a young woman of the name of Morris. . . . They killed at Mayfield's Station John Glen who had married the widow Mayfield, and three persons at Brown's Station a few miles from Nashville. They wounded John McRory, and caught and scalped three of Everett's children and killed John Everett. . . .

The Spanish intrigue died hard. At least the rumors of it did. They would linger for some years to come, and the name District of Mero would linger too, but mostly as a reminder of what might have been, maybe. For better or for worse—and plenty of folk still wondered which—the Cumberland settlements were wedded to the United States.

Scarcely had the maneuvering ended when Andrew Jackson was wedded too. There should have been nothing remarkable about that, to be sure. The prospering young attorney was an extremely eligible bachelor, none more so on the Cumberland. It happened, though, that he married another man's wife.

9
Not Precisely
Made in
Heaven

FROM the first, circumstances promised no easy course for the romance of Andrew Jackson and his Rachel. The gloomiest of soothsayers, all the same, would have thought twice before venturing to predict the long bittersweet saga that would come of it. In fact, love probably caught them both unaware, as love is likely to do.

Shortly after young Jackson arrived in the Western District he took lodgings at the Widow Donelson's big blockhouse. Colonel John had been dead three years then, killed either by Indians or white outlaws; some had it one way and some the other, and no one ever knew. But he had been waylaid on the road from Kentucky, riding south to the Cumberland in preparation for moving back to stay, and after his death Mrs. Donelson had gone ahead with the move. Her husband had done well in the last two years of his life and young John was following in his father's footsteps very ably, so there was no pressing need for her to take in lodgers. What with the ever-present threat of Indian war parties, though, an extra man with a rifle and a brace of pistols was always welcome. The arrangement was hardly a convenient one for Jackson, since the Donelson place was more than ten miles from Nashville, and on the other side of the Cumberland River at that. But no doubt he was well aware that, even with the colonel dead, the Donelsons were a large, well-to-do, and influential clan, well worth cultivating.

It was not long before the presence of the Widow Donelson's daughter Rachel became an added attraction. "As gay, bold and handsome a lass as ever danced on the deck of a flatboat . . ." wrote the ubiquitous Judge Haywood, perhaps going a bit overboard in recalling that Rachel had come down the Tennessee in her father's *Adventure* at the age of thirteen. Somewhat more to the point, a girl cousin of Rachel's own generation called her "irresistible to men," and went on to sigh over her raven hair, her splendid figure, the dimples that lent charm to her ready smile.

At the time, however, she was doing no dancing and very little smiling. Jackson soon had the story from his fellow lodger John Overton, with whom he shared a bed in the Widow Donelson's office, as Cumberland folk called their guest cabins. Rachel was in disgrace. Lewis Robards, the husband she had married at seventeen up in Harrodsburg, Kentucky, had recently banished her from his bed and board: sent her home accused of a too-warm dalliance with another man. Overton himself was a newcomer from Harrodsburg. He knew the Robards family well; so well in fact that Lewis's mother, putting no stock in her jealous son's charges, had asked him to sound Rachel out on the possibility of a reconciliation. Undoubtedly Overton made a convincing advocate for the wronged young wife. Too, the aura of sadness that surrounded her may have touched Rachel's robust beauty with a new spiritual quality, very appealing to a lonely young man far from his old Waxhaw stamping ground. They were bound to get well acquainted anyway, sharing the same household as they did.

Then one day Lewis Robards came riding down from Kentucky, filled with contrition and eager to claim his bride again. Rachel was willing, and the reconciliation proceeded so handily for a while that the couple even planned to build a place of their own and stay on the Cumberland for good. The Indian menace was especially bad at the time, however. It kept them confined to the Donelson blockhouse, and soon they were bickering again. Things went steadily from bad to worse. They reached such a pass, finally, that John Overton had to take his friend Jackson aside and tactfully break the news: this time he—Jackson—was the cause of Robards' jealousy.

How that hit him, Jackson never said. Whatever his feelings toward Rachel Robards at that point, he kept them to himself. It would be best, Overton advised, if he left the premises at once.

Jackson agreed. He moved into Kaspar Mansker's station, several miles away. But a meeting between him and the jealous husband probably was unavoidable. And meet they did. Robards was truculent, ready to fight on the spot. Contemptuously Jackson declined. He suggested an encounter with pistols and seconds would be more appropriate for gentlemen, if Robards really wanted satisfaction. Apparently he did not; at least not all that badly. Thus one version of the story. According to another, Jackson simply proposed to crop Robards' ears with a butcher knife unless he stopped his jealous vaporings. On that frontier, and from a man of Andrew Jackson's forthright temper, it was not necessarily an idle threat.

Intimidated or not, Lewis Robards left soon afterward for Kentucky. Some quoted him as declaring he had had a bellyful of the Cumberland and would never be back. Yet his reconciliation with Rachel had not gone completely sour. He had her promise at parting that she would rejoin him in Harrodsburg, and inside of a week or two she packed up and followed him. It seemed a proper ending. Her brief, pointless friendship with Andrew Jackson could have gone nowhere anyway, and it was over now forever. Well, perhaps not quite forever, after all. It was late May or June when Rachel left her mother's home. July came, and with it a letter for the Widow Donelson. The marriage was over, wrote Rachel; this time the break was past healing. She wanted to come home.

The man who saddled his horse and traveled up the Kentucky Road to get her was Andrew Jackson.

From this distance in time it seems strange that he should have taken the mission upon himself, and stranger still that Mrs. Donelson should have let him. The Cumberland crawled with brothers and male cousins of Rachel's. Any of them could have undertaken to bring her home without the risk of provoking a violent confrontation with Lewis Robards or talk of scandal by loose-tongued neighbors. Nevertheless, Jackson went. There was no confrontation. But, before the end of July, court records at Harrodsburg noted the filing of a complaint by one Lewis Robards: his wife Rachel had "eloped . . . with another man."

Friends of Andrew Jackson—most notably John Overton—made much of his bitter self-reproach for having been, however inadvertently, the cause of Rachel's woes. No doubt he did reproach himself, but by this time he could hardly have been deluding himself. His feeling for Rachel Robards no longer stopped at friendship; he was in love. All the same, their trip from Kentucky was no elopement. Once back on the Cumberland, Rachel went to live with a married sister and Jackson went about his business. Some accounts have Robards hastening down from Harrodsburg for a last effort at a reconciliation. If indeed he did it was a waste of time, for Rachel would have none of him. Even then, apparently, he said nothing of having taken legal action against her. It seems odd that he did not—the more so because the same accounts claim there was another clash between him and Andrew Jackson. In any case, he gave up after a while and returned to Harrodsburg.

The last green weeks of summer mellowed into the gold and russet splendor of fall. Nothing more was heard from Robards. Neither Rachel nor Jackson had any inkling of his court complaint. Then travelers from Kentucky began to bring rumors that he was about to descend on the Cumberland yet again. No conciliation this trip, either; he was vowing to carry his wife away by force if necessary. That was too much for Rachel. She would run before putting up with another Robards ordeal. The Donelsons had friends in Natchez and she prepared to visit them.

Another friend of the family, a Colonel John Stark, happened to be in Nashville loading flatboats for a downriver trading venture. When asked about a passage for Rachel, however, he was reluctant to say yes. The river route to Natchez was an arduous two-thousand-mile haul beset by the myriad perils of storm, high tide, low water, snag, reef, sawyer, riffle—plus hostile Indians and equally savage river pirates. Stark pointed all that out. He could not be responsible for Rachel's safety, he insisted. Still she was determined to go, and Stark then pleaded with Andrew Jackson to come along, presumably as her special protector. Again it was John Overton who wrote the story. But he wrote it thirty-odd years after the fact, when Jackson was a presidential candidate with the scandalmongers trying to make much of his youthful pursuit of Lewis Robards' wife. The truth was that a woman aboard a flatboat was no great rarity. Coming down the Tennessee River with her father eleven years earlier, Rachel had survived worse hardships and hazards than Colonel Stark had any reason to anticipate. It is unlikely that he was very worried, or pleaded very hard with Jackson—or needed to. When his little fleet pushed off early in 1791, both Rachel Robards and Andrew Jackson were passengers.

Some three months later Jackson rode up the Chickasaw Trace

to Nashville, completing the Cumberland flatboatmen's customary round trip in about the customary time. All had gone well, he reported. He had left Rachel comfortably established in the Abner Greens' home near Natchez. The Donelsons were pleased to hear it, of course, but he found them seething over recent news from another quarter.

Lewis Robards had a divorce, granted by the Virginia General Assembly at Richmond (Kentucky still being part of Virginia, though not for long). The procedure was fully in accord with the law of the time, which usually granted divorces only by legislative action. What the Donelsons resented was not the divorce itself but Robards' grounds for it. In charging Rachel with desertion he also alleged that she had "lived in adultery with another man" ever since leaving him.

Jackson exploded. In a towering Jacksonian rage he swore he'd go hunting Robards, have a retraction out of him at pistol point, maybe this time have the ears off him for good measure. He might have, too, but then came a cooler second thought. As a result of it he soon went pounding back down the Chickasaw Trace, armed with the Widow Donelson's permission to sue for her daughter's hand.

Andrew and Rachel were married in August, in the Greens' parlor. They were both twenty-four years old. There was already a good log house on the land-grant acreage Jackson had got from Governor Don Esteban Miró. It stood high on a bluff overlooking the confluence of Bayou Pierre and the majestic, far-rolling Mississippi, a situation both beautiful and secluded, and there for two months the lovers honeymooned. It was October before they returned to the Cumberland and a round of riotous merrymaking in their honor. From one of Rachel's brothers Jackson purchased a plantation named Poplar Grove in Jones Bend. No shadow appeared to threaten their happiness.

Cumberland folk were not put off by the unfortunate circumstance of a courtship carried on amid the wreckage of Rachel's first marriage. Until the Great Revival swept the west in the early 1800s, backwoods Americans were not the straitlaced, purse-mouthed bigots they have too often been painted. Frontier life was by nature a make-do proposition. That was true of moral attitudes as well as more practical matters. A man and a woman with a fancy for one another very frequently had no preacher handy. They might in fact have to do without one for a long time, too long a time to wait, and if they solved their problem in their own way other folk were not disposed to be holier than thou about it. As for the Jacksons, they were two attractive young people, generally well liked and plainly in love. Besides, Lewis Robards had been a stranger, an outsider—and very possibly, from his actions, a sonofabitch to boot.

Thus no one was inclined to make any fuss when the true facts regarding Robards' divorce finally came to light.

It had been no divorce at all. The General Assembly of Virginia had granted Robards only *the right to sue for a divorce* on the grounds submitted, and he had neglected to avail himself of that right until late in September 1793. Which meant that, legally speaking, Rachel had for a fact spent two whole years "living in adultery with another man." It was some months later still before faithful John Overton unearthed the truth, and then only by accident while looking up the records of other legal proceedings in which he was interested.

There was nothing to be done about it by then, of course. Friends advised another wedding immediately. A second ceremony, they pointed out, would at least be legal; the first one clearly had not been. Jackson refused, with some heat. He and Rachel were married in the eyes of God, and that ought to be sufficient. It had better be, he added; he would know what to do about any man who cared to mention the word adultery in his hearing. But no man did, and presently he calmed down and he and Rachel were married again, and it is not recorded that any untoward incident marred the second tying of the knot.

The marriage was not precisely made in heaven, though. One way or another the specter of an irregular union would haunt the Jacksons all the days of their lives. It would be the death of Rachel at last, and Andrew would kill one man because of it and come close to killing others. It is not given to a man to foresee such things at twenty-five, however, and rightly so.

10

Judge
Jackson

STATEHOOD came to Tennessee in 1796. It came not without some struggling at Philadelphia, where Federalist congressmen saw no reason why the Union should welcome seventy thousand unrefined new citizens from the backwoods, certain to hold with the radical new ideas on democracy being preached by the likes of Thomas Jefferson.

It came as no great boon to the folk of the Mero District, either.

The old Spanish intrigue was dead, save perhaps for a reflex twitch or two. Still the issue of Spain's domination of the Mississippi River remained and steadily grew thornier with swelling flatboat traffic down the Cumberland. More and more, these days, the frontier began to see Spanish war as a likelier solution than Spanish alliance—and the federal government, to the Cumberlanders' way of thinking, seemed lacking in the necessary spinal stiffness. That was one thing. For another, there were the old Indian troubles. Those were over by 1796, true; they had been ended forever two years before. But it rankled that the Mero militia had had to do the job on the sly, and quite illegally.

It was a business wryly typical of all the white man's dealings with the red. For years, peace hopes had rested on treaty after treaty. As early as 1783 the first one had put a stop to the Chickasaws' raiding on the Cumberland. By its terms they kept their ancient tribal lands from the Duck River to the mouth of the Tennessee and thence westward to the Mississippi, plus some of the good hunting ground between the Tennessee and the Cumberland. It was a fair treaty and the Chickasaws never broke it, though it stopped white encroachment for only a little while. Over the years there were many similar agreements with the Cherokee too: a people who had been peaceful, or wanted to be, since the days of Chief Attakullakulla. Still there was no peace, not even when the irreconcilable Dragging Canoe died and other chiefs took over the Chickamaugas' strongholds. Andrew Jackson undoubtedly spoke for a majority of his neighbors when he wrote scathingly of a proposed new peace effort in 1791: "Why do we now attempt to hold Treaty with them, have they attended to the last Treaty. I answer in the negative. . . ."

Jackson knew better, or should have. It was the white man who broke the treaties, always. He himself, adding to his land holdings at every opportunity, was as guilty as the next man. The pattern had been set when the settlers' first crossing of the Cumberland broke Richard Henderson's Sycamore Shoals treaty. Each succeeding pact legalized the breaking of an earlier one. Then it was promptly violated in its turn, and the poor savage had no recourse but the rifle and the tomahawk. All of which had no real bearing whatsoever on the District of Mero's eventual resolve to put an end to the Indian troubles once and for all.

There was a complication in that President George Washington, personally, had forbidden any further incursions into the Cherokee tribal lands. He had even threatened to send federal troops to put teeth in the order. The nation's first administration thus was virtually the last to concern itself with the Indians' rights. But not even the hero of the War for Independence was a man big enough to stand in the way of manifest destiny. Nowhere west of the Allegheny Mountains was there any doubt where that destiny pointed.

Volunteers from East Tennessee and Kentucky rode into Nashville in pursuit of an Indian raiding party, so they said. The Mero militia had mustered and was ready. Together they staged a swift, clandestine foray against the Chickamaugas' hidden town of Nickojack. With them rode a young man who had been a prisoner there and knew the secret trails. In the dark of a September night some swam the Tennessee River, some crossed on makeshift rafts of cane, and some waited on the bank to pick off stray fugitives. Caught with no guards out, the Indians never had a chance. A surprise attack through the drifting mists of early morning speedily turned from a battle to something more like a turkey shoot. Warriors not cut down at the first onset ran for their lives along with squaws and children. Nickojack and its neighboring town of Running Water were burned, the Chickamaugas' power broken forever. So one-sided was it that the victors rode back to Nashville with total casualties of only three wounded and one dead. The dead man was killed in camp on the homeward march, but not by any Indian. For reasons of his own he elected to sleep in a tree one night and was injured fatally when he fell out of it.

Territorial Governor Blount issued a tongue-in-cheek reprimand to General James Robertson, who had planned his militia's expedition but discreetly kept it unofficial by staying home himself, and the affair ended there. Nothing about it was calculated to impress the men of the District of Mero with any need for membership in the United States or any benefits therefrom. Even after a constitutional convention duly carried out the necessary amenities, Tennessee became the sixteenth state of the Union over the District of Mero's emphatic veto. Davidson County voted nay by five to one.

But a lone county on the Cumberland had no more say about the course of manifest destiny than the President. Statehood, freedom from the fear of Indians, and the steady improvement of the old Avery Trace—now called the Cumberland Road—brought hopeful new settlers in numbers that began to look like prosperity. No pioneers, these people; they were land breakers, not land winners. And already, so quickly could conditions change, the Cumberland had no land left simply for a bold man's taking. North Carolina, like most states, had paid off her veterans of the late war with parcels of western land, and enterprising speculators and big land companies bought them out in wholesale lots. The would-be freeholder looking for a patch where he could build a cabin, sow a corn crop, and raise a family would buy it, these days, or else keep moving west. To neglect the legal formalities was to risk being run off as a squatter. Hundreds of thousands of acres of Indian treaty land were bought and sold freely, often by men who never had set eyes on it, never been anywhere near it. But "let the buyer beware" was a maxim clearly understood and generally honored by both parties to a deal. Past history nourished an abiding faith that time would bring everything out right: in the end the Indian would have to go. And so in the end he would, and did. For the speculator it was a time when old investments paid off handsomely and new ones promised rewards more golden still.

It was a time when a man could overreach himself, too, and come a cropper. Andrew Jackson almost did.

Marriage had sharpened the edge of Jackson's hunger for wealth and position. Poplar Grove no longer suited him; his Rachel should have a more elegant home by far. He bought a larger plantation nearby, named Hunters Hill, and there on a knoll with a sweeping view of the Cumberland he ordered work begun on a new house. No plans or pictures of it exist today, but all accounts insist that it was built of sawed lumber throughout. If so, it was truly an example of opulence for a region where even the well-to-do were content with squared-log houses and would be for some years to come. But there was no limit to Andrew Jackson's ambition, and he was a young man impatient for achievement. He visualized a store on the Cumberland too, and in time perhaps others in various locations. He engaged an overseer for Hunters Hill. "Put your Negroes Under him," wrote the friend who recommended the man, "and keep out of the field yourself. . . ."

Therein lies a clue to changing conditions on the Cumberland. All the early settlers affluent enough to own slaves had worked right along with them in the fields, as they had been accustomed to do back on the Watauga and the Holston. Now, though, a new and more gracious way of life was taking shape and with it a new frontier gentry was rising. It was more roughhewn than its Tidewater Virginia and Carolina ancestry, no doubt, but not a whit less proud.

To finance his high-flying ambitions Jackson found it necessary to dispose of some of his extensive land holdings. On a trip to Philadelphia in 1795 he sold thirty thousand acres of his own, and fifty thousand more which he held in partnership with John Overton. Typical of the times, the latter parcel was Cherokee treaty land, had anybody cared. But, as usual, no one did. The buyer was David Allison, a wealthy eastern merchant and speculator, who paid with ten thousand dollars in personal notes. This was the customary business procedure in an economy still lacking a banking system of very widespread stability. A man's word had, literally, to be his bond. But his note, if he had a reputation sufficiently good to back it up, could serve as cash. David Allison boasted such a reputation, and Jackson had no trouble in exchanging several thousand dollars' worth of the notes for supplies to stock the new Cumberland store. Routinely, the heads of two Philadelphia mercantile houses with whom he dealt requested his endorsement on the notes. Routinely, he signed and headed homeward, happy in the thought that he had taken another long step toward prosperity.

Presently he was neck-deep in public affairs. His Davidson County neighbors started it by electing him as their representative to the constitutional convention about to be called to order. They may have felt slightly let down when it was, for Jackson immediately took issue with them by standing forthrightly for statehood and the Federal Union. He was credited, in fact, with being the first man to suggest "Tennessee" as the new state's name. Apparently there were no hard feelings, however, for he was elected without opposition as Tennessee's first member of the national House of Representatives, and later served out William Blount's unexpired term as senator, when Blount fell afoul of senatorial rules of conduct and was forced to resign.

The young man in a hurry was spreading himself too thin, as indeed he would be prone to do for the rest of his life. Even before the constitutional convention met in January of 1796, he had word that Allison had defaulted on the first of his notes. The Philadelphia merchants wanted their money, and since Mr. Allison's notes bore Mr. Jackson's endorsement, they presumed Mr. Jackson was prepared to pay . . . ?

Mr. Jackson was in a bind.

The several notes had been written so that they fell due at intervals over a four-year period. As each one did, the debt grew. David Allison went to debtors' prison, a ruined man. It became clear there was no hope he could ever pay. Somehow Andrew Jackson managed to, just barely. The new store went by the boards. Lock, stock, and barrel, Jackson traded it for thirty-three thousand acres—land again; always and forever land, on the frontier—and sold them to an East Tennessee man named James Stuart for twenty-five cents an acre. But he had to take most of it in another note. This one was signed by William Blount, who happened to be in debt to Stuart. And soon Blount, too, was in financial straits. The fact was, hard times had come to the United States. The depression that had wiped Allison out was spreading westward across the mountains, pinching many a man who had considered himself comfortably well off. Blount was not ruined like Allison, but he was unable to pay when Jackson presented his note. It had to be discounted, on terms so low that all hope of profit disappeared. By this sort of frenzied finance, frontier style, Jackson continued to meet his obligations—just barely.

He had other troubles. Brooding over the blemish on their marriage, Rachel began to fall into spells of melancholy. She fretted over her husband's long absences in Philadelphia on his country's business. Jackson's letters to several of his many in-laws during this period were filled with expressions of his concern for her state of mind. What with that and his financial worries, he finally left the Senate in the spring of 1798. It was his intention, he assured Rachel, to "retire . . . from publick life." Undoubtedly he meant it, at the time. He flung himself furiously into the management of Hunters Hill. A cotton gin was purchased and installed there. A distillery was added to the premises. A new store opened for business on the bank of the Cumberland. More of the Allison notes fell due and Jackson paid them—still not easily, but he paid them.

Then "publick life" beckoned again: this time election to the Tennessee Superior Court. It would send Judge Jackson out to ride the circuit, just as Public Prosecutor Jackson had ridden it ten years before. He knew Rachel would be unhappy about that. But he also knew it would mean new stature for him in his chosen profession. He wanted that. His years in Congress had been peculiarly lacking in satisfaction to one of Jackson's aggressive temperament. He had done nothing of any great moment there, attracted no attention save for "the queue tied with an eelskin hanging down his back" and his "manners of a rough backwoodsman." As a Superior Court justice in his own state he would be a person of undoubted consequence: still a rough backwoodsman, maybe, but respected by his kind. He accepted the appointment, after a "retirement" of just six months.

Andrew Jackson made a good judge, right for his time and place. His sketchy grasp of legal technicalities might be faulted, but his uncompromising dedication to fairness, never. The tradition of his customary charge to juries hearing lawsuits in his court has become a classic: "Do what is right between these parties. That is what the law always means." It was an elemental notion of justice, very much in tune with the frontier's elemental values. Tennessee folk liked Judge Jackson. It was lucky for him they did, for he promptly

embroiled himself in an elemental frontier feud. And it was altogether in character for him to choose as an adversary the foremost
hero in all the state. That was Governor John Sevier, the renowned
Nolichucky Jack himself.

The match was in no way even on the face of it. For all his
rapid rise in Republican Party politics, Jackson was a comparative
Johnny-come-lately with his reputation still to make. Sevier's was
long since made, his popularity impregnable. He had been Nolichucky Jack, riding with his Carolina neighbors to whip a British
army at King's Mountain, when a teen-age sprat named Andrew
Jackson was doing little more to win the nation's liberty than
decline to clean a redcoat officer's boots. Sevier had been a scourge
of the Cherokee and the Chickamaugas long before young Jackson
ever decided to leave the Waxhaws. It was a safe bet that any male
citizen of Tennessee could have recited Nolichucky's record without a moment's pause for thought: thirty-five Indian fights and
never a defeat. It was John Sevier, practically single-handed, who
had kept the ill-starred state of Franklin afloat for its whole stormy
three-year life. Sevier had commanded the East Tennessee militia
throughout the strenuous territorial days. And when Tennessee
got her statehood Sevier, again, was the people's choice for governor. Not once but three times running they had elected him. Three
consecutive terms was all the new state constitution allowed a
man, else he might have claimed the office indefinitely.

At some point during this career John Sevier had participated
with other influential East Tennesseans in certain deals involving
public lands. Nothing unusual in that; who, after all, had not suc-
cumbed at some time or other to the prevailing land fever? In this
case, though, someone had been guilty of dishonest manipulations
with forged land warrants. The details would make tedious reading
today, but there is little doubt that Sevier was involved—and by
no means innocently. Nothing came of the affair, nevertheless,
not even when Andrew Jackson—a yearling congressman at the
time—ran across some clues to it and agitated for an official investigation. But Sevier thought him a busybody, quite understandably, and so the seeds of hard feeling began to take root.

Stepping down at the end of his third term, Governor Sevier
proposed to take command of the Tennessee militia, with the rank
of major general. It was an honor to which the aging warrior—he
was fifty-seven—considered himself entitled: a fitting capstone to

an illustrious lifework. Jackson's decision to seek the commission too must have struck him as the sheerest sort of effrontery. It was true that Jackson had been a member of the militia for some years. He had joined as judge advocate of the Davidson County regiment, with the rank of captain. But his military attainments were still far in the future. His soldiering experience at the time, and in comparison with John Sevier's, was trivial. But the choice was made in the democratic way, by a vote of all militia officers, and—no doubt shockingly, to Sevier—their ballots added up to a tie. That gave the deciding vote to Governor Archibald Roane, Sevier's successor and Andrew Jackson's very good friend. He voted for Jackson, to nobody's surprise, and John Sevier had another score to settle with the lanky upstart from the Cumberland.

He was not beaten, not a bit of it. One term out of office made him eligible to run for governor again, and he came roaring out of retirement to challenge Archibald Roane for reelection. Jackson, stumping hard for his friend, attempted to bring up the matter of the alleged land frauds once more. All it got him was a harsh lesson in political reality. A popular hero's moral probity or lack of it counted as nothing against his panache—and Nolichucky Jack Sevier had panache to burn. He descended on settlements the length and breadth of Tennessee as he had once descended on hostile Indian towns. He rode the stony ridges and the backwoods creek bottoms, the ancient Indian war trails and the newly rutted wagon traces. He rattled the big cavalry sword he always wore and spoke ringingly of old glory days not too long past. He won the election hands down.

With becoming modesty, for his part, Andrew Jackson forebore to flaunt his general's title. Publicly he remained Judge Jackson except when official functions of the militia required his appearance in full-dress regimentals. The feud might have died for lack of nourishment but for the gamecock dispositions of both men, and the fact that the regular term of Superior Court took the judge to Knoxville, the capital, in the fall of 1803.

One afternoon he adjourned court as usual and left the courtroom for his lodgings at a local inn called the Indian King. There probably was no more on his mind than supper and the daily letter to Rachel he would write later. But there on the courthouse steps stood Governor Sevier, engaged in spirited give-and-take with a large crowd of bystanders. The legislature happened just then to be carrying on an inquiry into the by then somewhat shopworn land-frauds scandal, and Sevier was vigorously denying any wrongdoing on his part. Jackson paused to listen. Seeing him, Sevier promptly launched into an anti-Jackson tirade to which the judge replied in kind, frontier fashion. One word led to another. Most accounts say the governor made some intemperate remark about the Jacksons' marriage, at which Jackson whipped up his heavy walking stick and charged with murder in his eyes. Sevier drew his sword and defended himself. But other men ran between the two, dragged them apart after a brief, violent scuffle, and bore them off on their separate ways.

That was all for the time being, but it was far from the end of the matter. Before dark that same evening a friend delivered Jackson's challenge to the governor's residence.

It proved the opening gambit in a markedly uncordial exchange of pleasantries that lasted more than a week. Sevier accepted the challenge and suggested pistols. He was sure, he sneered, that Jackson was too oafish a fellow ever to have learned a gentleman's skill with the sword. He also pointed out that Tennessee had a law against dueling. Quite obviously he, the governor, could not be expected to break it. Therefore the encounter must take place elsewhere.

Many states had such antidueling laws, and in practically all—Tennessee included—they were flouted openly and often, with little fear of legal retribution. Indignantly, his ardor for battle still white hot, Jackson accused the governor of dodging the issue. He, Jackson, was ready to fight anywhere—Georgia, North Carolina, Virginia, Indian Territory—"if it will obviate your squeamish fears." He threatened a public declaration of His Excellency's cowardice unless His Excellency got down to business without further ado. Tartly Sevier replied that the seconds should go ahead with arrangements as to time and place. Still, nothing happened. His own second, a young militia officer by the name of Sparks, failed to get in touch with Jackson's man. Privately, as he confided to a few intimates, Nolichucky Jack was growing heartily sick of the whole affair. What, he complained, had he to gain by fighting Jackson? His personal courage was beyond doubt; he had spent a lifetime proving it, more than amply. As a family man he had no right to risk his life in a reckless duel. He was getting a little old for such capers anyway, while Jackson, at thirty-six, was in the prime of life.

Mutual friends called on Jackson and tried to make peace. Jackson was adamant. Rachel's good name had been sullied; he could neither forgive that nor ignore it. Come what might, John Sevier must fight him.

Meantime, word was getting around. The brawl on the courthouse steps had been witnessed by a great many people. The tale had been bandied about to a great many more, all over Knoxville and its environs. That Nolichucky Jack had talked out of turn was common knowledge, and his reluctance to face Judge Jackson was rapidly becoming as self-evident as the judge's eagerness. Popular sentiment began to swing Jackson's way. He had offered to resign from the Superior Court bench if need be, rather than back away from his challenge. Now he changed his mind about the resignation and held court all week. On Sunday he sat down in his rooms at the Indian King, sharpened a quill, dipped it in pure vitriol, and scratched out an ultimatum to Sevier. The reply was still unsatisfactory. On Tuesday the Knoxville *Gazette* printed a paid notice over Andrew Jackson's signature, detailing the full extent of the governor of Tennessee's poltroonery.

Jackson was not there to see Knoxville's reaction. Having handed in the notice on Monday, he picked up his friend Dr. Thomas Van Dyke, an army surgeon stationed with the garrison at nearby Kingston, and the two of them rode the ten miles or so to Southwest Point at the junction of the Clinch and Tennessee rivers. By the terms of a treaty still in force, that was nominally Cherokee territory, thus forestalling at least one of the governor's "squeamish fears." Jackson and Van Dyke made camp and waited. They waited five days, so it is said. They had given up, saddled up, and mounted for the ride back to Knoxville when Sevier appeared at last with an entourage of several men at his back.

The confrontation that followed was a lively one by all accounts, if not quite according to the *code duello*. Both Jackson and Sevier dismounted, drew pistols, and loudly dared each other to fire away. Neither did. Instead they commenced to bawl insults back and forth. After a while they stopped that, due to the soothing offices of Dr. Van Dyke and Sevier's second. Both men put their pistols back in their saddle holsters. Then, without warning, the altercation began again. Jackson lunged at Sevier, shouting that he was going to cane him. Sevier drew his sword, frightening his horse so badly that it bolted and took his pistols with it. By that time, though, Jackson had turned and drawn one of *his* again. Hurriedly scrambling behind the nearest tree, Nolichucky Jack let loose a torrent of abuse, damning him for a coward to shoot an unarmed man—at which point the governor's teen-age son George Washington Sevier drew a pistol and leveled it at Jackson. Whereupon Dr. Van Dyke drew on George Washington. But through all this, by some fortunate miracle, no one pulled a trigger. An impasse of sorts thus being established, cooler heads finally were able to prevail. The pistols were put away. Someone caught Sevier's horse for him and he remounted. After some further discussion, everyone agreed no good would come of prolonging the meeting. Sevier and his people rode off.

Till they were out of earshot, it was said, judge and governor never stopped damning one another's eyes.

The feud was destined to go on with unabated bitterness as long as both men lived. There would be no more talk of dueling, though. Indeed, after such an encounter as theirs mere bloodletting would have seemed an anticlimax. Even Andrew Jackson, never his whole life long given to any overt signs of a sense of humor, seems to have realized that. In time, too, it probably dawned on him that he had been lucky: the man who killed a popular idol like John Sevier could surely count his own political career in limbo.

As it was, if neither he nor Nolichucky Jack came out of the affair with any great credit, neither was hurt much either. No doubt it was the best possible ending.

11

The Wayfaring
Stranger

INTO Nashville one late May day in 1805 rode a wiry stranger seeking Judge Jackson. He came by the road from Lexington, Kentucky, but his journey had been far longer than that. It had started nearly three months earlier with his departure from the Senate chamber in the new national capital on the bank of the Potomac River in Virginia. His designs had led him to Philadelphia and thence westward across the Alleghenies to Pittsburgh at the forks of the Ohio. He had then floated downstream, with stops for leisurely visits in towns along the way, before leaving the river at Louisville to strike southward through Kentucky. It was something of an afterthought that brought him to the Cumberland.

The stranger was a cultured and knowledgeable New Yorker of forty-nine. Much of what he had seen in the west impressed him deeply. Some did not. In "Wieling, sometimes erroneously spelled Wheeling," he was pleasantly surprised to see several well-dressed women. But Louisville, where George Rogers Clark had built his fort on Corn Island, struck him as quite unprepossessing. His opinion of Nashville was not recorded, though at this point in his travels he would have known about what to expect there.

The town still sprawled loosely around the same spacious square on its bluff above the Cumberland River. A stone courthouse had replaced the small log structure of Andrew Jackson's early days, and only a few cedar trees remained of the many that once had crowned the bluff. The stumps of others, though, still had not been grubbed out of the ground. From one corner a dirt road slanted steeply down the face of the bluff to Johnson's Landing at the water's edge, with its old log fort now falling into ruin and its meager huddle of shanties catering to the boisterous river trade. The square itself was considerably more substantial. A number of its buildings were of brick or stone and some were two stories high. Almost all boasted wooden awnings beneath which idlers could take shelter from the sun. A large open-sided shed served as a marketplace for the farmers roundabout. There was a groggery presided over by one de Monbruen, a son of the old French *coureur de bois* who had once shot buffaloes for their tallow around Big Salt Lick. There were also three large taverns: Talbert's, Winn's, and the spanking new Nashville Inn.

Possibly the stranger stopped to rest and refresh himself in one of these places. He must at least have paused somewhere to ask directions to Judge Jackson's, unless he already had them from the ferryman who had carried him across the river. Whether or not he identified himself, it is unlikely that his arrival in Nashville went unnoticed. He was no man to be overlooked, in spite of his scant five feet and two or three inches. Sometime later a prominent contemporary would describe him, in the much too florid phraseology of those days but with obvious admiration too, as ". . . a man of erect and dignified deportment; his presence is commanding, his aspect mild, firm, luminous. . . . His eyes are of a dark hazel, and from the shade of projecting eye bones and brows, appear black; they . . . beam with the most vivid and piercing rays of genius. His mouth is large; his voice is clear, manly and melodious. . . ." This was no ordinary stranger, clearly.

He was in fact the recent Vice President of the United States and as such by all odds the most distinguished political figure yet seen on the Cumberland. It was entirely incidental that he was a fugitive from justice, too: under indictment for "the illegal tendering of a duel" in New York and for murder in New Jersey, where the duel had taken place.

His name was Aaron Burr.

The indictments notwithstanding, Burr's western journey had soon blossomed into a triumphal tour. The west was Republican country, by and large. Out here the Federalist Party was very much

in the minority, and its late great spokesman Alexander Hamilton
had been heartily disliked. Most of the trans-Allegheny region still
was frontier, or had been within the memory of folk still hale and
active. Physical courage was admired, and men were accustomed
to settling their own differences among themselves. Feeling that
way, they were not disposed to think the less of anyone for calling
his enemy out and killing him in a fair stand-up fight—as Aaron
Burr had killed Hamilton in the duel at Weahawk above the Hud-
son River not quite a year past.

If the affair had ruined Burr's political fortunes on the eastern
seaboard, then the west promised opportunities for a swift rebuild-
ing. He had left Washington with that in mind. Everywhere along
the way he had talked with old friends of his senatorial days, and
with new ones met for the first time. He had been sought after,
entertained, wined and dined by the prosperous and the politically
powerful. He had been followed, cheered, lionized by crowds of
common folk who chafed in resentment of an eastern establishment
far away and seemingly oblivious of their problems. It was much
the same spirit of restlessness and frustration that had led the
District of Mero, not so long ago, to look toward Spain as a potential partner. It was enough to set fire to a less volatile imagination
than Aaron Burr's. Beyond a doubt, he rode into Nashville that
May day filled with the heady exhilaration of great plans on their
way to ripening.

When he rode out again it was not to Hunters Hill, for the Jacksons no longer lived there. The dark threat of financial insolvency
still hung over Judge Jackson's head—the "Judge" a courtesy title
only, now, for he had resigned from the Tennessee Superior Court
a year ago. It was the old story of an urgent need to devote his full
energies to his plantation and to various other commercial ventures
that seldom did better than break even. He had recently had to sell
Hunters Hill and move to another, less pretentious place called the
Hermitage, on Stone's River. No sawed-lumber mansion, this, but
a two-story log blockhouse no better than most of his neighbors'.

But no hint of such private troubles would show, of course, in
the welcome Burr had from the craggy squire and his lady. It was
as warm as he could have wished. Tennessee owed Aaron Burr a
special debt of gratitude, and no man in Tennessee had more reason than Andrew Jackson to cherish Burr's friendship.

The attachment was little more than casual on Burr's part. His trip to Nashville was a sort of last-minute digression, made only because friends in Kentucky had happened to mention the major general of Tennessee militia as a man to be reckoned with one day. But Jackson remembered the fight for Tennessee's admission to the Union nine years before. Federalist opposition in the halls of Congress might have kept her out, but for the unsparing help of an influential Republican senator from New York by the name of Aaron Burr. More, when Jackson appeared in Philadelphia as a green young congressman from the new state, Senator Burr had gone out of his way to be kind. In particular, perhaps, Jackson recalled an invitation to a state dinner given by Burr in 1797. Years afterward he was heard to comment more than once on the rare wines served that night. Andrew Jackson had a long memory, for favors as well as injuries. Now he could repay the old debt with a spirited display of hospitality, and did, and the middle Cumberland was not backward about joining in.

On May 29 Davidson County's elite turned out en masse for a dinner in Burr's honor at the Nashville Inn. Jackson was the first to rise and propose an extravagant toast to the distinguished guest. The day's festivities stretched out through a long afternoon and evening, and included, in Burr's own words, "the most magnificent parade that had ever been made at that place." The distinguished guest delivered an oration, no doubt a ringing patriotic expression of the sentiments his audience had come to hear and cheer. No doubt, too, the whole occasion partook of the rough-and-tumble fun of a backwoods gala, with gallons of good Tennessee whiskey poured down thirsty gullets, all the burning political issues of the day thrashed out—not without some stomp-and-gouge differences, perhaps—and linsey-woolsey homespun, sober broadcloth, silks, satins, beaver top hats, fancy bonnets, and rivermen's wool hats with turkey feathers, all mingling in happy confusion in the courthouse square.

The following days brought more dinners, barbecues, and similar fetes. Everyone, Burr reported in a letter to his adored daughter Theodosia, "seemed to be contending for the honour of having best treated . . . Colonel Burr." The colonel—whose title was bona fide, earned during the late War for Independence—stayed on for five days as the Jacksons' guest. Sandwiched in among the social occasions there was ample time for serious talk with his host. And talk was Aaron Burr's real reason for being there.

No one to this day has ever uncovered the true extent of Burr's western ambitions or the precise details of any plan he had for attaining them. Perhaps he himself was not quite sure, was simply an opportunist bent on going as far as luck, nerve, and the ability to sway men's minds would take him. In that spring of 1805 it appeared he was generously endowed with all three.

Before leaving Washington he had approached any number of possible confederates. George Merry, the British ambassador, was one, and with him Burr laid a very specific proposition on the table. Given a half-million dollars of His Britannic Majesty's money, he would undertake to organize and outfit an expedition and personally lead it down the Ohio River to separate the western states and territories from the Union. It was a plan shrewdly calculated to appeal to British interests in North America, and Merry had been impressed sufficiently to pass it along in a confidential report to Prime Minister Pitt. The answer still was pending. In the meantime Burr had made similar overtures to the Spanish ambassador, whom he found considerably less receptive. Boldly playing both ends against the middle, he had also conferred with all manner of his own countrymen, both inside and outside government circles. Some were wealthy men, able to furnish the financial backing he needed. Some held influential posts in the Jefferson administration. Some were no more than adventurers like himself. The plans Burr unfolded to them all were alike in broad outline, though they differed greatly in detail. To some he had held out the promise of British help, to others of Spanish. Various other versions merely proposed armed filibusters to seize either the Spanish Floridas or Mexico, where memories of the old conquistadors held out the promise of rewards in hard yellow gold.

Projects like this would sound nowhere near as radical in 1805 as they do today. There was a burgeoning expansionist sentiment, in the west especially, that saw nothing wrong about such adventures. The idea of secession from the Union was no shocking thing either, in the climate of the time. The New England states had entertained it very seriously for a while, and in fact still did. (Briefly, before the fatal duel with Hamilton, Burr's name had been linked with that too.) And even so potent a policymaker as President Thomas Jefferson was on record as approving peaceful separation for any of the western lands where the people wished it —though he had changed his views somewhat since laying out

fifteen million dollars to acquire Louisiana from Napoleon Bonaparte.

Whatever else one might think of him, then, Andrew Jackson's
guest could hardly be called a traitor. The ominous word "conspiracy" had not yet been applied to any of his designs, as it would
be later. His dream of an independent nation to be set up somewhere, with himself as King Aaron I and his daughter as Princess
Theodosia—if indeed he ever harbored it—had been confided to
not a soul as yet. Certainly he mentioned no such flamboyant
foolishness to his hard-nosed host. Nor did he say anything about
foreign backing; Jackson's aversion to both Spaniards and Englishmen was well known.

What Burr did discuss was a perfectly respectable undertaking
which might, depending on future developments, serve as a spring-
board for—well, for almost anything. As with all his plans, the
known details are vague. In essence, however, he was thinking in
terms of a new settlement on the Ouachita River in southwestern
Louisiana. The land was a large tract known as the Bastrop Grant,
a holdover from the days of Spanish sovereignty, and he had already looked into the possibility of buying it. The necessary
money, he said, would be no problem.

He was very sanguine about finances, always, was Colonel Burr.

Apparently the settlement he described to Jackson would center
about an organization not unlike the old minutemen of Lexington
and Concord fame: a picked force of stout patriots armed and
trained as a sort of free-lance military reserve, ready at need for
instant action. As Aaron Burr saw it, both the need and the opportunity were at hand, or soon would be. He spoke of the feeling
in Washington—shared throughout the western country, and he
knew it—that war with Spain was not only inevitable but very
close. Once it came, Burr's troop of hardy settlers on the Ouachita
would be transformed overnight into a spearhead lunging at the
very heart of Spanish America: a fighting vanguard for the regular
army troops to follow. That seems to have been the gist of it, anyway, no doubt presented with all the persuasive conviction at which
Burr was adept. Mexico was his objective; it appears he made no
secret of that, and it was of course plain that Aaron Burr as Mexico's
conqueror would be in a fair way to mend his tarnished political
fortunes. But that scarcely could be held against him. Andrew

Jackson, no military hero by any means as yet, probably was flattered that so eminent a man as Burr should solicit his advice.

Well, he owned, the thing might be brought off. He wondered, though, whether Burr had considered all its aspects. Shorn of the military overtones, the venture was primarily a land settlement scheme, another form of speculation, actually. Jackson had learned a good bit about speculations, the pitfalls as well as the potential profits. All in all, he thought the scheme impractical. As a fellow patriot, though, he could not but applaud Burr's motives.

At some point in their conversations Burr brought out his clincher. He had not come west as a private citizen, exactly. Everything he planned had the unofficial blessing of Henry Dearborn, President Jefferson's secretary of war. The moment the expected hostilities broke out, that blessing would become official: Burr was promised a commission, the command of troops. He undoubtedly offered that as confidential information, but it put a wholly different face on the matter, as Jackson would understand? And Jackson did. "By the Eternal"—it was his favorite oath and we may assume he used it now—he never had hung back when his country needed him, and never would. Spanish war, was it? The Tennessee militia would be ready. Burr and Mr. Dearborn could rely on that.

It was all Burr asked, all he had expected. The lean Tennessee strongman was in his camp. And in splendid company too. "It will be a host of choice spirits. . . ." He may have spoken the very words. He wrote them sometime later, in any case, but to another man.

The visit lasted five days. "I could stay a month with pleasure," Burr told Theodosia in a letter. But he still had much ground to cover, other men to see, other plans to make. With the courtliness that always came naturally to him he took his leave of Andrew and Rachel. In a final gesture of Tennessee hospitality Jackson put a pirogue and a riverwise boatman at his disposal, and Aaron Burr was off down the Cumberland for Fort Massac on the Ohio River. There he would spend four days in earnest conference with General James Wilkinson of the regular United States Army, another old friend. No third person was ever to know all they said to one another, but they certainly dealt in projects darker and more suspect than any that were hinted at the Hermitage. Afterward Burr headed on down the Ohio and the Mississippi in considerably higher style than the Jacksons had provided on the Cumberland. Things were looking up for Aaron Burr. He rode an army keelboat with crimson sails and an honor guard of ten soldiers and a sergeant, and in his pocket were letters of introduction to certain powerful citizens in New Orleans whose interests and his own were very likely to coincide. All this was courtesy of Jamey Wilkinson, for whom things were also looking up. He was not only the army's ranking officer now, but governor of all the upper Louisiana Territory too. Come the pinch, though, Andrew Jackson would prove the truer friend.

By early August, Burr was back on the Cumberland again, once more established in the office at the Hermitage. "For a week I have been lounging at the house of General Jackson, once a lawyer, after a judge, now a planter . . . one of those prompt, frank, ardent souls I love to meet." So he wrote in another of his countless letters to Theodosia, and went on to tell her of two of Rachel's young nieces, fellow guests who "contributed greatly to my amusement, and have cured me of all the evils of my wilderness jaunt. . . ."

Jaunt, indeed! What he dismissed so lightly was in fact a lone ride of four hundred-odd miles up the Natchez Trace. It was never by any stretch of the imagination a pleasure trip, and at that season of the year the Trace harassed travelers with muggy swamp heat and clouds of ravenous mosquitoes in addition to the more noxious human predators who infested it in all seasons. But no one ever questioned Aaron Burr's courage or his hardihood. He rode, besides, armed with the awareness of a great destiny as good as won. It was a weapon more potent than pistols.

He was justified in thinking so, at least, for New Orleans had been the climactic triumph of his whole western tour. He had hobnobbed there with the cream of society, with aspiring politicians, with businessmen of far-reaching influence and adventurous vision. The good sisters of Ursuline convents, captivated by the Burr charm, had promised to pray for his success. Considering that the object of his ambitions was a Catholic country, it was no small coup. Members of the Mexican Society, a group of Americans openly dedicated to wresting that province from Spanish rule, had sought his counsel and his good offices. He was very willing to give both, no doubt of that. In fluent French, with wit and ingratiating savoir faire, he had won the hearts of Creole aristocrats who made no secret of their discontent with a New Orleans under the aegis of the upstart United States. To all these diverse groups he had listened with a sympathetic ear. What commitments he may have made to certain people we do not know, but there is evidence that he discouraged no one's hopes. In the lush clime of the old French-Spanish city, its atmosphere heady with the smells of intrigue and cabal, nothing could have seemed impossible to a man like Burr. Not even a realm for King Aaron I? Possibly that little conceit was born in New Orleans that summer.

The Natchez Trace may have taken more out of Burr than he let on to Theodosia, however. This time he was content to linger at the Hermitage in comparative quiet for ten days. Then the pressure of things to be done drove him on again: up into Kentucky for a meeting with the rising young attorney Henry Clay, out to St. Louis for another secret session with Jamey Wilkinson, from there to Vincennes in Indiana Territory and an audience with Governor William Henry Harrison. As fall days began to shorten, his way finally led eastward once more: to Philadelphia, Washington, and the ultimate perfecting of his grand design.

He would be back.

12

Horseflesh and Pistols

ONE THING, and one only, Andrew Jackson and Aaron Burr had in common. Hard-pressed by the need for money though both were, neither was letting it cramp either his ambition or his style of living. In Washington, outwardly undismayed by the news that the British government wanted no part of him after all, Burr went on planning, recruiting, raising money somehow, somewhere. At home on the Cumberland, Jackson grimly strove to keep his leaky credit afloat in a sea of debt while still indulging his passion for thoroughbred horseflesh.

The buyer of Hunters Hill had fallen behind in his payments. He offered to make up the arrears in slaves, but Jackson already had a flatboatload of slaves on their way to the New Orleans market, along with shipments of barrel staves and cotton. Cash was what he needed now. He had opened another store at Clover Bottom, on Stone's River just upstream from the Hermitage. He had also built a racecourse adjoining and was partner in a boatyard on the river. All this had been done with borrowed money and the profits, so far, were slow in coming. Furthermore, history appeared to be repeating itself in that two Philadelphia merchants were writing pointed letters concerning accounts long past due.

On the pleasanter side, though, Jackson had a new racehorse of imposing lineage: a big bay stallion named Truxton. Irksome financial worries were not enough to keep him from the serious business of training Truxton for a match with Mr. Comfort Lazarus's gelding Greyhound.

Ironically, even that held the threat of imminent bankruptcy. He had acquired the stallion only because the former owner, a Major Verell, was also neck-deep in debt. It might have struck any other man than Jackson as a bad omen, at the very least, since a good share of Verell's difficulties stemmed from having backed his horse too generously in an earlier loss to the same Greyhound. But Jackson had seen that race and liked Truxton's looks. He would back his judgment of horseflesh against any man's, and promptly did. He proposed a horse trade, sweetened it by offering to assume more than a thousand dollars of the major's debts in addition—and Truxton was his. Still backing his judgment without a qualm, he arranged a rematch with the Lazarus horse for a side bet of five thousand dollars. And by the time the horses went to the post at the Hartsville course, thirty-five miles up the Cumberland from Nashville, he had another wager down, this one for fifteen hundred dollars "in wearing apparel." Had any neighborhood wag ventured the obvious joke about the squire of the Hermitage being reduced to betting his shirt—no one did, so far as is known—it would have been almost literally true. Jackson was getting in very deep, quite possibly faced ruin if his horse lost.

But Truxton won.

Jackson was not afraid to ride his luck. He spent part of his winnings to add Greyhound to his stable, accepted a challenge by Captain Joseph Erwin to race the gelding against Erwin's Tanner, and won again. Stung, Captain Erwin flung out another challenge: his stallion Ploughboy against any horse Andrew Jackson owned, the race to be run later that fall at Jackson's own Clover Bottom course for a two-thousand-dollar side bet. This was not to be taken lightly, for Ploughboy was a racehorse widely celebrated as the best in all the District of Mero. Nevertheless, Jackson accepted the challenge. Under the code he lived by, it was unthinkable that he should not.

He was still in luck. He named Truxton as his horse, but Ploughboy pulled up lame on the day of the race, had to be withdrawn, and Erwin paid a forfeit of eight hundred dollars as agreed. This was perfectly legitimate and according to custom. It should have caused no hard feelings on either side. Unfortunately, it turned out otherwise.

The trouble began with some loose tavern talk by one of Andrew Jackson's friends, inferring that Captain Erwin had tried to pay off in fraudulent notes. Apparently it grew out of a simple misunderstanding, and as soon as Jackson got wind of it he set the record straight. It was true, said he, that there had been a slight difference of opinion about the nature of Erwin's notes, but he had never questioned the captain's integrity and they had no quarrel with one another. Erwin agreed with that explanation and the affair might have ended there. But exaggerated stories continued to circulate until finally Charles Dickinson, Erwin's son-in-law, took it upon himself to blame Jackson for them. Jackson advised him curtly to stop listening to lies. He disliked Dickinson anyway, the young man having once, in his cups, made some sneering allusion to Rachel's previous marriage. Though he had apologized later, the slur was not forgotten. So there was bad blood between the two, and it went on simmering through that winter of 1805/6 as partisans of both sides kept the affair of Erwin's notes alive with remarks that grew less temperate at each exchange.

It was not only partisans, either. Insults flew back and forth between Jackson and Charles Dickinson, mostly carried by a busybody young friend of Dickinson's named Thomas Swann, till it seemed one or the other must surely challenge. Just in time, however, Dickinson was called to New Orleans on business.

Even that failed to help matters, for presently Swann appointed a second to carry *his* challenge out to the Hermitage. Jackson thought that presumptuous; eventually he rode into Nashville and gave the young man a public caning for it. Still Swann insisted on his duel. Again Jackson declined. He did not, said he, know Mr. Swann to be a gentleman. However, he said, he was ready to go to any solitary thicket of the young man's choice and there shoot it out with him—on the strict understanding that such an encounter was in no sense a duel. Apparently Mr. Swann had no stomach for such raw frontier heroics, and no more was heard from him. But the feud smoldered on, dragging others in. Jackson's good friend John Coffee found cause to challenge another Dickinson crony and took a pistol ball in the thigh when they met. Regrettably, though, the Dickinson man fired before the word was given, an unpardonable breach of dueling etiquette that afforded no satisfaction to either side. General James Robertson, now getting on in years at sixty-four, was so upset by the mounting ill will around him that he wrote Jackson a long letter urging that things had gone far enough. He cited Aaron Burr: "I suppose if duelling Could be Jestifiable it must have bin in his case and it is beleaved he has not had ease in mind since the fatal hour. . . ."

Far away in the east, Colonel Burr did indeed lack "ease in mind" that winter, though for reasons other than Robertson assumed. They would become a *cause célèbre* on the Cumberland sooner than anyone could have guessed.

In the spring another meeting between Truxton and Ploughboy was arranged, for a side bet of three thousand dollars. But the money was the least of it. Feelings on both sides were so edgy now that the race was an out-and-out grudge match.

April third, the appointed day, dawned darkly under lowering clouds. That was an omen for the Jackson camp, perhaps, for this time it was Truxton that came up lame. The horse limped badly on a hind leg hurt some days before. Friends of Jackson congregated at the stable with long faces. There was nothing to do, they advised, but call off the race and pay the forfeit. Jackson thought it over, saying nothing, his face as grim as the sky overhead. He knew Truxton's condition better than anyone, but there was more involved here than his horseman's judgment. There was stiff-necked pride, too. The race, with the atmosphere of feud surrounding it, had aroused great interest all over the middle Cumberland. An army of horsy gentry was already gathered at Clover Bottom, and very few of them even pretended to be neutral. That undoubtedly helped to shape a decision typically Jacksonian: his horse would run.

Word spread through the crowd and was received with mixed emotions. Both factions had come amply supplied with bettable property: slaves, horses, deeds to 640-acre tracts of land. The betting went slowly, however, Jackson men covering only a few thousands of dollars of Ploughboy wagers. Even that was as much loyalty, perhaps, as any real hope of winning.

Following the custom in those Cumberland meets, the race would be run as the best two heats out of three, each heat being two miles long. That too seemed to favor Ploughboy. A lame horse might last for one heat, if he could run at all; but two or more . . . ?

It appeared Truxton could run, lame or not. He broke in front at the start of the first heat, held his lead, and won handily. He pulled up limping worse than ever, though: apparently badly hurt now. Ploughboy's backers, momentarily downcast, saw that and were reassured. And headstrong Jackson was committed now. It was too late to change his mind and pay the forfeit.

The horses went to the starting line again. A ruffle of drums sent them flying into the second heat, and as it did the clouds opened up in drenching rain. What if anything that had to do with it—whether Truxton found the heavy going more to his liking than did Ploughboy—was no doubt argued in paddock and tavern taproom for months afterward. For again the big bay stallion broke in front. Again, incredibly, Ploughboy failed to catch him. Soaked to the skin but three thousand dollars richer, and far richer still in vindicated pride, Andrew Jackson matter-of-factly noted the winning time: three minutes, fifty-nine seconds "without spur or whip."

This time there was no question about Captain Erwin's notes. Erwin's son-in-law, though, was of a mind to pay Jackson in a different coin. Charles Dickinson returned from New Orleans soon after the middle of May. The very next issue of Nashville's *Impartial Review and Cumberland Repository* carried a long personal notice over his name. In it "the Major General of the Mero district" was characterized bluntly, if somewhat redundantly, as "a worthless scoundrel, a poltroon and a coward." The notice also informed any interested parties that Dickinson planned to leave shortly for Maryland. The inference was too plain to be missed. If the major general was man enough to challenge, he had better not be wasting time.

That he must challenge was a foregone conclusion, of course. And so, of course, was Dickinson's acceptance.

They met on May thirtieth, a Friday, near Harrisons Mills on the Red River, just across the Kentucky line. It meant a long ride from Nashville, to which Andrew Jackson objected heatedly. But Dickinson, like Governor Sevier before him, would not break Tennessee's antidueling law. Jackson snorted in disgust; the law was broken so often it was meaningless. He objected, also, to a week's delay in getting on with the business. After all, Mr. Dickinson had professed some urgency about a trip to Maryland, had he not? But for reasons of his own, Dickinson would not be hurried. Possibly he thought the waiting might shake his adversary's nerve, for it was said he was offering bets to all comers in Nashville's courthouse square that he would kill Jackson "at the first fire." He certainly had excellent grounds for self-confidence, in any case, for many people claimed he was the best pistol shot in Tennessee. It was common knowledge that he could put four balls out of four into a playing card at dueling range, and for many years a story insisted that he left Jackson a series of such reminders, tacked to trees along the Kentucky Road.

Jackson left the Hermitage shortly after sunup on the day before their meeting. To Rachel he said only that he had business in Kentucky and might be away for some days. She knew about the trouble with Dickinson, though. Of course she knew; it had been gossiped around Nashville for months. And so she must have realized, too, that it was more than hard feelings over a horse race sending the two men out to kill each other. One day the old, malignant shadow on her marriage would break Rachel Jackson's heart. No doubt it loomed darkly indeed that morning.

In Nashville Jackson joined his party. General Thomas Overton, John's brother and a brigadier in the Tennessee militia, had agreed to act as his second, and three other friends went along. Their later accounts indicate that the daylong ride through the spring countryside was a pleasant one, in spite of their mission and the very slim chance it would not end in tragedy. Jackson talked volubly for much of the way, and perhaps it was natural that his thoughts seemed to dwell on his friend Aaron Burr, that other celebrated duelist. He discussed Burr's western project at some length, still seeing scant hope that anything would come of it. He expressed his oft-quoted opinion of his friend's judgment, or lack of it. "Burr is as far from a fool as any man I ever saw," he declared, "and yet he is as easily fooled as any man I ever knew."

Burr had recently written him from Washington. The little colonel still was convinced that war was inevitable, though he conceded frankly that President Jefferson was secretly maneuvering for peace at all costs. Burr expected Spain—or possibly even France —to begin hostilities with an attack on New Orleans, in which event General Jackson and his frontier militiamen would be the nation's stoutest defenders. He was very flattering about that: "I have often said that a brigade could be raised in West Tennessee that would drive double their number of Frenchmen off the earth. . . ." And so, if Jackson would send him the names of his most

trusted officers he would undertake to see that they received pre-
ferment from Secretary of War Dearborn at the proper time.

Swallowing the flattery hook, line, and sinker, Jackson had sent
the list of names. One wonders which man, actually, was "as
easily fooled as any. . . ."

The party spent that night at a tavern near Harrisons Mills.
Nothing was said of the morrow's business; if Jackson's nerves were
bothering him he gave no sign of it. After supper he smoked a
leisurely pipe and swapped small talk with other guests, then went
to bed. Before sunrise next morning his party and Dickinson's met
as agreed, in a small clearing among poplar trees on the bank of
the Red River.

This duel would be no *opéra bouffe* parody like that other affair
with Nolichucky Jack Sevier. For this one, the arrangements were
carried out with scrupulous correctness according to the *code
duello*. The distance was twenty-four feet. The two principals were
to take their places at their respective marks, pistols held at their
sides with muzzles toward the ground. Both signifying their readiness, the second chosen by the toss of a coin would call out the
single word, "Fire." Each man could then fire or hold his fire, at
will. But if either fired before the word, or failed at any time to
toe his mark, both seconds were pledged to shoot him down. The
pistols were Jackson's, a matched set of flintlocks firing one-ounce
balls. As the code required, the two seconds made certain that
they were properly loaded and primed.

So at last the adversaries faced one another. Charles Dickinson
was young, only twenty-seven; handsome, smartly turned out in a
short blue jacket and gray pantaloons; above all, supremely sure of
himself. He had joked with his party on the way to the field, had
told his young wife at parting to expect him home that same evening. Jackson was older by twelve years, and somewhat taller: a
grim, gaunt figure in loose frock coat and pantaloons of dark blue.
It was a fairly usual thing in these meetings, once the common-
sense advice of friends sank in, for both men to fire into the air,
shake hands, and agree that the demands of honor had been
satisfied. Not here, though; not this time. Between this pair there
was only cold, raw hate.

Dr. Hanson Catlett, Dickinson's second, had won the toss for
choice of position. General Overton, winning the next toss, would
give the word.

He put the formal question: "Gentlemen, are you ready?"

Dickinson answered instantly: he was. A little more slowly, Jackson said he was too.

Overton's voice was loud and clear: "Fire!"

Dickinson brought his pistol up, aimed, and fired in one swift, smooth motion. Jackson staggered slightly, his left hand moving convulsively toward his chest. He caught himself, though, and did not go down. He was neither a fast shot nor an exceptionally good one. Well aware of it, he had made up his mind beforehand not to be rushed into firing too hastily. Now, very deliberately, he raised his long right arm and leveled his pistol. Dickinson had recoiled a step, jaw sagging in chagrin.

"Back to the mark, sir!" Overton cried sharply.

But the lapse was due only to momentary confusion, not cowardice. Dickinson stepped back to the mark, folded his arms and waited. Jackson pulled the trigger.

There was no flash, no roar nor gush of powder smoke; nothing but a brittle metallic click as the hammer of his pistol caught at half-cock. Coolly, implacably, he thumbed it back, aimed again, pulled the trigger again. That time the pistol fired, and Dickinson fell.

The code forbade either duelist to approach the other at such a juncture. While the Dickinson people knelt beside their man, Jackson and his party turned and walked to their tethered horses. Not till they were on the point of mounting did Overton notice the blood soaking his friend's clothing. Brusquely Jackson acknowledged that he was hit. Knowing his adversary's skill, he had more than half-expected to be.

Long afterward, looking back with his grimness not a whit softened, he added: "But I should have hit him if he had shot me through the brain."

13

The Grand
Design:
First Stage

CHARLES DICKINSON died that night, comforted at the last by his friends' assurances that Jackson too was dying. They were very nearly right. Dickinson's aim had been truer than he knew, thrown off only slightly—so most accounts agree—by the loose fit of Jackson's coat. The ball lay so close to his heart that surgeons despaired of removing it. In the end they did not dare to try, and he would carry it for the rest of his life. But he did not die.

His recovery was slow, however. He lay, restlessly bedridden at the Hermitage, throughout most of the early summer. Quite likely he was in no condition to take much notice of current events. In retrospect, certainly, it appears he was unaware of the public's changing temper as regarded Aaron Burr. Or it may have been only rugged loyalty to a friend, refusing to credit what was after all no more than rumor and innuendo. But there was plenty of that, both east and west, arising from various dark sources. Some of them remain mysterious to this day.

Perhaps Aaron Burr himself, that man "as easily fooled as any . . ." had talked too much, too indiscreetly, to too many of the wrong people, during the previous year's western junket. Loose talk was not normally among his failings, but it was possible. And perhaps one of the wrong people was the shadowy Stephen Minor of Natchez, down the Trace. It seems to have been something of an open secret that Minor, despite his United States citizenship and his considerable wealth and prominence, had close Spanish ties of long standing. Now his name and Burr's were being linked in tales out of Natchez and New Orleans—to what purpose no one was really sure. Many thought it was Minor who had first set the rumor mills to grinding. Grinding they were, at any rate, and very ominously too. It had been going on for months.

Long before the end of winter, the *United States Gazette* back east in Philadelphia had published a piece that posed a whole clutch of disturbing questions. The paper had wanted to know about Colonel Burr and his "revolutionary party on the Western waters." It demanded the truth about a report that several "States bordering on the Ohio and Mississippi" were about to set up a new and separate government. It referred to another report that army forts and arsenals all the way down the Mississippi to New Orleans would be turned over to Burr and his revolutionaries. It asked, finally: "How soon will Colonel Burr engage in the reduction of Mexico by granting liberty to its inhabitants and seizing on its treasures, aided by British ships and forces?"

This was strong stuff: words with the bark on, as the saying went. And, since its first appearance, the piece had been picked up and reprinted by a great many other journals. One was the *Gazette* in Lexington, Kentucky—close enough to Nashville, surely, to have caused a deal of talk there. Yet Jackson either had not heard it or had chosen to ignore it. Now, slowly convalescing as the months of summer passed, he was discovering that he had a new and unsuspected affinity with Aaron Burr.

If the duel with Hamilton had been Burr's big mistake, his own with Dickinson was proving scarcely smaller. The dead man had been popular: possessed of all the social graces, of excellent family, an accomplished lawyer and one-time protégé of Chief Justice John Marshall of the United States Supreme Court. Sympathy went out to the grieving young widow, all the more because she was carrying Dickinson's unborn child. The funeral had been attended by an immense crowd, and afterward a mass meeting had petitioned the editor of the *Impartial Review* to publish a special memorial issue as a gesture of respect for the deceased. Nothing so wrong in that, perhaps—except that it would also, if indirectly, be a gesture of censure for Andrew Jackson. Still, some old friends— former friends now, maybe—had put their names to the petition.

The long feud with Governor Sevier had left Jackson with a good many political enemies, besides, and it appeared they were making the most of this chance to cut him down to size.

The detail of the pistol that stopped at half-cock was fanned into a hot little controversy. Captain Erwin and others declared publicly that in all fairness Jackson should not have been allowed to aim and fire after that. Both General Overton and Dr. Catlett denied any violation of the code: their principals had agreed specifically, beforehand, that half-cock was not to be considered a "fire." Erwin men retorted that the agreement had not been put in writing, hence meant nothing. The debate itself meant nothing: a splitting of hairs, no more. But it left a good many folk, not necessarily partisans of either side, with the feeling that a truly forebearing man, even wounded himself, would not have shot down a disarmed and helpless enemy.

No doubt it occurred to Jackson that people had said similar things, or worse, of Aaron Burr. They were saying worse now, the rumors continuing to pile up as black and thick as thunderheads in the summer sky.

Toward the end of August, Burr was back in the west again. This time he was accompanied by a secretary and a Frenchman, a Colonel Julien de Pestre, apparently a sort of military aide-de-camp. Reports described the former Vice President as "traveling incognito." If so, he was singularly inept about it, for his activities seemed in no way secret. He was said to be recruiting keen young men around Pittsburgh for—well, for what? Nobody appeared to know. But he, or agents of his, were ordering quantities of stores—barreled pork, flour, cornmeal and the like—sufficient to supply a small army. Some of it was to be delivered at various points along the Ohio River, and some at Natchez. Near Pittsburgh, too, Colonel Burr had dined with a landowner by the name of George Morgan and indulged in table talk of so startling a nature that Morgan had later confided deep misgivings to some of his friends, who in turn confided them to others and finally set them down in a letter to Secretary of State James Madison. What all the talk boiled down to, though, was that Colonel Burr had not actually *said* much of anything. "More was to be concluded from the manner . . . and hints given, than from the words used. . . ."

Whatever he was up to, Burr never stayed in one place very long. At Marietta, Ohio, he reviewed the local militia and placed an order with a boatbuilder on the Muskingum River for a fleet of shallow-draft flatboats. Obviously they were intended for a descent of the Ohio—but to where, and to what purpose? He also was a guest at the rococo mansion of Harman Blennerhasset on an island in the Ohio. Blennerhasset was a young expatriate Irishman with a charming wife and, most of his neighbors thought, considerably more money than good sense. Just the sort of hare-brained fellow, they thought, to take up with any kind of escapade imaginable. Few of those neighbors doubted young Blennerhasset was among Aaron Burr's partners in—well, the question persisted: in what? Was it significant that soon after Burr's visit a series of articles appeared in the *Ohio Gazette,* arguing for separation from the Union of all the western states? As was quite common, the author used a nom de plume, calling himself "Querist." But it seemed to be no secret that "Querist" and Harman Blennerhasset were one and the same person. Mr. Blennerhasset's capacity for indiscretion was, in fact, boundless. Enlarging on his theme in conversations with acquaintances, he was said to be boasting privately that the separation he advocated would be accomplished under Burr's leadership "in nine months"; that Burr already possessed the means of tying President Jefferson "neck and heels"; that Burr could "with three pieces of artillery and three hundred riflemen defend any pass in the Alleghenies. . . ."

Meantime, Burr was moving on. Late in September he appeared once more at the Hermitage, and was welcomed there as warmly as ever. Andrew Jackson, now up and about again, quickly spread the word that he expected his friends would not hang back in paying their respects to the visitor. If some of the rumors had reached his ears—and undoubtedly they had—the stubborn quality of his friendship was more than equal to any doubts they raised. Quite by chance, too, Burr arrived in Nashville about the same time a postrider spurred his lathered horse up the Natchez Trace with news infinitely more urgent than all the rumors put together.

The prospects for war with Spain had taken a sudden upturn. A hostile Spanish force stood at the Sabine River, the disputed boundary between southwestern Louisiana and Mexico. Spanish patrols had crossed the river in arrogant violation of United States territory. American citizens had been seized, the flag willfully dishonored. Louisiana's Governor William C. C. Claiborne was mustering his militia at New Orleans and General James Wilkinson was in Natchez on his way from St. Louis to take personal charge of the garrison at Natchitoches, the army's farthest outpost in the disputed region. The war Aaron Burr needed was at hand, clearly. What was more, Jamey Wilkinson was in position to trigger it with a shooting incident any time he chose—and Wilkinson was Aaron Burr's chief confederate.

Undoubtedly Burr forebore to mention that last to his host. Andrew Jackson was no admirer of Jamey Wilkinson, as Burr well knew. But Jackson needed no prodding from Burr, or anyone, to react to the Spanish threat. In the martial atmosphere created by his order alerting the Tennessee militia, and the general indignation over the Spaniards' villainy, Burr's own warlike designs could not but be applauded. It was no time to be questioning the motives of a patriot. Jackson's enemies held their peace, and so did any who may have had their doubts of Colonel Burr.

But Burr tarried only a short time around Nashville. Soon he was flitting back and forth about Kentucky with his customary energy: planning, recruiting, tying up loose ends. There was much to do. His Spanish war had caught him behind schedule. Time was of the essence now, and it was passing, and still he had his problems. Overall, though, the grand design appeared to be shaping up. Back came a letter to Andrew Jackson after a while. Burr enclosed a draft for thirty-five-hundred dollars and ordered five flatboats to be built and provisioned at the Clover Bottom boatyard. The business was more than welcome, Jackson's finances being what they were, and martial enthusiasm still ran high among his friends. One of them, a genial sportsman named Patton Anderson, began to enroll volunteers for a troop to embark with Burr.

Then on a crisp November day while the clatter of adzes and mauls rang out across Stone's River, and Anderson drilled his would-be adventurers on the racecourse infield, a stranger presented himself at the Hermitage.

The stranger's true identity has been a mystery virtually from that day to the present. A few casual historians have tried to explain him as a friend of Jackson's, which he patently was not. Some have given him a name, Captain Fort, which apparently was what he called himself. Most have theorized that he was a "natural son" of Aaron Burr, which he may have been. Burr, whose reputation as a rake was considered notorious by some New Yorkers, is known to have fathered at least one bastard son there.

Whoever he was, at any rate, the young man evidently seemed a pleasant sort. He said he was on his way from the east to join Aaron Burr, and that sounded plausible enough. The Jacksons invited him to stay the night, which he did. As the evening wore along, it became apparent that he knew a good bit about Burr's western project and was not averse to talking.

One is tempted to imagine the pair of them sitting up late that night: the lanky squire of the Hermitage jackknifed into an easy chair, smoking his pipe and saying little, blue eyes quizzically probing from under shaggy brows as he sized up his garrulous guest. Like most of its kind, the blockhouse consisted of a single big room on the first floor, with a huge stone fireplace in one wall. It was November, probably chilly; there would have been logs blazing in the fireplace, the smoky light pulsing along hewn ceiling beams in the shadows overhead. Rachel would long since have said her good-nights and retired. And perhaps Captain Fort grew a trifle self-important, as young men can. Perhaps he had one too many whiskey toddies, loosening his tongue.

It may have come about that way. However it did, the captain presently made some careless reference to a scheme to divide the Union. If Jackson had listened with only half an ear till then, suddenly he was all attention. He asked questions, and Fort answered them with easy glibness. He spoke of a lightning descent on New Orleans: the city seized, the port sealed off, then a swift conquest of Mexico. Do all that, he said, and the western states would readily fall into line. Jackson's dander rose. His questions came more harshly: how was this to be accomplished? Still glibly, Fort spoke of federal troops whose general was in collusion . . .

Abruptly the young man realized he had said too much. He attempted to drop the subject, shrug the whole thing off. He protested that he actually knew nothing. Wilkinson? No, he was not acquainted with the general. Burr? He knew Colonel Burr only slightly, could not say that he was in the scheme, if indeed there was a scheme at all.

Too late! Andrew Jackson was aware that Burr and Jamey Wilkinson were friends. He knew they had had dealings of some sort the preceding summer. And he knew, finally, of the long-standing suspicions held by many westerners regarding Jamey Wilkinson's too-cozy relations with Spanish authorities in America. Add all that to the tales floating about the Ohio Valley and he could guess the truth, or as near it as made no difference.

Captain Fort departed the next morning, probably somewhat crestfallen, certainly with no cordial farewells to gladden his journey. Where he went and what ultimately became of him history does not say.

Andrew Jackson plunged into some vehement writing.

To Aaron Burr went a letter flatly declaring their friendship at an end unless or until Burr cleared himself of all suspicion of treason. To Daniel Smith, United States Senator from Tennessee, went another, laying out the situation as Jackson understood it and urging quick federal action to head off any possible coup. Burr was not mentioned by name, however. It may have been a natural disinclination to get a friend into trouble on hearsay evidence— but also, perhaps, it was beginning to dawn on Andrew Jackson that his own relations with Burr might well come under fire now. As a possible hedge against that, he dashed off a letter to President Jefferson himself, pledging the services of the Tennessee militia against attack from any quarter. Then he followed it with still another—to Governor Claiborne at New Orleans, warning against a possible attack "from Spain." He was voicing the old western bugaboo here, the years-old fear that Spain might pinch off New Orleans and close the Mississippi River in a two-pronged movement from Mexico and the Floridas. Yet the thought that all this could wind up beside the point, after all—that Burr's plans might be, as he had claimed, under the tacit aegis of the War Department—must still have troubled Jackson, for he added that he would "delight to see Mexico reduced," but was prepared to "die in the last Ditch before I would see the Union disunited."

Having thus covered his flanks about as well as a good military man could, he settled back to await developments. Burr was the first to answer. His letter gave his solemn word of honor that he planned nothing harmful to the United States, and Jackson was half-convinced. But if he was reluctant to believe ill of Aaron Burr, he could not quite forget that Burr and General James Wilkinson were good friends. And of Wilkinson, Andrew Jackson was not only willing but eager to believe any sort of villainy. Besides, the news drifting into Nashville continued to be less than reassuring.

Early in November Joseph Hamilton Daviess, United States

district attorney for Kentucky, had petitioned the Federal Court at Frankfort for Aaron Burr's arrest on a charge of treason. The court had refused, finding the evidence too flimsy. Burr had heard of it, however, and insisted on a formal hearing to clear his name. It turned out to be abortive. After requesting two delays, Daviess finally was forced to stand up in court and state that his best witness had decamped, leaving him in the lurch. The fiasco made him a laughingstock, while Burr was roundly applauded by the crowd. Still, the accusation had been made; that ugly word "treason" had been applied openly to Aaron Burr's activities for the first time, and the doubts it raised were not easily put to rest.

Doubts were not conviction, nevertheless. Jackson gave no orders to stop work on the flatboats at Clover Bottom. Patton Anderson went on with his recruiting of volunteers.

Soon after the middle of December, Burr appeared at the Hermitage again, accompanied by a Kentucky associate named John Adair. Jackson happened to be away from home on business, and Rachel's greeting was distantly polite but no more. She very pointedly did not ask the callers to stay overnight; Burr had to take lodgings at the Clover Bottom Inn and wait there for Jackson's return with what patience he could muster. Adair left him and headed down the Natchez Trace, apparently to enlist help for Burr's designs in that direction.

At that point Aaron Burr must have been feeling travel-worn and more than a little harassed, whether or not he showed it. Troubles were beginning to press in on him. Too much talk had circulated for much too long, leaving too many people wondering what he was up to. In Cincinnati a ragtag crowd had gathered outside his tavern to serenade him with a rendition of the "Rogue's March" as he dined with friends. He had remarked, not losing a jot of his aplomb, that he always enjoyed music with his meals. But there were worse things happening. Farther east, on both banks of the Ohio, Harman Blennerhasset's "Querist" articles had been stirring up hornets' nests of public indignation ever since their first appearance. Just a few days before Burr's arrival on the Cumberland, in fact, Blennerhasset and the eastern recruits already gathered on his island had had to push off hurriedly in five of the flatboats from the Muskingum yard, only hours ahead of a mob of Ohio militiamen and surly hangers-on. Balked of its prey, the mob had tramped roughshod through the Blennerhasset gardens, ransacked the Blennerhasset mansion, then broken into Blennerhasset's wine cellar and wound up gloriously drunk.

Cooling his heels at Clover Bottom, Burr probably was slow to hear of that latest development. When he did it made little difference anyway. Ready or not, the time had come for a descent of the Ohio River; he had already sent word to that effect. And in spite of the discouragements that beset him, he still had no reason to think his case desperate. A few allies had let him down, true, but he had others who remained staunch. Most important, he still had James Wilkinson and Jamey still had the army, face to face with the Dons at the Sabine, primed to make war at his convenience.

When Andrew Jackson got around to calling, that too was encouraging. The meeting was a prickly one at first, though. Jackson had even brought his friend John Coffee with him, possibly as the witness he might need later to absolve him of any taint of conspiracy. But Aaron Burr made a good advocate for himself. He had charm, personal magnetism, the persuasive gift of logic of the accomplished lawyer he was. He swore again that everything he planned to do had the approval of federal authorities. He clinched it, no doubt with a bit of a flourish, by producing a blank commission signed by Thomas Jefferson.

Jackson owned himself satisfied.

That hurdle behind him, Burr took the time to pen a soothing letter to Senator Daniel Smith, repeating the same assurance he had been giving Jackson, that he planned only to lead a corps of volunteers against Mexico upon the outbreak of war. But in the unlikely event of peace instead, he wrote, he would simply go ahead with his settlement of the Ouachita lands and make the best of a planter's life. He could not resist adding a wistful postscript: "I have been persecuted, shamefully persecuted. . . ."

Only two of the boats he had ordered were ready. He indicated they were all he needed, and Jackson refunded some fifteen hundred dollars for the three not built. Stockly Hays, a seventeen-year-old nephew of Rachel's, had planned to leave for school in New Orleans as a passenger with Burr, and neither Rachel nor Jackson had any objections. Shortly before the day of embarkation, however, the latest news from Louisiana came up the Natchez Trace to Nashville. It was shocking: General Wilkinson had concluded a peace treaty with His Excellency, the viceroy of Mexico. By its terms both nations agreed to honor the Sabine River boundary.

Both armies were pulling back, thus establishing a neutral zone along the river. The war, in short, was over before it had begun.

Burr took the disappointment as stoically as he had taken every other setback. He remarked only that he was "sorry for it," and thought the general mistaken in electing not to fight. Privately he must have been badly puzzled too, for it appeared Jamey had let their big chance slip. The march on Mexico would have to be abandoned now—though no doubt it was always possible that Jamey had some new stratagem in mind. Burr had gone too far to stop now, regardless. There was no course left him but to proceed with his ostensible voyage to the Ouachita. Several horses and quantities of stores already had been purchased. They were loaded aboard the boats. A score or so of young men from the neighborhood still were determined to go along. But with the prospect of military glory dimmed, Patton Anderson and his Cumberland rifles decided to stay home.

In the early-morning gray of December twenty-second the two flatboats were poled out into the current from the Clover Bottom shore. They swung slowly down Stone's River and out into the Cumberland to begin the long downstream drift to the Ohio. Aaron Burr's clouded destiny was very nearly played out now, and the folk of the District of Mero would see him no more. They were still to be caught up in the furor of his passing, though.

The good-byes were accomplished with no great fanfare.

14
The Grand
Design:
Finis

RUMORS followed Harman Blennerhasset's people down the Ohio like hounds yelping after a panicky fox. For the first stages of their flight the little band traveled by night, risky as that was on a river lacking any semblance of navigation aids and strewn with the lurking hazards of snags, sandbars, and sawyers. For a while, too, all hands toiled at the oars to stay ahead of pursuit. There was none, actually, but they did not know it, and their furtive passage only bred new apprehensions along the way.

At Jeffersonville in Indiana Territory a few other boats with more recruits joined up, giving rise to tales of an armada manned by as many as a thousand desperadoes. Joseph Hamilton Daviess was at Louisville when the expedition passed there. He reported that he counted sixteen vessels, mostly big keelboats and flats. The discomfited district attorney was not exactly an objective witness, but his story was conservative by comparison with some others. Many people claimed their sleep was disturbed by volleys of musketry as the boats stole past in the dead of night. At least one excited citizen heard a cannon fired, so he said. The flotilla tied up briefly at Clarksville and was visited by curious townsfolk. Several remarked on the absence of any women or children: strange, they thought, in a party of peaceful settlers. Others saw a box carried on board one of the boats, and deduced from its size and shape that it might contain muskets. Pittsburgh, far to the

rear, sent tales of stagecoaches arriving from the east crowded with "Yankees," all of them asking about "a rendezvous with Comfort Tyler." Mr. Tyler, already on the Ohio with Blennerhasset, was known to be a Burr lieutenant: one of the western project's most vigorous recruiters, in fact.

How much talk reached the middle Cumberland no one knows. Undoubtedly some did. And no doubt some was accurate, or reasonably so. A great deal was purest moonshine, too—but who was to tell the difference? Andrew Jackson's stature in the neighborhood and his well-known hair-trigger disposition would be enough to discourage impertinent comment, Aaron Burr being a friend of his. Resentment over the duel with Dickinson still smoldered, all the same. One suspects that many a Jackson neighbor may have begun to look askance at the Hermitage as the western outpost of a conspiracy. The question refused to go away, somehow: *was* Colonel Burr what he professed to be, or was he not?

On Christmas Day, Burr joined the Blennerhasset party, on an island (long since washed away) at the Cumberland's mouth. Stockly Hays, incidentally, was the messenger who rode ahead to make contact and set up the meeting. The day was raw and blustery with gusts of rain. Gathering around their beached flatboats, the adventurers listened to a short address by Burr. Most were young men from respectable eastern families; there was not a real desperado in the lot. Many had joined up with only a hazy notion of where they were going, or why. Apparently some had been given to understand that they might be called on for military service, and some had not. Aaron Burr offered scant enlightenment. The nature of their mission, said he, would be told them in due time. For the present, secrecy must be the order of the day because he had powerful and unscrupulous enemies working to defeat him. He moved through the crowd when he had finished, and made a point of shaking hands with every recruit in the Ohio River contingent. None of them had met him before. All told, one recalled later, the force numbered about a hundred.

Burr had not exaggerated about his enemies. But all he knew, all he could even guess, fell far short of the whole truth. He was already heading straight into disaster.

Jamey Wilkinson's peace treaty at the Sabine had not come out of a clear sky, precisely. In October, almost three months earlier, Burr's last letter from the east had reached the general at Natchitoches. It had been a long, weary time on the road, for the trusted courier who brought it had first sought Jamey in St. Louis, then followed him all the way down the Mississippi. Written in the private code Burr and Wilkinson always used, the letter was a strange one, full of an extravagant bravado that was not Burr's usual style. It also contained a couple of outright lies.

Burr wrote that he had obtained funds and

commenced the enterprise. . . . Everything internal and external favors views . . . Naval protection of England is assured. . . . England, a navy of the United States, are ready to join. . . . It will be a host of choice spirits. . . . Burr will proceed westward first August, never to return. . . . Burr guarantees the results with his life and honor, with the lives and honor and the fortunes of hundreds of the best blood in the country. . . . The gods invite us to glory and fortune; it remains to be seen whether we deserve the boon . . .

Wilkinson was not impressed. He doubted the blithe assurance of British help. Word of Prime Minister Pitt's death had reached the Mississippi Valley that spring; it was nearly certain that a new British government would be in no mood to meddle in a risky American adventure. For more than a year, anyway, Jamey had been mulling over some second thoughts about his own connection with the venture. The flood of scare talk and wild conjecture already let loose had shaken him badly. He knew that associates in New Orleans now had serious doubts, too. The whole tone of Burr's letter—what he read between the lines more than the text itself—convinced him that the project had become a forlorn hope at best. At worst, it might put a rope around a great many necks, Jamey's own included. The problem was, all at once, how to extricate himself while still salvaging what personal advantage he might.

Those skeptical westerners who questioned Wilkinson's loyalty happened to be right. He had been Agent 13 on Spain's secret payroll for years past, his oath as an officer of the United States Army notwithstanding. He was, in fact, a traitor of such grand scope and versatility as to make Benedict Arnold the merest tyro alongside him. The big difference was that nothing could be proved against Jamey until long after his death. He had had no scruples about betraying his country to Spain, or Spain to Aaron Burr when that looked profitable. He had none about betraying Burr either, if that was the way the wind blew now.

It appeared that was indeed the way the wind blew. For most of the long night after he decoded Burr's letter, the general considered ways and means. In the morning, his mind made up, he confided to his second-in-command at Natchitoches that there was a treasonable plot afoot with Aaron Burr as its ringleader. The plot was far advanced already, he said; he had uncovered it only when Burr had tried to enlist *him,* and dealing with it was going to take all the resources at his command. But first the army must be freed of the Spanish menace at its front. For Jamey Wilkinson, the man with a foot in each camp, that posed no great difficulty. He was aware that the Spanish authorities were as eager for a peaceful compromise as he was. Then, once negotiations were underway, Jamey spent several more days in deep thought before dispatching a message warning President Jefferson of a large revolutionary army advancing down the Mississippi. With it went a copy of Burr's damning letter, carefully edited to remove all references to Jamey's own involvement. Never one to overlook the chance for a dishonest dollar, the general next sent a similar copy to the viceroy of Mexico and demanded a reward in keeping with his service in scotching Burr's Mexican designs.

His Excellency was no fool. He declined to pay. Very likely Thomas Jefferson was not fooled either, but the occasion for destroying Aaron Burr once and for all was too good to be missed. Burr was an old rival; there was no love lost between them and had not been for a long time.

On November twenty-seventh the President issued a proclamation announcing the existence of an illegal enterprise "against the dominions of Spain," and sternly warning all participants to "withdraw from the same without delay, or . . . answer the contrary at their peril." Western communications were slow, however, especially by the roundabout way down the long, thinly populated reaches of the lower Ohio and the Mississippi. Thus it was Burr's bad luck that the proclamation never overtook his little flotilla. It did not arrive in Nashville until almost the end of December. Burr's name was not mentioned in it. But that made little difference, what with all the earlier talk.

"Last night at the hour of nine commenced the burning of the Effigy of Colo. Aaron Burr," reported the *Impartial Review* on January third.

There had been just time for the news to get around by word of mouth; time for indignant citizens to pack the courthouse square, and for emotions to blaze up as hotly as the flames that consumed the straw man. The ghost of Charles Dickinson was there, too. His friend Thomas Swann and his father-in-law, Captain Erwin, harangued the crowd around the bonfire, and both named Andrew Jackson as Burr's ally. With the hue and cry raised openly, other friends of the dead man no longer hesitated to stand up and be counted.

Fortunately for the civic peace, no doubt, Jackson was not present. He already knew the score against him, having heard from Secretary of War Henry Dearborn some days before. "The merest old-woman letter you ever saw . . ." he called it contemptuously. But no wonder. The evidence suggests that Henry Dearborn was one of Burr's conspirators, and he may have had the personal word of Burr that Jackson was another. Without committing himself, therefore, he was trying to pass along the warning to hunt cover. Piously he cited eastern rumors claiming that Burr's adventurers expected to be joined on the Cumberland by General Jackson and two regiments of Tennessee volunteers. It was a situation, he wrote, in which the general might find it possible to put a stop to the whole business if he acted speedily.

The general was having none of that. He fired off a truculent answer accusing Dearborn of "dishonor, dishonesty . . . and want of candor," and declaring that he, Jackson, had no reason to care how the secretary chose to defend himself "before the world." Having got that off his chest, Jackson went about clearing his own name in the best possible way: with action instead of words. Hurriedly mustering several companies of the local militia he rode off at their head to scour the lower Cumberland for the fugitive Burr. It was too late, of course; Aaron Burr was already past Fort Massac, on down the Ohio and out into the Mississippi. But the manhunt kept folk satisfied for the week or two till the storm subsided. Then even the most prejudiced of hotheads began to realize it had been pretty much a teapot tempest after all. There was not and never had been any real prospect of treason, war, and rebellion on the Cumberland. And thus it ended.

Meantime, as everyone knows, Aaron Burr floated placidly down the Mississippi to his fate. He was arrested at Bayou Pierre but escaped and fled toward Spanish Florida; was recaptured, carried east, and tried for treason; was acquitted in court but found guilty forevermore in the harsher court of public opinion; passed finally into a bitter and disillusioned obscurity. Whatever it was he actually dreamed and schemed and plotted for, however he might have been remembered had luck not turned against him at the last, his worst sin probably lay in misjudging his own times and the temper of his countrymen.

As for the score or so of Cumberlanders who went off with him from Clover Bottom, no one knows. Some of Burr's eastern recruits stayed on in Louisiana or Mississippi and some made their various ways home again. It is a good guess that some of the Cumberland lads, too, eventually tramped back up the Natchez Trace with nothing to show for their excursion save the awareness of having taken part in history—if they *were* aware. Come right down to it, a flatboat trip to New Orleans was nothing so earthshaking for a Cumberland riverman to brag on.

The drama had one more role in it for Andrew Jackson. He was summoned to Burr's trial at Richmond, Virginia, as a government witness, though he never testified—not formally in court, that is, but he testified: loudly and clearly in the streets and taverns of the city, to everyone with the time and the inclination to listen. Characteristically, the man from the Cumberland made no secret of his belief that General James Wilkinson, not Aaron Burr, was the real traitor in the case. "A double traitor!" he declared of Jamey, and added ". . . pity the sword that dangles at his felon's belt, for it is doubtless of honest steel!" When the occasion arose, he made no secret, either, of his feelings about the lack of that same steel in Thomas Jefferson's backbone. While he waited impatiently through one court delay after another, there arose the latest incident in the long-running controversy over the British navy's stopping and searching of American ships on the high seas. In June, off the Virginia Capes, His Majesty's frigate *Leopard* fired a broadside into the United States's *Chesapeake*, then laid her aboard and seized four seamen alleged to be British deserters.

Jackson, a rampant Anglophobe since boyhood, was beside himself. When it became clear that there would be no warlike reprisals despite a storm of public indignation, he announced his intention of airing some opinions from the steps of the Virginia State House. He did, as soon as court adjourned that day. He aired them for the better part of an hour, to a large and militant crowd. "Mr. Jefferson," he said in part, "has plenty of courage to seize peaceable Americans . . . and persecute them for political purposes. . . . But he is too cowardly to resent foreign outrage on the Republic. . . ."

Mr. Jefferson, very anxious for Aaron Burr's conviction, made a point of keeping in close touch with the government prosecutors at Richmond and knowing all that went on there. Presently he sent a trenchant suggestion from Monticello: the testimony of the major general of the Tennessee militia could be dispensed with.

Andrew Jackson went home to the Hermitage.

15

Antebellum

ANDREW JACKSON would go home to the Hermitage many times in the stormy years ahead, and many times go forth again to battle, refreshed by communion with the land and the people he loved. Inevitably, though, the Jackson who went on to wider fame as soldier and then as statesman would belong less to the Cumberland than to the nation.

A curtain came down, somehow, with his bloody brawl in 1813 with the Benton brothers, Tom and Jesse, in a hotel on Nashville's courthouse square. It was a backwoods donnybrook, altogether in character for the man who had once dispatched a bully with a fence rail and threatened to cane Nolichucky Jack Sevier, but it was also the last of such didos. Destiny had larger plans for Andrew Jackson. The shoulder smashed by Jesse Benton's pistol ball still was far from healed when the general led his militiamen to victory over the Creek Indians at Horseshoe Bend in Alabama.

It was a second chance for a man already passed over once and for all by history, or so it seemed. Jackson had mustered his Tennessee militia at the outbreak of the War of 1812. He had put his men aboard flatboats and taken them down the rivers to Natchez, two thousand strong and itching to fight the British. But Jamey Wilkinson still was the American commander in the west. The Tennesseans cooled their heels for a spell, then Jackson was curtly informed of orders from Washington to disband his troops. Just that and nothing more. They were unpaid, had neither supplies nor rations, were eight hundred miles from home, and their country had no use for them—or for their general either. It was on the dismal homeward march up the Natchez Trace, doggedly plodding along on foot because he had given up his horse to a sick soldier, that Andrew Jackson won a nickname. "Tough as hickory!" his men said of him, approvingly, and Old Hickory he would be from that time on.

The second chance was all Jackson needed. Having disposed of the hostile Creeks, he marched into Spanish Florida and occupied Pensacola. There was nothing in his orders authorizing that, to be sure. The British had naval forces based in Pensacola, though, and it always had been Jackson's conviction that Florida ought to be United States territory anyway—and before long it was. So he drove the British out, then turned and marched swiftly for New Orleans. And now, all at once, destiny was running his way irresistibly. It was late 1814, England's main offensive thrust had shifted southward, and Jamey Wilkinson was gone from New Orleans. Now the city would be saved by Andrew Jackson or by no one.

He did save it. With his motley crowd of Tennessee and Kentucky frontiersmen, Creole free lances, Jean Lafitte's pirates, and a sprinkling of Choctaw braves and free black men, he utterly routed an army of seasoned British regulars that had stood up to the cream of Napoleon Bonaparte's Grande Armée on the fields of Europe. The battle, it turned out, was strategically pointless; the war already had ended, though the news came late. But that mattered not at all. What mattered was that it was a grand victory, a mighty psychological lift for a young nation that had been feeling pretty sorry for itself. It was also a shining milestone on the glory road that ultimately took Andrew Jackson to Washington as the seventh President of the United States.

Little happiness he had from that, though, for he went to the Executive Mansion a widower. The old scandal of the Jacksons' irregular marriage was a burden Rachel had borne with stoic patience for thirty-five years, but the bitter calumny attending the presidential campaign of 1828 made it too heavy to bear longer. Jackson never forgave his political enemies for that, and for eight long years he was a President distinguished as much for the stature and the venom of those enemies as for the loyal friends he kept. In sum, he was an uncompromising, hickory-tough old man who never dodged a fight and never yielded. When he died at the Hermitage on a warm June Sunday in 1845, Americans would look behind them at the tumultuous years they came to call the Age of Jackson and realized their nation had changed past any going back.

Sometime during those years, the Cumberland ceased to be frontier.

As early as 1814 the *Pittsburgh Navigator and Almanac* described Nashville in terms too enthusiastic to be applied to any common river town. The *Almanac* was a combination travel guide and pilots' handbook for the Ohio and Mississippi rivers and their navigable tributaries, compiled by an extraordinarily zealous young Pittsburgh man named Zadok Cramer. Noting that the town was in "a flourishing state of improvement," he went on to explain:

> ... it has a respectable banking company; a cotton manufactury ... a ropewalk, a powder mill—and a cotton gin—all in handsome operation. Wm. Carroll & Co. in connection with Mr. Cowan of Pittsburgh, have a nail manufactury and an extensive ironmongery store. And the citizens generally are turning their attention to the establishment of such manufacturers as will tend to render them independent and happy. . . .

Cramer mentioned Nashville's two hundred or more houses, many of them "large, elegant buildings of brick." He had words of praise for the two churches, the courthouse, the jail, the Reverend Thomas Craighead's Davidson Academy. But river commerce was his *Almanac's* reason for being, and he found that thriving too:

> There is a line of barges constantly running from Nashville to New Orleans, loaded down with the rich products of Tennessee and up with sugar, coffee, rice, hides, liquors, dry goods, etc., conducted principally by Mr. Spriggs, a most active and industrious trader, and . . . among the most expert conductors of a barge, of any person on the river. These . . . give employment to a number of active, hardy men. . . .

Zadok Cramer's "barges" were the long, narrow, double-ended rivercraft more commonly called keelboats and remembered nowadays chiefly for the legendary exploits of Mike Fink: bullyboy, folk hero, and roughest toughest keelboatman of them all. Whether or not the real Mike Fink lived up to all that, there is no evidence to show he was ever on the Cumberland. Others of his strong-backed, half-horse half-alligator brethren were working the river a good while before 1814, though. Records kept at Johnson's Landing ten years earlier have a pair of keelboats arriving there with goods for one of Andrew Jackson's stores, and a harpsichord and some other fancy furniture he had bought for Rachel in Phila-delphia. Apparently it all came the long way 'round: first overland to Pittsburgh, then down the Ohio and up the Cumberland. Despite the extra mileage, it would be a more practical route than the all-overland trek by wagon. But it was not cheap. Jackson's freight bill added up to more than sixteen hundred dollars—which in-cluded the cost of enough whiskey to keep fourteen keelboatmen in fettle during the upstream haul on the Cumberland. A miserable, draft-animal drudgery it was, too: all hands walking their boat into the current for hours on end, shoulders braced against heavy poles and feet treadmilling from bow to stern down a cleated gang-way—or else going over the side to drag her through the shallows at the end of a cordelle. Sixteen days and twenty gallons it took, Cumberland's mouth to Nashville.

The middle and lower river provided business enough to attract more entrepreneurs than Cramer's Mr. Spriggs. John Coffee, An-drew Jackson's partner in the Clover Bottom boatyard, had at least two keelboats, the *Adventure* and the *Resolution*, trading with New Orleans by 1803. A few years later another Nashville firm was advertising a boat large enough to handle ninety tons of cargo: perhaps a leviathan for her time. There were still others as time passed and the District of Mero—the old name was slow to die—grew and prospered.

Going down to New Orleans to join her husband after the mo-mentous victory in 1815, Rachel Jackson traveled by Cumberland keelboat, and wrote home that she arrived in "the tollerable time of 25 days." In fact, that was better than "tollerable" for a passage that sometimes took much longer. And the full round trip, coming back upstream by oar, pole, and cordelle—only occasionally helped out by sails when the wind happened to be right—might be a matter of three months or more. Zadok Cramer was well aware of the time factor, too. He concluded his flattering observations on

Nashville with the hope that a day was soon to come "when the citizens . . . will see a steam boat winding her way up the Cumberland in all the majesty . . . of her internal and secreted power." It could be done, he advised; nothing was needed "but the spirit of beginning."

The admonition probably was unnecessary. Nashville citizens could sniff the winds of change as well as any, not to mention the sweet smell of potential profit. When the fine new steamboat *General Jackson* slid into the water at Pittsburgh early in 1818, Nashville money had built her, Nashville men owned her, and Nashville was her port of registry. She shunned the Cumberland on her maiden voyage, all the same, and arrived at the New Orleans levee with a full cargo of flour, Monongahela whiskey, and other goods from the upper Ohio. Then when she tried to head for Nashville on her return trip, low water stopped her at Cross Creek, nearly a hundred miles short. It was hardly an auspicious beginning for steam navigation on the Cumberland.

The *Jackson* failed to make her home port for almost a year, in fact, and even then it took a strong assist from nature to get her there. Again low water held her up, this time at the lower end of Harpeth Shoals. She lay at Harpeth Island for several days, till her captain gave up and had most of the cargo out of her and into barges for delivery to his consignees in Nashville. Then at the last minute a high tide came rolling down the river and she steamed triumphantly through the Shoals in all her twin-stacked, whistle-blaring, gingerbread glory. "A sight so novel at this place has attracted large crowds of spectators," remarked the *Nashville Whig and Tennessee Advertiser*. It was probably an understatement. Others who remembered the great day—it was March 11, 1819—were far less restrained in telling how thousands poured in from all the countryside to marvel and to cheer. Progress had come to the Cumberland on the thrashing buckets of paddle wheels, and trailing clouds of black woodsmoke.

It kept coming. The *Rifleman* tied up at Nashville early in 1820; then a few months later the *General Robertson;* then in quickening succession the *Cumberland,* the *General Greene,* the *Nashville,* the *Pennsylvania,* the *Red Rover* . . .

Misadventures came, too. The *General Robertson* blew a boiler at Eddyville on her second trip up the river, killing several passengers and two members of the crew. It gave folk along the lower

Cumberland a nine-day topic of doleful conversation, but no more. Riding any contraption that ran on high-pressure steam was bound to be a pretty chancy proposition, and everybody knew it. But one couldn't turn one's back on so amazing a performance as New Orleans to Nashville in twelve days flat. Progress indeed, and with a capital P at that! The *Rifleman,* obviously one of the first of the flash packets, chalked up that passage in 1822.

Harpeth Shoals remained a hazard always irksome and occasionally lethal, as they would for virtually as long as steamboats plied the Cumberland. A sudden drop in the river could catch a boat there with three feet of water or less, and when it did she stuck hard and fast; either ripped her bottom out, stayed hung up till a high tide came along to float her off, or had to be "hogged" through. Hogging was a simple if strenuous procedure in which the whole crew—deckhands, roustabouts, frequently deck passengers too—went over the side to shovel away mud and gravel and literally "root her out like a hog," as the saying put it. Then with the assistance of a stout hawser run from the capstan to some handy tree on the bank, with boilers popping and groaning under full heads of steam and paddle wheels churning up cascades of lather, she either wallowed through into deep water or she didn't. Inconvenient as they might be, such crises could be taken in stride as part of the game, and were. At her best the steamboat had a fine, free, hell-for-leather flair about her that was not to be matched till that other machine-age masterpiece, the steam locomotive, came chuffing and bellowing on the scene. Meantime, from the overblown elegance of Lucullan dinners in ornate gingerbread saloons to the main decks where poor folk bedded down on hard planks and took their chances with the trampling feet of roustabouts hustling freight at every muddy little country landing, the steamboat served up a rich slice of assorted Americana, on the Cumberland no less than the larger Ohio and Mississippi.

It was steamboatmen's nature to be venturesome. By 1828 nervy pilots were pushing the smaller packets upstream as far as the mouth of Caney Fork, and even turning some way up that stream if they happened to catch a favoring tide. A few years more and the bolder pioneers were feeling their way farther still through the Cumberland's crooked bends and chutes and riffles: past Martinsburg just over the Kentucky line, through the tricky Wild Goose Shoals to Rowena Landing, finally to Point Isabel where the river's north and south forks met. They could go no farther; Smith's Shoals and the falls made sure of that.

President-elect Jackson stepped aboard a steamboat at his own Hermitage landing to leave for his inauguration in 1828: in its own small way, a historic first. But that was the least of it. The election of 1828 was not only the first to send a westerner to the White House, but a historic first in crudity and vilification as well. Slanderous references to Rachel Jackson as "a convicted adulteress" were only part of it. Political foes went to outrageous lengths to portray Jackson as a murderer, a bloodstained ogre. One widely circulated handbill pictured six coffins, to remind voters of six mutinous militiamen he had executed during the Creek War. Another showed the general, unmistakable in full army regimentals, personally hanging an unnamed opponent from a handy tree. "Jackson is to be President, and you will be HANGED," proclaimed the caption. Jackson was the people's choice, nevertheless. He defeated incumbent President John Quincy Adams by an electoral vote of 178 to 83. And it quickly developed, then, that Andrew Jackson himself was the greatest historic first of all. Daniel Webster, the senatorial giant from New Hampshire, voiced an apprehension prevalent in Washington when he predicted the new President "will bring a breeze with him. Which way it will blow, I cannot tell." The senator was right. A breeze not only blew up from the Cumberland, it rapidly approached gale force.

The times simmered in a ferment of restlessness and controversy anyway. It was an attack of national growing pains. And into the midst of the ferment strode a leader whose like the nation never had known before, a living symbol of the emergence of the power of the common American; sometimes good, very often bad; still, overall—*progress!*

The Indian, once claimant to all the fine hunting grounds south of the Ohio River, suffered his final deprivation. No matter that it came long after he had put aside the rifle and the tomahawk to put his trust in white men's law instead. White men's law was not for him. Chickasaw, Choctaw, Cherokee, and Creek, all were herded into a limbo far across the Mississippi. It was the final victory in Andrew Jackson's long, implacable warring with the red man, but Dragging Canoe had foreseen it years ahead of Jackson's time. Eliminating the poor Indian, though, was but a detail in the large-scale scene. Jackson brought down the national bank with equal, uncompromising finality. South Carolina states' righters tested the presidential mettle and got *their* swift comeuppance. The Republic burgeoned in heady awareness of its manifest destiny: a brand-new term to conjure with. Out in the far southwest the one-time Cumberlander and Jackson comrade-in-arms Sam Houston led a valiant little army of Texans in rebellion against Mexico. "There, you see?" cried old, ailing Aaron Burr when the news reached New York City. "I was right. I was only thirty years too soon." Among other bitter memories, perhaps Burr recalled how the Cumberland had once hailed him as a hero, and how quickly that had changed. "What was treason in me," he observed querulously ". . . is patriotism now."

Just so. In 1845 Andrew Jackson's deathbed was made softer by the knowledge that Sam Houston would bring Texas into the Union as its twenty-eighth state. And when it developed that

that meant war with Mexico, Tennessee reacted with such enthusiastic truculence as to earn the permanent nickname of Volunteer State. In June of 1846 the First Tennessee Regiment paraded through Nashville before boarding a steamboat for the front. As the soldiers swung jauntily past the famous Nashville Female Academy, five hundred pretty students stood watching, starry-eyed. And one, a niece of General Zachary Taylor, stepped forward to hand the commanding officer a battle flag with a motto embroidered by the senior class. Weeping for the "fallen brave," it declared, was preferable to the living presence of "men too timid to strike for their country."

Spartan women, indeed! And would the young ladies, growing matronly in another fifteen years or so, remember . . . and feel the same? No doubt they would and did. By and large, though a reasonably small number of "fallen brave" never came back from Mexico, Cumberland folk found the times good.

Nashville thrived. Since becoming Tennessee's capital in 1843 it had grown apace, had a population crowding seventeen thousand as the decade of the 1850s opened. The city accommodated travelers in six hotels. It was the home of five newspapers, a respected medical journal, and a temperance organ. Long ago its people had spilled across from the Cumberland's south bank to the north, and spanned the river with a covered wooden bridge supported on massive stone abutments. The first bridge over the Cumberland anywhere, it was already growing old; come 1860 it would be replaced by a new suspension bridge of iron. Nine colleges flourished within a fifty-mile radius of Nashville. Every last one of them, according to a local booster, was "the equal of Old Harvard." The city had two theaters and attracted such stars of the day as Jenny Lind, Phineas T. Barnum's Swedish Nightingale, and the great Norwegian violin virtuoso Ole Bull. Grand Opera, too, came up the Cumberland by steamboat, in the persons of Arditi's original Italian Company. One runs across hints that such foreign cultural treats were not always wholly satisfying, however. Two concerts by Jenny Lind drew only fair newspaper reviews, and apparently Grand Opera was simply too far over Nashville's head. The editor of the *Gazette*, for one, felt constrained to lecture his readers on the correct attitude after a performance of *Lucia di Lammermoor*: "Those who attend . . . must not find fault. . . . If a man in his death agony is heard to sing, the hearer must not become disgusted. . . ."

On the whole, the city's elite preferred diversions less exotic: grand balls, sumptuous dinners, and the like. Growth and the rising level of opulence had not quite submerged old frontier values. Airs might be affected, and on occasion were, but the fare tended to be plain and hearty. A dinner served by Dr. and Mrs. Felix Robertson, for example, had for its twin *pièces de résistance* a savory Tennessee ham at one end of the table and a large roast of beef at the other, together with a selection of local vegetable dishes and a lavish array of pies and cakes for dessert. Felix, the son born to Charlotte and James Robertson on the eve of the furious defense of Freeland's station fifty-odd years before, had grown up to become one of Nashville's leading citizens and its most prominent physician. He may very well have looked down his nose at such ostentation as the banquet given by a local politician to celebrate his election to the United States Senate. The menu on that occasion consisted exclusively, so we are told, of dishes prepared in a fashionable New Orleans restaurant and sped to Nashville by fast steamboat.

One wonders about that. The record run of the old *Rifleman* had been beaten long ago by fancier, flashier packets; and one after another down the years their records, too, had fallen. But the absolute, irreducible minimum time, set by the *America* in 1849, still was five days, fifteen hours, and thirty minutes. It was long enough, surely, for even the most flavorful French cooking to lose something in transit. All in all, bread broken with Dr. Robertson probably was better.

High life and cultural attainments like Nashville's could never have existed, of course, without the solid foundation of economic prosperity. The Cumberland provided it. Upstream along the river's great middle bend were Gallatin, then Lebanon, then Carthage at the mouth of Caney Fork, each town a center of that rough-genteel agricultural aristocracy peculiar to the antebellum south. From their landings, and from smaller ones scattered in between, packets headed down the river "flat out," as steamboatmen said, with deck cargoes of cotton bales stacked several tiers high. Farther upstream were landings at Granville, Gainesboro, and Celina, where the Obey River flows into the Cumberland a few miles south of the Kentucky line. The rolling Tennessee bluegrass had given way to rougher country by that point in the river's course, and farther upstream the land grew rougher still. Settlement had come slowly to this region. Instead of plantation mansions, the traveler saw plainer houses with fewer acres around them. Yet it was country that provided ladings of burley tobacco, shelled corn, pickled pork, good sour mash whiskey, hogs, cattle, horses, and mules on the hoof. Even thus early there was industry too, for a pair of paper mills operated on this stretch of the upper river. All this added up to profitable steamboat cargoes. A survey taken in 1847 showed freights worth a good round thirteen million dollars passing through Nashville every year. The men who totaled up the figures were hardheaded railroad promoters. Before the 1850s ended they would be laying iron rails into Nashville to get a new era under way.

Conditions downriver were as good. James Robertson is supposed to have been the first man to smelt iron at Cumberland Furnace, sometime before 1800. If he was, he realized slight gain from it. But the ore was there, and more skillful ironmasters followed him. Over the years the first crude charcoal-fired furnaces had grown into impressive numbers of modern smelters, forges, and rolling mills scattered almost the whole length of the lower river. The Highland Rim iron they turned out was prized throughout the east for its superior qualities as the boiler plate so essential to the onrushing Industrial Age.

All this added up, if not quite to a promised land, at least to a reasonably happy and prosperous one. But there was also slavery. The "peculiar institution" had been driving its wedge between north and south for most of the nineteenth century, and it was the Cumberland's geographic luck to be caught in the middle. If the "tug" ever came, Cumberland country would be torn apart—like Tennessee, like Kentucky, like the nation itself—between free country and slave, Union and Secession, Republican, Whig, Democrat, and whatever. The irony was that few Cumberland people, slave owners or not, cared all that much about the black man's bondage. They were for it, mostly; that is, they took a dim view of turning the slaves loose, whether they owned any or not. But hardly any would have split the Union over it, had they had their way.

Presently, though, some South Carolina hotheads had to go and fire on Fort Sumter. President Abe Lincoln promptly issued a call for seventy-five thousand volunteers, presumably to chastise the guilty south. . . . And the "tug" had come.

iii

Look Away, Look Away...

16

The
Innocents

THERE was something wryly fitting in the presence of Felix Zolli-coffer and his four thousand Tennessee volunteers on the upper Cumberland. They were amateur soldiers and he was an amateur general, and this still was very much an amateurs' war. Few among even the West Pointers who had learned their trade in Mexico, or fighting Indians, could begin to guess as yet at its potential for bloodshed and ruination.

The war still was very new as the year of 1862 opened. Its first battle had been fought six months earlier at Manassas, Virginia, far eastward across the mountains, and the Union army had got the drubbing of its life. Perhaps that was not as fortunate as it seemed from the Confederate point of view. It fostered the danger-ous myth that one good old southern boy was worth ten "pasty-faced mechanics" from the north; that southern chivalry had but to spring to arms to stamp the forces of tyranny into the dust; that the whole business was knightly and glorious, besides.

Such notions were destined to prove pretty frail once the going got really rough. Meantime, General Zollicoffer was every inch a true believer: just the man to do his duty or die trying. He was a long-time resident on the Cumberland, a Nashville newspaperman popular enough among his fellow citizens to have represented them in Congress at one time. His military experience was somewhat less impressive, comprising a brief spell of Seminole War service in Florida years before. He was immensely personable, though, a bit of a firebrand by nature, and a southern patriot of unexcelled ardor—for all of which, it appears, his men idolized him. He would have to count heavily on that, for he had drawn the assignment of holding the upper Cumberland against Union forces that outnumbered him by two to one, at least. There were diplomatic complications too. Kentucky was a border state—neutral—whatever that might mean in a war with no real place for neutrals. Practically speaking, it meant little more than that Kentuckians with aggressive political convictions were free to follow them into one camp or the other. Yet there was always the ticklish possibility that whatever Kentucky finally did, officially, might well depend on how badly her official feathers were ruffled, and by whom.

Theoretically this appeared to be the case. Actually, Kentucky's neutrality had been a dead issue almost from the first. The Union already had violated it more than once, and Zollicoffer at once proceeded to do so. Stationing a small holding force in Cumberland Gap, he moved the balance of his army out to Mill Springs on the south bank of the Cumberland. Nevertheless, he took pains to send Kentucky's Governor Magoffin a polite letter of apology: "Tennessee feels and has ever felt toward Kentucky as a twin sister. . . . If the Federal forces will now withdraw from their menacing position, the force under my command shall be immediately withdrawn. . . ." Then, having made his manners, he bent the rules of neutrality a little further by circulating a proclamation that demanded blatantly, "How long will Kentuckians close their eyes to the contemplated ruin of their present structure of society . . .?"

The federal forces, encamped around Lebanon in central Kentucky, showed no inclination to withdraw. Neither did they make any motions toward the front, however. In fact, Union strategy still wavered between Nashville and East Tennessee as primary objectives. But Zollicoffer was unaware of that and presently, emboldened by the enemy's inaction, he commandeered a wheezy old stern-wheeler steamboat, ferried his army across the river, and went into camp at Beech Grove.

It was strictly against orders, an amateur's ploy. South of the river, Zollicoffer had occupied a coign of vantage from which he could strike swiftly to counter Union crossings either upstream or

down. On the north bank, he stood an excellent chance of being
trapped between the river at his back and the stronger Union force
in front. General George B. Crittendon, his superior officer at East
Tennessee headquarters in Knoxville, promptly sent a courier
galloping with orders to fall back to Mill Springs at once. Yet when
Crittendon followed a few days later he found the army still at
Beech Grove. It was a better campsite than Mill Springs, Zollicoffer
explained blandly, and so he had felt justified in staying there at
least until they could talk it over. Moreover, he added, his recon-
naissances indicated that the Federals had accepted the challenge
of his Cumberland crossing. They were now advancing, which in
his opinion made the very thought of a retreat not only unsoldierly
but ungallant as well.

George Crittendon was a forty-nine-year-old professional from
the regular army. His thoughts on his subordinate's opinion have
not been preserved, perhaps fortunately. But the Union advance
already had him in a tactical bind. Rather than try to retire then,
and risk being caught in an awkward straddle of the river, he
deemed it best to stand and fight.

And then—it would be a common enough occurrence in this war,
the Good Lord knew—the rain began.

It rained hard for days on end, turning roads into morasses,
filling the Cumberland and every tributary bankful in swirling
flood tides. To Crittendon, grimly preparing for his last-ditch stand,
that held out the possibility of a stroke to swing the odds in his
favor. The Union army was divided, coming on along both banks
of Fishing Creek which flowed into the Cumberland some way
north of Beech Grove. With the creek running too full to be forded,
Crittendon reasoned, neither contingent would be able to reinforce
the other. He could attack the nearest by surprise, crush it, then
deal with the other at his convenience. It seemed a good plan;
better by a long shot than meekly waiting for the enemy's blow
to fall. His staff agreed. The orders went out.

Shortly after midnight on the morning of January nineteenth
the noncoms turned their men out for muster in the rain and the
chilly Cumberland River mist. They were Tennesseans mostly,
with a heavy sprinkling of Secesh-sympathizing Kentuckians: raw-
boned farm boys, mountaineers, upper-river men. Some had
brought their own hunting rifles. A good many of the rest carried
ancient army-issue flintlocks dating from the War of 1812, so hard

up for arms was the Confederacy already, and the war hardly started yet. It was a corn pone and fatback army, two brigades of it: eight infantry regiments, a battery of light field guns, and a cavalry battalion to do the scouting. There was nothing wrong with its fighting spirit, though it is doubtful that many of the men could have said what it was they proposed to fight about. This country of theirs was stony poor, root-hog-or-die poor, not plantation country at all. Hardly one of them came from a slave-owning family, or would ever own a slave himself, or ever aspire to. And probably not one, if asked, could have explained the doctrine of states' rights with any clarity. It was significant of their confused loyalties that the Union army they would shortly face had a regiment of their neighbors, *literally* their neighbors in some cases, and men as like them as like could be save for Union sentiments as against Secessionist. War—this war anyway—made strange enemies.

In the inevitable confusion, sleepily grumbling, stumbling, swearing, the soldiers formed ranks and started forward to their first battle. For most of them, one way or another, it was going to be the last one too. Nine miles up the road was an inconsequential hamlet known as Logan's Crossroads, and the sleeping Union camp.

The rain pelted down. It was slow going in the slippery, shin-deep mud; slower still when cannons and caissons mired to the wheel hubs, and men had to turn to and spend their strength to help the floundering horses. Time passed, and with its passing the chances of a successful surprise attack grew slim.

The chances never had been truly good, in fact. The Union commander was Brigadier General George H. Thomas, another hard-bitten professional whose special talent for standing fast was not yet appreciated, but prodigious all the same. "Old Slow Trot," his men called him, and it was a fact that speed was not his forte and never would be. But Thomas was methodical, not prone to make mistakes. As dawn came on behind the storm wrack, he had his pickets out and a troop of cavalry patrolling the road. It was not long before the staccato popping of rifle fire told both sides that their advance guards had found each other.

Now Crittendon had a decision to make. Forge ahead as planned? Or call it a lost opportunity and fall back to some defensible position? No; a retreat by untrained recruits could turn too easily to rout. He ordered a charge, Zollicoffer's brigade spearheading it.

They went in yelling, in fine fettle still: plenty of what European military experts would have called élan and these country boys knew as plain old grit. The Yanks, hit as they swarmed out of their tents and formed up, were knocked off balance at first, rolled back through the camp in a savage, trampling melee. But nine mud-slogging miles had taken a little too much out of Zollicoffer's stalwarts. The charge faltered; its momentum died; the battle spilled untidily out into the surrounding fields and thickets and fencerows, each army as green and battle-innocent as the other— but both giving all they had. When a group of hard-pressed Confederates took shelter on their bellies in a shallow gully—a common-sense maneuver worthy of tested veterans—a downy-cheeked Union major mounted a rail fence, indignantly berated them for cowardice and invited them to stand up and fight "like men." The Union was beginning to rally now, the odds swinging relentlessly against the attackers. Flintlock rifles, soaked by the rain, missed fire more often than not. The men armed with them had to give ground or hunt cover, cursing in frustration. For every blue-clad soldier who went down, another seemed ready to step into the breach. It was no illusion, either. Union reinforcements were splashing across Fishing Creek, not too swollen to be forded after all. Later, a court-martial would hear testimony that General Crittendon was "almost beastly drunk" during the battle. If so, one can see his point. Just about everything that might conceivably have gone wrong for him had.

Then suddenly, for the Confederates, the battle fell apart completely. General Zollicoffer lost his bearings in the rain and fog and noise, and all by himself went galloping into the enemy lines. It was his bad luck, also, to be nearsighted. Apparently he never realized the soldiers around him were not his own, for he was bellowing orders at them when a Union colonel rode up and shot him out of the saddle.

Some of his people saw him fall. He wore a white rubber raincoat too conspicuous to be mistaken, but in the prevailing confusion many thought the fatal shot had been fired from their own lines. Someone raised an angry cry: "Betrayed—!" Others took it up and passed it on. Swiftly as flame in a train of gunpowder, panic exploded through the weary ranks. Men turned and ran. They burst in among units of the other brigade, who caught the contagion and ran too. They threw down rifles and knapsacks, abandoned their artillery, left regimental colors in the mud, and never stopped running till they reached the Cumberland. The Union pursuit, delayed because prudent General Thomas made his men stop to replenish their cartridge boxes, found the Confederates' Beech Grove camp empty save for the gear and provisions left behind. The men had fled across the river in the same old steamboat commandeered by Zollicoffer for the original crossing. It was growing late in the day by then, and still raining. Peering through the murk, the Yanks saw fire lay a crimson smear over the water. The last boatload of fugitives had run her aground on the south bank and put the torch to her.

The remnants of Crittendon's army virtually melted away around him on the retreat to Knoxville. It is unlikely that many of the men thought of it as desertion. They lived in this country. They had gone off to war and now they had come home, was all.

17
The Guns
of Donelson

THE Cumberland was not destined to be a lucky river for the south.

Even before he heard the bad news from Mill Springs—or Beech Grove, or Fishing Creek; the battle would come to be known by all three names—General Albert Sidney Johnston had been fretting over his problems as supreme Confederate commander in the west. The defense line Johnston had cobbled up from Cumberland Gap to the Mississippi was woefully thin at best, much of it held together by little more than the proverbial spit and baling wire. Now Crittendon's defeat left its eastern end all unstuck, and no part of what remained was more vulnerable than the lower reaches of the Cumberland and her big sister the Tennessee. Cutting deep into the western Confederacy as they did, both rivers made logical targets for Union invasion. Worse, their sole defensive works were Forts Henry on the Tennessee and Donelson on the Cumberland, neither one a bastion to inspire confidence. Because of Kentucky's troublesome neutrality, both forts had been built on Tennessee's side of the boundary line, fifty miles upstream from the respective river mouths. It was by no means the ideal location in either case. Worse still, construction was far behind schedule, and the engineer officer sent down from Nashville to expedite matters reported gloomily that he had completed a thorough examination ". . . and do not admire the aspect of things."

Worst of all, perhaps, were the tales of a new breed of mechanical monster prowling the waters for the Union. The ironclad gunboat, it was called: not precisely a secret weapon to be sure, but nothing like it had been seen before on any western river, and the unknown was always ominous.

Rightly so, too. For the ironclad gunboat was an early manifestation of something this war was going to prove, and that was the capacity of the "pasty-faced mechanics" for creating national muscle. A remarkable Indiana Yankee by the name of James B. Eads—steamboatman, engineer, inventor, among other things—had come up with the original idea and sold it to the Department of War. Then, given a government contract to build eight of the craft, he had gone ahead and put all eight in the water inside a hundred days.

Each was essentially a squat, shallow-draft steamboat some hundred and seventy-five feet long by fifty in the beam, with sides and ends slanted sharply inboard to deflect enemy shot. Each was heavily armored forward, though not aft, with two-and-a-half-inch iron plate bolted to thick hardwood timbers. Each was highly maneuverable, could work up to a top speed of eight knots, and carried four heavy-caliber guns to a broadside, plus three more pointing forward and two astern. What Eads had created, in short, was a flotilla of strictly utilitarian fighting machines, ugly as sin but bristling with lethal potency.

With such leviathans stacking the odds against them, it was small wonder that Confederate commanders on the Cumberland and the Tennessee were gripped by a defeatist malaise as the early weeks of 1862 slipped by. Their pessimism was justified, or so it seemed. On February second, four of the new ironclads—*Cincinnati, Carondelet, St. Louis,* and *Essex*—steamed up the Ohio River and turned into the Tennessee. Behind them came three conventional wooden gunboats and a flotilla of steamboats packed with Union troops. On February sixth, after some days of preliminary jockeying, the ironclads pounded Fort Henry into submission in a brisk two-hour cannonade. Ulysses S. Grant, the Union brigadier commanding, put troops ashore to storm the fort's landward works, but they never fired a shot; the works had already been abandoned. Jubilantly he closed his report on the operation with a brash prediction: "I shall take and destroy Fort Donelson on the 8th. . . ."

The date was arrant braggadocio, maybe, but Grant was dead

serious. Rain held him up so that it was the twelfth, four days late, before he moved out for Donelson. When he did it was at the head of fifteen thousand troops marching overland to the Cumberland, while ten thousand more went by steamboat the long way 'round. He left another two thousand-odd as a garrison for Henry, but available on short notice should he need them. He didn't expect he would. But the ironclads had dropped down the Ohio to Cairo, Illinois, to refuel and repair battle damage. Only *Carondelet* was on the Cumberland when he got there.

The Confederate high command, all this while, had agonized in a dither of misgivings. The defeatist sentiment persisted. No one from Albert Sidney Johnston down believed Fort Donelson could be defended successfully. But with Henry gone, it was plain that Johnston's whole defense line was doomed. His only recourse, as he saw it, was to shorten his front by pulling the main Confederate force under General William J. Hardee back from its position at Bowling Green, Kentucky, to some safer haven south of the Cumberland. But that, in turn, meant Donelson must be held at least long enough to keep Grant off Hardee's flank till the pullout could be completed. To that end, Johnston had begun to shuttle fresh troops into the fort even before the fall of Henry.

Military protocol being what it was, however—and still is, come to that—some comic-opera complications arose. With the new brigades came new brigadiers, who brought touchy questions as to who outranked whom. The result was that Donelson had four changes of command within a week: a trifle many even for so democratic an organization as the Confederate States Army.

Colonel John W. Head of the Thirtieth Tennessee Regiment had been the original commanding officer. He was replaced by General Bushrod Johnson: one-time West Pointer and one-time civilian schoolmaster, with a bulging savant's brow and the large, sad eyes of a man beginning to suspect this war had pitched him in beyond his depth. His command responsibilities were short-lived, however. Next came General Gideon J. Pillow: possibly an improvement, though a slight one. Pillow was a West Pointer too, a Mexican War veteran, and a hard-nosed fighting man besides—or at least he possessed the knack of sounding like one. "Drive back the ruthless invaders . . . and again raise the Confederate flag over Fort Henry!" he exhorted the garrison in his opening address. Almost immediately, though, he was heard declaring loudly, if more modestly, that "with God's help" he would never surrender Donelson. But by that time General John B. Floyd was on hand with *his* brigade. Floyd was a political general pure and simple: a past governor of Virginia and past secretary of war under President Buchanan— but no soldier and never would be. Between his arrival and Pillow's, Simon Bolivar Buckner had come in also: another West Pointer, Mexican War veteran, and once head of the militia in his native Kentucky. But the time of his arrival had denied Buckner his turn at the command, for he was junior to Gideon Pillow.

The situation made for some abrasion of egos, all the more since no two of the four brigadiers were very far apart in seniority. Floyd, for example, outranked Pillow by only a month or so. To make things more prickly still, Pillow and Buckner heartily disliked one another, nursing an old army feud that had started during their Mexican War days and continued through civilian life later.

Nevertheless, the additional brigades brought the garrison to a strength of more than seventeen thousand: quite enough to give Ulysses S. Grant all the fight he could handle. Some sound hard work had made a difference too; Donelson was no such sitting duck as Fort Henry had been. The prevailing Confederate pessimism and Union exuberance over an easy first victory tended to blind both sides to a pair of rather obvious facts. For one, Henry had been all but indefensible to begin with, being situated on ground so low that a rising Tennessee tide had flooded part of its battery even before the federal attack. Only nine of fifteen guns had remained above water long enough to fire a shot, and of the nine only two were of sufficiently heavy caliber to stand up to the ironclads. Yet even at such a disadvantage—fact number two—Henry's gunners had scored damaging hits on all four gunboats, and put *Essex* right out of action with a shell through her boiler. A lucky shot, perhaps. All the same, it suggested the ironclad gunboat just might not be invincible.

As for Donelson being no second Henry, Grant began to realize that at once. His first attacks on February thirteenth were repulsed, bloodily, warning him the place was going to be tough. Its landward defenses extended in a three-mile arc along the west bank of the Cumberland. They were anchored at the northern, downstream, end by a high bluff with heavy batteries dug into sandbagged emplacements. On the bluff, too, stood the barracks and officers' quarters of the fort proper. At the southern end the defense arc enclosed the small town of Dover, with a landing where steamboats could bring in stores, munitions, and any necessary reinforcements from points upstream. In between was mostly high, broken ground, thickly wooded, in which the defenders had dug rifle pits and thrown up earthworks. They had felled trees in front of the works, too, their tops pointing outward and their branches trimmed and sharpened to form abatis threatening attackers with impalement. The more vulnerable salients were backed by hidden batteries of field artillery, besides. And on top of all that, it began to dawn on Grant that until ten thousand of his troops coming around from Henry by steamboat arrived—they hadn't yet—his force was probably outnumbered.

Characteristically, he wasted no time worrying about it. A bold and resourceful defender might have sortied and mauled him badly, even routed him. But John Floyd was no more than a civilian trying to play general, Grant knew. Grant had soldiered with Gideon Pillow in Mexico, as well, and had scant respect for him either.

Everything considered, though, it seemed advisable to let the ironclads do the job here as they had at Henry. *Carondelet* still was the only one on hand, but her opening probes of the batteries on the bluff appeared encouraging. In two days she had fired off more than a hundred rounds, disabled a Confederate gun and killed a battery commander—considerably less damage, actually, than Union observers estimated—while taking only two hits in return. True, one of those had come near crippling her. A massive solid shot from the top of the bluff, it had plunged downward through her plating, smashing the timbers underneath to send deadly splinters flying, then carried on into the engine room where it barely missed the steam drum, battered down a bulkhead, tore up some piping, and ricocheted among the startled firemen, as an officer put it afterward, "like a wild beast pursuing its prey." But maybe that had been another lucky shot; on the whole, Donelson's gunners hadn't looked nearly as good as Henry's. *Carondelet* anchored out of range downstream while her crew tended their wounded and got busy on emergency repairs. The land forces dug in and waited.

Before dark Flag Officer Andrew Foote came breasting the Cumberland current with three more ironclads, *St. Louis, Pittsburgh,* and *Louisville,* followed by the wooden gunboats *Conestoga* and *Tyler.* Prospects were looking up.

That night it rained again. The weather thus far had been mild and springlike, but it changed abruptly as the wind veered around and blew out of the northwest, bringing bitter cold. The rain turned to driving, stinging sleet. Outposts on both sides crouched in their rifle pits, shivering and miserable. Scarcely one of these youngsters, Yank or Rebel, was a seasoned soldier, but the Yanks had the harder time of it. Carefree in their utter greenness and fooled by the balmy temperature—wasn't Tennessee the sunny Southland, anyway?— many had thrown away overcoats and blankets during the march from Fort Henry. Now they paid the price of that foolhardiness, for the lines were too close together to permit campfires. All night long, in fact, both sides kept up intermittent fusillades of gunfire; perhaps it was one of the few ways a man could try and forget the cold. But there were some who simply gave up and drifted off to sleep, to be found in the morning stiff and stark.

Daylight came at last: Friday, February fourteenth. The skies cleared and it was a lacy valentine of a day, the brown hills along the river turned pure white, every tree and bush and clump of weed sheathed in glittering ice. Not that anyone had the time or the inclination to pause and mull over so pretty a piece of whimsy, for there was smoke downstream, and the thump and chunk of reciprocating steam driving paddle wheels. Grant's riverborne ten thousand had arrived. The garrison left behind at Henry had marched in during the night, also. Now it was Donelson's turn, as old campaigners liked to put it, to "look the elephant in the eye."

For this fort General Grant proposed a variation on the tactics that had sufficed for Henry. Instead of lying off and shelling the defending batteries to rubble, the ironclads would simply pound them hard while running past. Whether the enemy was destroyed or only outflanked would be immaterial; the ironclads, having proceeded upstream to Dover, could then cut the Confederates' line of retreat southward and at the same time shell them out of their shore works from the rear. If it worked the Rebs would have no choice but to surrender, sparing the Union army a nasty bloodletting.

Commodore Foote agreed. But after talking in the meantime with Commander Henry Walke of *Carondelet,* he insisted on a brief delay in order to prepare his gunboats for the set-to. That high, arching shot from the bluff into *Carondelet*'s innards had made its point. The preparation consisted largely in heaping spare anchor chains, lumber, and bags of coal on the ironclads' upper decks to provide extra armor of a sort. By a little before three in the afternoon the work was finished, the flotilla had steam up, and Foote reported himself ready. By that time, too, the fresh troops were all off the steamboats and deployed around Donelson's landward works.

The delay had allowed plenty of time for word to get around, inside the fort as well as out, that the action was about to start. Civilians from Dover, drawn by an edgy fascination with the Union's river-prowling monsters, vied with Confederate soldiers in scrambling for choice viewing spots. Many of those soldiers, and a good few of their officers, too, left defensive positions virtually unmanned in their determination to miss nothing. It made less difference than it might have, for their opposite numbers in the Union lines were every bit as eager to find front-row seats. Had it occurred to anyone to liken the Cumberland's west bank to the tiers of old Rome's Colosseum—apparently it didn't—the comparison would have been an apt one. Near-unanimous opinion, regardless of personal sympathies, already had cast the garrison of Donelson in the Christian martyrs' role.

General Floyd stood among his aides on the fort's ramparts. A telegraph instrument had been set up there and an operator crouched over the key, ready to send battle tidings clicking down the line to Nashville. *Carondelet* poked her blunt snout around a bend downstream and a rustle of excitement ran through the group. Donelson was doomed, Floyd muttered nervously.

A young captain named Bidwell, commanding a battery of thirty-two-pound smoothbore cannons some way down the face of the bluff, kept an eye on his half-trained cannoneers and fretted inwardly that they might break in panic before the enemy ever came within range. Up at the top of the bluff, Captain Reuben Ross requested Gideon Pillow's permission to open fire with his rifled hundred-twenty-eight-pounder. Curtly the general gave it.

Carondelet came on around the bend, turned broadside and angled across the stream toward the near bank. *Pittsburgh* followed, taking station on her starboard quarter. Behind *Pittsburgh* came *St. Louis*, Commodore Foote's flagship, and then *Louisville*.

The thin-skinned *Conestoga* and *Tyler* lurked a thousand yards in the rear, under orders to stay out of the in-fighting, to load their big eight-inchers with explosive shells and fire high.

Captain Ross's first shot splashed into the water, short. The range was a mile and a half.

Slowly the four ironclads came on, struggling to get into formation abreast as Foote shouted orders through a megaphone from *St. Louis's* armored pilothouse. It was hard going. A tide had swollen the Cumberland for some days past but was falling now, the current running strongly in a narrowing channel that cramped the space for maneuver. The range closed to a mile.

Observers disagreed later whether *Pittsburgh* or *St. Louis* fired the first salvo for the Union. Whichever it was let go with all three bow guns. Instantly the rest of the flotilla fired also, practically as one. All four ironclads went on firing, alternating solid shot and explosive shells as fast as crews could load and gun captains prime,

aim, and jerk the lanyards. *Conestoga* and *Tyler* opened up, arching their long-fused shells high overhead. Sprays of dirt and rock flew from the bluff.

Miraculously, not a hit was scored. And the Confederate gun crews, green as they were, stood fast. Their inexperience told, though. Captain Ross's rifled cannon jammed when overanxious men tried to load a solid shot without first sponging out the barrel. Frantic efforts with the rammer failed to budge the thing and so, heedless of the hot metal whistling down all around them, the whole crew clambered out of their sandbagged emplacement to go rooting among the debris at the bluff's edge. They were looking for a suitable log that might prove stouter than the rammer, and they found one. They lugged it back, trimmed it roughly to size and thrust it down the cannon's muzzle. All heaving together, up on the parapet in plain sight of the Yankee gunners downstream, they drove the stubborn shot home by main strength, and swabbed the barrel free of its caked powder residue, and got back into action.

After all that they deserved to draw first blood, and did. The shot took *Carondelet* squarely in the bow, smashed one of her anchors, caromed high, and carried part of a smokestack into the river.

Still the ironclads came on, firing steadily. But more Confederate guns began to answer as the range shortened. A squat, massive columbiad bellowed and spat out its ten-inch shell. A pair of thirty-two-pounders on top of the bluff joined in. But the rifled gun up there fired once more and was through. Inexperience again: a gunner left the priming wire in the vent, the blast bent and fused it there, and the big gun was spiked as effectively as any Union saboteur could have wished. The ironclads kept coming, black and ominous, in line abreast, smoke-wreathed, spewing flame: a sight to shake even the stoutest hearts. And so it did.

Colonel Nathan Bedford Forrest, commander of the garrison's cavalry units, turned to an aide who had been a clergyman in civilian life. "Parson," he pleaded, "for God's sake, pray! Nothing but God Almighty can save the fort!"

General Floyd scribbled his first battle report to Albert Sidney Johnston: "The enemy are assaulting us with the most tremendous cannonade from gunboats abreast the batteries. . . . I will make the best defense in my power. . . ." Nervously the telegrapher tapped it out. Then, close to panic, he added an impromptu observation of his own: the gunboats had passed the batteries "and are right on us. . . ."

Well, not quite—but now the range was five hundred yards, and still closing. Halfway down the bluff Captain Bidwell had his eight thirty-two-pounders firing at last, the incessant cannon crashes rolling and reverberating along the high, snow-covered riverbanks. Another message from John Floyd clattered down the line to General Johnston: "The fort cannot hold out twenty minutes. . . ."

Down on the river, though, the ironclads were having their troubles. The Rebel smoothbores and the big columbiad were scoring hits. Later, one of the many Union soldiers who watched would write down his impressions: "Thick and fast came the shots and bombs from the batteries, crashing on the iron plates, skipping across the waves, going clean through the smokestacks, tearing down the rigging. . . ." Later, too, one ironclad's captain would report how the fierce head-on fire cracked the gunboats' armor and peeled it away "as lightning strips the bark from a tree."

A forward gun on *Carondelet* blew up, strewing her deck with wounded men. A spark got into loose powder and flame spurted up through the choking fog of smoke. As men struggled to rig the pumps, a roundshot screamed in through a forward gunport and took the heads right off three gunners in a row. These Union sailors were no more seasoned than their adversaries ashore. Soldier volunteers, mostly, they never had bargained for this kind of slaughterhouse war. There was near-panic till their regular navy officers got them in hand again. The fire was put out, sand sprinkled over decks made slippery by spilled blood and brains. Still firing, the ironclads forged ahead. The range closed to three hundred yards, to two hundred and fifty . . .

As it shortened, however, much of their fire went high, arching far over the bluff to fall harmlessly in the trees beyond. The Confederate gunners, by contrast, were shooting now with uncanny accuracy. *Pittsburgh* took a shot in the bow, right on the waterline, and then in quick succession another. *St. Louis* began to swing broadside to the swift Cumberland current, out of control from a direct hit in the pilothouse that killed her helmsman, shattered the steering wheel, and cut down Commodore Foote with splinter wounds in arm and ankle. Repeated hits already had wrecked *Louisville*'s pilothouse. A repair party ran aft and worked heroically to rig a jury steering gear, but bursts of shell fragments from *Tyler* and *Conestoga,* far downstream and badly off-target, rattled like deadly hail on the deck around them, driving them to cover. Then *Pittsburgh,* unmanageable with so many tons of water pouring into her forward hold, yawed sluggishly and barged into *Carondelet.* Damage was slight, both ships rebounding and falling apart at once. But *Pittsburgh* went staggering off downstream, and Commander Walke suddenly perceived his *Carondelet* was all alone with enemy shot and shell still beating the river to froth around her.

Just that quickly, it ended. Commodore Foote dragged himself to his feet in the shambles of *St. Louis's* pilothouse and ordered the signal given to retire. It was hardly necessary. *Pittsburgh* and *Louisville* were hulks drifting with the current and the flagship was in little better shape. *Carondelet* covered the retreat, backing down to keep her armored bow presented to the foe. She kept firing, too, but more to wrap herself in concealing smoke than in any further hope of hurting Johnny Reb.

Johnny, for his part, was throwing hats and caps in air and cheering himself hoarse in the sweet intoxication of victory won when he'd had no business winning. Not so General John Floyd. Apparently still pinching himself lest the whole thing turn out to have been a dream, he reported only that the ironclads had been damaged and driven back, and he believed the fight was over for that day. One wonders what Albert Sidney Johnston thought, especially when he shortly received another telegram, dispatched in blithe disregard of protocol, by an exultant Gideon Pillow: "We have just had the fiercest fight on record between our guns and six gunboats, which lasted two hours. . . . No damage done to our battery and not a man killed. . . ."

In any case, General Johnston already had answered those earlier panicky communiqués from Floyd and his telegrapher. Assuming Donelson to be as good as lost, he had ordered Floyd only to get his troops safely back to Nashville if possible.

It was not going to be much of a victory at that.

What followed was all sad anticlimax: the same tale that would grow old and dismal before this war was over, of opportunities fumbled away and men's courage gone for naught. A Confederate sortie in force on the following night, designed to break out into the road to Nashville, was timed and executed perfectly—at first. Taken completely off guard, the Union forces were rolled back;

the escape route lay wide open. But Gideon Pillow stopped to send off another of his dramatic victory messages: "On my honor as a soldier, the day is ours. . . ." Then, inexplicably, he decided a Union counterattack was imminent and ordered his troops into defensive positions. Simon Bolivar Buckner objected. The original plan called for Pillow to lead the bulk of the troops through the breach and away, with Buckner's brigade covering the retreat. Buckner insisted vehemently that he was ready and able to do that; there was no reason to change the plan. Still Pillow demurred. Finally they appealed to General Floyd and Floyd ran true to form, backing and filling till Union regiments rallied and stormed back to close the gap—and the last chance for an orderly withdrawal was gone.

In the bleak early-morning hours of Sunday, February sixteenth, the Confederate brigadiers met for a last council of war in the snug parlor of Dover's mayor. (He happened also to be a major on General Pillow's staff.) Nothing had really changed for Donelson; the fort still was capable of standing a long and bitter siege. But the old defeatist malaise would not down, and surrender was in the air. No one argued against it very seriously. Again, though, the comic-opera touch: the command seemed all at once to become an intolerably irksome responsibility. Plaintively John Floyd reminded the others of his rather doubtful position with the Federals. As President Buchanan's secretary of war, he had been accused of preparing for secession by transferring excessive quantities of arms and munitions to arsenals in the south. At the time, Congress had considered bringing charges of malfeasance in office. As a prisoner of war, now, might not Floyd find those charges revived? And in the heat of wartime passions, how far might the vengeful north not go?

"Gentlemen," he protested, "it wouldn't do."

General Pillow, then? But Pillow had made those vainglorious brags never to surrender Donelson. "Liberty or death!" he had shouted, in plain hearing of the assembled garrison. A good deal of the fire had gone out of Gideon Pillow since then, true. Still . . .

Eventually the talk and the arguing had to end.

"I turn the command over, sir," said Floyd to Pillow.

"I pass it, sir," said Pillow to Buckner.

"I assume it," said Buckner glumly, and called for pen, ink, paper, and a bugler to sound the parley.

18

The Tattered
Stars
and Bars

IT would be a memorable surrender, though not as any model of military decorum. The brief grace period before General Buckner opened the prescribed amenities saw a notable rush to get out of Fort Donelson while the getting was good. Gideon Pillow went first, crossing the Cumberland in a leaky scow found for him by an aide. So great was his hurry that he left even his personal body servant and his saddle horse behind. John Floyd left soon afterward and rather more comfortably, aboard the steamboat *General Anderson*. She had just pulled in from Nashville with four hundred fresh troops who would now, to their intense disgust, only swell the Union's bag of prisoners. To Floyd's credit, he got part of his brigade—a regiment of fellow Virginians—off with him. To his vast discredit, he left a regiment of Mississippi boys howling in disappointed fury on the landing. They had held off a mob of other would-be fugitives while the Virginians embarked, on the assumption that they were to be next, so the spatter of rifle shots that sped the *Anderson* on her way was perhaps excusable. But most of the garrison was denied even that slight satisfaction. They had fought well, those southern cannoneers and riflemen. They figured they had whipped the Yankees, and could hold them off indefinitely from now on. They expected to do just that, and the news that their generals had sold them out sparked such resentment that the bearer of Buckner's white flag had some difficulty getting through the lines.

Fiercely scorning the whole notion of surrender, Colonel Nathan Bedford Forrest led his cavalry out to cut their way to freedom or die trying. As it happened, they were not called on to do either. They had to wallow "saddle blanket deep" through a chilly Cumberland River backwater—almost every trooper with a grateful infantryman up behind him—but they never saw a Union soldier, never had a shot fired at them, and eventually rode off to fight another day. Union generals would come to rue that, for Nathan Bedford Forrest was just the man to make himself the nemesis to a whole succession of them as long as this war lasted.

At some point in the confusion, Donelson's third brigadier also decamped. Bushrod Johnson simply walked out of the fort as the victorious Federals moved in. No one saw him go, or challenged him. He kept walking and got clean away.

Escapes were beside the point, however.

The point about Fort Donelson's fall was made, unmistakably, when General Grant scribbled out his reply to Simon Bolivar Buckner's request for surrender terms. No terms, said Grant. It would be "unconditional and immediate surrender," or "I propose to move immediately upon your works. . . ."

One feels for Buckner, surely one of the most put-upon of Donelson's many luckless warriors. In vain he protested the reply as "ungenerous and unchivalrous." It was, especially from an old friend and fellow officer to whom he had once lent money. But he surrendered; he had already committed himself, so to speak, as a defeated man. And practically overnight—as soon, that is, as the journalists could file their stories and the bulletins go up in newspaper offices across the north—the Union had more than just a new victory to celebrate, more even than a new hero who had won it. The Union had a brand-new catchphrase to fire the imagination. It was a phrase worth memorizing and repeating, and folk did by the thousands. It said something about this war and the Union's stomach for it that had not been said before, and needed saying. It tickled the public's fancy, besides, to reflect that the initials U.S. stood for "Unconditional Surrender" and "Ulysses Simpson," Grant's given names, at one and the same time. Which seemed eminently fitting. Come to think of it, some pointed out, U.S. also stood for "United States." Maybe a good omen for the future had been given, down there on the Cumberland.

The New York Times went so far as to announce that the end of the south's rebellion was at hand: "After this it certainly cannot be materially postponed. . . ." It could be and would be, the *Times* notwithstanding, yet the Confederacy was never to recover fully from the loss of Donelson. Nashville, unfortified and virtually defenseless once the fort had fallen, was surrendered without a fight a week later. Albert Sidney Johnston elected to make his counterstroke, not on the Cumberland but at Shiloh on the Tennessee. He died there, and a great many others died there also, and the only outcome was that the war went on. . . .

Among other things, that brought steamboats churning up the Cumberland once more: fleets of them, in numbers surpassing the palmiest of prewar days. During the navigation season, meaning whenever tides on the lower river permitted, as many as forty or fifty packets a week arrived at Nashville. Sometimes they lay at the levee so many deep that latecomers waited days on end for the wharf space to unload. It was a far, sad cry from good old times come back, though. The packets might be yesterday's favorites, many of them, familiar names and all; but now the sole owner was the federal government and the traffic was all military. Yet this section of the Cumberland was mostly Confederate country at heart, never mind how the armies fared. There was little enough folk could do save snipe at the passing steamboats from the bank, sometimes. In fact there was a good bit of that, and once in a while the boldest spirits even found ways to make themselves more than merely pesky. Someone did at Palmyra on the lower river, where a gunboat and several army transports were ambushed and badly knocked about by artillery hidden somewhere in the town. Nobody ever identified the guilty parties—or the heroes, depending on one's point of view—but the navy declared they were civilian guerrillas, and reacted promptly, in no uncertain terms. More gunboats steamed up from Smithland and shelled Palmyra flat. Not a house was left standing, according to the report of the lieutenant in charge. Similar treatments were administered as necessary to other towns upstream until in time—again, as Cumberland tides permitted—the gunboats clamped an iron grip on the upper river all the way to Point Isabel, soon to rename itself for Union General Ambrose Burnside. Thus the Cumberland, however unwillingly, became a Yankee river for the duration.

Nashville chafed under the rigors of military occupation, but bustled like an anthill too. Nashville was shabby in peeling paint, its citizens in threadbare clothing and cracked shoe leather. But Nashville was arsenal, storehouse, forward bastion, and staging area for Union armies grinding relentlessly into the farther vitals of the south. It was slow progress against great difficulties, sometimes stopped cold in its tracks, often beset by incredible ineptness. Still, in the end, it was unstoppable. And in the end, the war came roaring back to Cumberland country.

It was as good as the end, anyway: the waning months of 1864 with the south already spent. Atlanta had fallen and William Tecumseh Sherman was about to start across Georgia for the sea. But against all reason the Army of Tennessee deliberately turned its back on Sherman to gamble on a drive northward to the Cumberland, or even to the Ohio, or as much farther as desperate and determined men might carry on. The Army of Tennessee had grown lean and hard and learned the facts of war since Donelson and Shiloh. It had fought a bloody stalemate at Stone's River, seen the just rewards of victory thrown away after Perryville and Chickamauga, known defeat at Missionary Ridge and Atlanta. It was not a lucky army. Thus far it had marched behind three leaders. Braxton Bragg, the disciplinarian, it had bitterly detested. Cautious Joe Johnston it had loved. One way and another, neither had quite measured up. Now the army followed the Kentucky-born Texan John Bell Hood.

The war had used Hood cruelly. His left arm hung limp and lifeless, destroyed by a wound at Gettysburg. Chickamauga had cost him his right leg, so that he had to ride strapped in the saddle. With all that he was a young man still, only thirty-three, and there burned in him a furious fighting spirit not a whit dampened by his body's maiming. The southern society lady Mrs. Mary Boykin Chesnut had known him in Richmond, where he spent some weeks convalescing after Chickamauga. Suffering had left its mark. His face, she confided to her celebrated Civil War diary, was "the face of an old Crusader." But she was deeply impressed, too, by "the light of battle in his eyes."

Looking backward, one is tempted to see Mrs. Chesnut's John

B. Hood as a man almost eerily right as the leader of a forlorn last hope.

Forlorn it certainly was, virtually foredoomed to failure. Yet Hood's march into Tennessee began with the sort of opportunity generals dream about, for he caught the Union forces opposed to him in a near-fatal split. General John Schofield with some twenty-two thousand men was at Pulaski, more than sixty miles south of Nashville where George H. Thomas was hurriedly trying to assemble the bulk of his scattered Army of the Cumberland. Somewhat tardily, Schofield saw his peril and started northward by forced marches. But Hood, maneuvering skillfully and swiftly, outflanked him, cut him off, and trapped him at Spring Hill on the Duck River. The trap was, or should have been, airtight: no way out of it at all. Hood's army was not a great deal larger than Schofield's, but he was in position to make the Federals fight his battle on his terms, chop them up, and eat them piecemeal.

Then, somehow, the trap was never sprung.

The question of what went wrong is one the Civil War buffs still ponder. At the time Hood raged savagely against the ineptness of the generals of his staff. He raged against his army, shamefully accusing it of a lack of fighting heart. He raged, in short, against everybody but himself. "I had hoped," he lamented in his memoirs, ". . . to be able to profit by the teaching of my illustrious countryman. . . ." He meant Stonewall Jackson. But history was not going to remember John B. Hood as another Stonewall Jackson, and what might have happened makes a pointless speculation anyway. What did happen was that no one blocked the Columbia pike, running straight northward past Spring Hill all the way to Nashville. Schofield slipped his army through in the dead of night, wagon train and all, marched it past the twinkling campfires of Hood's whole army, and hustled it up the pike so swiftly the men alternately walked and double-timed. Nathan Bedford Forrest, commanding Hood's cavalry, loosed a reckless, last-minute attack on the column just as dawn broke. It was too little, and much too late. An infantry regiment in Schofield's rear guard turned and fixed bayonets. A battery or two of artillery turned too, and unlimbered, and Forrest's charging troopers were blown out of their saddles at point-blank range. By midmorning the weary Federals were deploying into entrenchments before the town of Franklin on the Harpeth River, only eighteen miles from Nashville.

The position was a strong one, as Hood saw when he led his own army up the pike a little after noon. His generals, smarting-mad though they were after the morning's recriminations, had their doubts about a straight-ahead frontal assault, and some ventured to say so. Hood ignored them. He knew all the military texts frowned on attacking an entrenched enemy unless one had the substantial advantage in numbers, which he lacked. He ignored that, too; he was no book general. One of his divisions had not yet come up. Neither had his artillery. He refused to wait. A cold fury possessed Hood. The November afternoon wore on and there were few hours of daylight left. He would not waste them. He would attack.

In silence, grimly, his generals rode back to their commands. "Boys, this will be short and desperate," one of them told his brigade as he ordered it forward. He was right. He would not live long enough, though, to take any comfort in the fact.

The battle flags were tattered, but they streamed out bravely. "For the moment we were spell-bound with admiration, although they were our hated foes," wrote a Union officer, recalling the grand spectacle as the Army of Tennessee formed ranks and began to move, flowing like a gray wave down the slope called Winstead Hill some two miles to the south, and on across an open, gently rolling field toward the waiting breastworks. Others in the federal lines would remember the coveys of quail that kept bursting up out of the brown November grass ahead of the oncoming ranks. Bayonets and rifle barrels gleamed coldly; the men stepped out with a steady, long-striding swing. But two miles made a long, long way for infantry to charge. Presently the Union artillery opened up with canister and grape. Men fell but the ranks closed and kept going; and then there was a long rippling crash of rifle fire, too, and the thing changed from grand spectacle to mass slaughter. Still the attack carried on. It broke over the Union emplacements, here and there along the line, and men fought hand to hand with bayonets and rifle butts. Driven back, the gray host re-formed and charged again, raising the high, defiant quaver of the Rebel yell. They did it as many as a dozen times, some of the Federals claimed afterward. And some remembered how at the end there were men who stumbled to their knees before the Union lines, utterly spent and pleading hoarsely, "For God's sake, Yank, don't shoot!"

It lasted an hour, or a little more. Even then it ended by fits and starts, slowly. The sun went down and still scattered little knots of men kept fighting in the dark. But long before that it was over. Hood had thrown away his bid for Tennessee.

Call it a drawn battle. Schofield had no reason for wanting to hold the field, at any rate. He pulled his army out that night, less two thousand casualties, and continued his retreat to Nashville. After a while Hood pulled together what was left of his battered Army of Tennessee and followed. The headlong attacks had cost a fearful price: more than six thousand dead and wounded. Of Hood's generals, five had been killed outright. Six more were wounded, one so seriously he would die of it, and another had been captured. But it was not in Hood's nature to turn back. At Nashville he would find a city the Federals had had two years to fortify. He was aware of that. He knew the Army of the Cumberland, once Thomas got it together, would outnumber his own more than three to one—and was well seasoned, rested, and superbly equipped besides. He knew enough to respect Major General George H. Thomas, too: the same solid, thoroughgoing man who had won that first battle on the Cumberland, at Fishing Creek back when the war was young.

Yet Hood pushed ahead, a man driven by a death wish, perhaps —or a vision of Valhalla. Weary as they were, his men would not shirk another fight. They were a scarecrow lot. Hardly a man boasted anything resembling a full uniform any longer, and all they had was ragged. A good half of the men went barefoot. The fine Indian summer weather of late November gave way to frost, and then to snow and sleet. Yet they followed Hood. He led them up into the low hills around Nashville's southern and eastern outskirts. There he put them to digging entrenchments in the frozen earth—not even Hood was sanguine enough to believe he could risk another attack—and waited for the enemy to come out.

His one long chance to catch Thomas in a bind went glimmering, though. Again it was a good effort, but too little and too late. Early in December Hood sent Colonel D. C. Kelly, one of Nathan Bedford Forrest's most capable cavalry aides, on a sweep around Nashville aimed at closing the Cumberland River to Union reinforcements. It started out very well indeed. Installing a battery of field guns on a bluff at Bell's Mills, twelve miles downstream, Kelly quickly snapped up a pair of steamboats bound for Nashville with military stores. It was sheer bad luck that he failed to carry out his primary mission, for a convoy with fourteen thousand Union troops had passed upstream no more than a day or so earlier. He proceeded to make a nuisance of himself, nevertheless. This Kelly, known as the "Fighting Parson" to his fellow cavalrymen, was the same aide whose prayers Forrest had so earnestly solicited during the attack on Fort Donleson. He was no man to be awed by ironclads, therefore, and this time he had more than prayers to work with. In a sneak raid by night, Union gunboats managed to recapture the two prizes Kelly had taken, but it was their last success. On December sixth the ironclads *Carondelet* and *Neosha* dropped down from Nashville to send the offending battery packing. Not once but twice they tried it, and both times Kelly's gunners ran them back upstream. For the next nine days the Cumberland remained blockaded. Then on the fifteenth the ironclads were back for another go, accompanied by five light gunboats called down from the upper river. Again Kelly was giving them a spirited knock-down-drag-out when a full division of Union cavalry moved in from the rear, and he had to limber up his guns and retire. General Thomas had taken his time, but he was ready now to have it out with Hood.

"Old Slow Trot" had grown in stature and in public esteem since Fishing Creek. These days he was the "Rock of Chickamauga," still no model of flair or brilliance but not one to make mistakes either. Early in the morning on that same December fifteenth, methodical as always, Thomas had paid his bill and checked out of his headquarters in Nashville's St. Cloud Hotel. He had called his staff together and ridden out with them to his waiting army. What followed has been called the most decisive battle of the war. Very possibly it was, when one considers that war's endless list of gory standoffs. The fighting lasted all that day and a long way into the next, and when it was finished the Confederate States' Army of Tennessee was finished too: nothing left of it but the wreckage of an army retreating southward as best it could.

The war was not quite over yet, but the Cumberland had soon the last of it.

19
The Piping
Times
of Peace

WILLIAM G. "Parson" Brownlow, the Reconstruction governor, rode into Nashville in 1865 like a Jove poised to hurl thunderbolts. The Parson—he had been one, for a fact—was a rabid East Tennessee Unionist who had once declared his readiness to "fight secession on the ice in hell." He had nearly come to that, too, having narrowly escaped hanging by a Confederate drumhead court-martial early in the war. The memory rankled, apparently, for he took over the Tennessee statehouse loudly vowing to show no mercy to men who had carried on rebellion, as he put it, "with all the malignity of fiends and cruelty of savages; who through rapine, arson, butchery, and perjury filled the land with mourning. . . ."

The land certainly was filled with mourning, and the first dismal months of defeat seemed to promise more, not less, under the conqueror's iron heel. One Confederate guerrilla, the notorious Champ Ferguson, was indeed tried, convicted, and hanged at Nashville that same year. But many believed Ferguson had been a Confederate spy on top of all his other sins. He was a man of violence anyway, a bushwhacker like most guerrillas, no matter which side they claimed to fight for, so that few people would deny he had blood enough on his hands to merit hanging. In the long run, though, the vast majority of ordinary folk, whether civilians or veterans who drifted home in ragged butternut or gray, found Parson Brown-

182

low's bite less ferocious than his bark. Shorn of the windy gas-
conade of him and his sort, and underneath all the corruption and
political chicanery that sprouted inevitably as an aftermath of war,
Reconstruction boiled down mostly to the dull, drab business of
getting everyday lives back into some kind of working order. It
was that way on the Cumberland as elsewhere. But Cumberland
country was more fortunate than much of the rest of the south. At
least it had been spared such devastation as, say, a Sherman
marching across it to the sea.

There were scars, of course, even in Nashville where no clash
of arms had taken place. The city showed the raw wounds of some
two hundred houses ruthlessly torn down to make room for the
emplacements deemed necessary for defense by Union engineers.
Whole blocks along streets once gracefully tree-lined stood bare
and ugly now, because Union occupation troops had needed fire-
wood. Some celebrated southern institutions like the Nashville Female Academy had closed their doors forever. Extreme low water
in the river revealed the charred superstructures of two steamboats
jutting above the current across from the Nashville wharves. They
marked the remains of the *James Woods* and the *James Johnson*,
converted gunboats burned and scuttled during the Confederate
retreat after the surrender of Fort Donelson. Some other scars, not
visible at a glance, were symptoms of evils more serious. Newspapers complained of flourishing drunkenness and crime. The
years of war had left the city with a rat population so teeming,
remarked one discouraged observer, it would have challenged the
talents of the Pied Piper of Hamelin himself. And at least one of
the city's more prosperous businesses was in itself a sad com-
mentary on the times. That was the factory of James Morton,
manufacturing the United States Army and Navy Leg, ingeniously
contrived ". . . of willow wood with India rubber springs . . . all
enameled on the outer surface with a flesh colored preparation. . . ."
There was a great demand for Mr. Morton's legs.

But physical ills could be mended, most of them, and in time
would be. It is worth mentioning, also, that by the war's end Nashville's official records bore witness to thirteen marriages of local
girls to Union soldiers. All thirteen bridegrooms, moreover, stayed
on as residents of the city or its environs. The war had fostered
something besides hatred, clearly.

The Cumberland itself took up much of the slack of readjustment.

She was still there, still flowing down to the Ohio as she always had. So was the land still there, the rich bottomland prized since the time of the Long Hunters. Still, there were mighty changes. One of the most drastic—or so it appeared at the time—was King Cotton's banishment from Middle Tennessee. That stemmed directly from the other far-reaching change wrought by the war, which was of course the black man's new freedom. Stripped of their work forces by the Emancipation Proclamation even before the coming of peace, the big plantation owners had had perforce to turn to other crops. Happily, the fertile bluegrass acres along the big bend of the Cumberland could raise fine wheat, corn, cattle, and hogs as readily as cotton, and with fewer farmhands. And in the beaten, hungry south food was the vital need anyway. Future years would prove that Middle Tennessee lost nothing by the changeover. Yet more perhaps than any other single thing, cotton had symbolized the aristocratic antebellum south, with all that was gracious and good about it—and the great deal that was sterile and decadent. Cotton was the product, above all others, that had made slavery a profitable institution. The old king's passing was a wrench, and he was missed.

Steamboatmen missed him very badly, for cotton had always been their mainstay. Cotton was the ideal cargo. It usually went to market during the months of high water on the river, when navigation was easiest. It was bulk freight, easy to handle and to stow, almost always bound on the lucrative long haul down the Mississippi to New Orleans. Now, increasingly, the steamboat operators had to scratch for whatever freights they could pick up. Increasingly, too, they were scratching in competition with the railroads that came poking their locomotives' iron snouts into town after town in what once had been steamboat territory exclusively.

On the lower river the competition gradually became a losing proposition. But railroads were slower to invade the basin of the upper Cumberland, where the country grew progressively more rugged and more sparsely peopled the farther one went past Nashville. With the dirt roads few and bad—often quite impassable in rainy weather—the steamboats remained unchallenged there, and would for a long time still. Their freight on the upstream run consisted largely of hardware, farm tools, and such other manufactured goods as folk still isolated in a remote back country needed. For the downstream run the roustabouts were called on to load a variety of stuff: hogs and cattle on the hoof, barreled pork and smoked side meat, molasses, eggs, hides, tobacco—all this brought in off the farms tucked away in stony hillside coves for miles around each landing. Items could run as small as bags of feathers or bunches of dried ginseng root gathered in the woods. It was all paying business, though; it all added up.

It was a neighborly, old-time sort of business too. A packet captain would order his pilot to head in for any tiny country landing on signal, maybe to take aboard no more than a crate of chickens, maybe to deliver the mail-order yard goods for some farm woman's new Sunday dress. And at the town landings an approaching packet's whistle still was enough to fetch whole populations hurrying, from shirttail boys and village ne'er-do-wells to the most august of solid citizens. Life revolved around the river. It was the highway to the world outside, the news-bringer, the assurance that some things remained steadfast, come what might.

In many ways those downhill years after 1865 were a halcyon time between the fading ordeal of the War Between the States and the oncoming century that would bring changes no Cumberlander could have dreamed of.

One change came early. Not even the upper Cumberland could remain untouched by progress; not with the postwar United States building and expanding at a clip never approached before. Presently the builders reached out for the virgin hardwood forests that had covered most of the region since times beyond knowing. Generations of settlers had scarcely disturbed the magnificent stands of cedar, oak, ash, hickory, beech, and walnut, once they had their modest acreages cleared and their cabins up. Before the war there had been little commerce in Cumberland lumber, either, beyond an occasional lot of ax handles or barrel staves going down the river as part of some mixed cargo. By the early 1870s, however, a new hardwood lumber industry was booming everywhere along the upper river. All the way from Carthage far up past the Kentucky line, mills were turning out rough-sawed lumber by the hundreds of thousands of board feet, while logs in quantities nearly as great were being rafted downstream without benefit of sawmills. For about ten years the steamboatmen enjoyed a promising new bonanza, since rough-sawed lumber provided bulk cargoes almost as satisfactory as those in the old days of cotton on the middle river. The years passed, though; the timberlands within easy reach of the Cumberland's mainstream were greedily cut over, and loggers began to work up into the more distant forests around Roaring River, Obey River, and Caney Fork. As they did, more and more of the timber they felled was simply rafted down those streams to the Cumberland and thence on to sawmills in Nashville. Once again the packets faced a losing battle for freights.

Rafting was essentially a throwback to old flatboat and keelboat days. It was a scorning of the Machine Age: men choosing to put their faith in the river's current and their own ability to offset her treacheries and dodges with brawn and river wisdom. Most of the time it took plenty of both.

Summer and early fall were the customary seasons for putting rafts together, in anticipation of the later fall rains that brought good tides down the river. There was a great deal more to the business than simply assembling the logs, chivying them into place with pike poles—a pike pole being the same instrument northern loggers knew as a peavey—and then chaining them fast. A rough kind of science was involved, for logs were not supposed to be taken if they were shorter than ten feet or longer than fifteen or so. Then the total quantity had to be calculated with considerable nicety according to the number of board feet wanted. The figure ran to about forty thousand, on an average, but could go as high as twice that. In practice this meant a raft some two hundred feet long by thirty or more in the beam: a mass of dead weight incomparably more cumbersome than any flatboat ever built. Yet a crew of only five oarsmen and a pilot could usually handle it. Of the oarsmen, three would man a long steering sweep projecting forward from the raft's bow, while the other two handled a similar sweep trailing astern. Pay was less than munificent, even for the times. An oarsman got fifty cents a day and keep, a pilot a dollar and a half and keep. For "keep" there was a rough lean-to providing shelter in the middle of the raft, with straw on which the men slept as time and duties permitted. Food was provided also, though each man was generally expected to cook for himself at a stove which often was little more than a grate fixed over a box of sand or a stone slab.

It is a pity there was no Sam Clemens to grow up along the Cumberland and write of it, or at the very least a John James Audubon to keep a journal of a trip down the river. Had there been such, some raftsman might have survived to stand as tall among American folk heroes as Mike Fink, the Ohio River keel-boatman, or Jim Bludso of Mississippi steamboat fame. He might well have been Cal Hamilton of Celina, a black pilot so universally admired by old-time rivermen that he must have been a giant among his kind. But the old-timers are gone now, and even their memories are fading fast. The raftsmen long ago followed flatboat- and keelboatmen into limbo, and no bard has left us a record of their feats or the details of their craft. Merely on the face of it, though, taking an inert, unwieldy mass of logs down the twisting and capricious Cumberland in all weathers and water conditions had to require skills of a high order. Surely no man today could do it. Even in rafting's heyday, membership in the fraternity probably was limited.

As with all travel on the river, everything depended on the tides. Once a raft was ready to go the crew stood by till a good high one came along; then the trick was to stay with it. If all went well, the downstream run to Nashville would average about forty miles a day. That was excellent going—but frequently all went far from well. In the early years it was customary to tie up at night and travel only by daylight. Later raftsmen took to running right through, which might shorten the time but certainly added to the hazards. In either case, the good tide could not always be counted on to last. It was capable of falling with incredible suddenness— "dropping the bottom out," as rivermen said—and when that happened it could buckle a raft's two-hundred-foot length badly enough to tear it right apart. Storms, contrary winds, all such everyday perils as snags, sawyers, and shifting sandbars were trials as great for raftsmen as for their steamboat rivals. And since no raft was anywhere near as nimble as even the slowest packet, the pilot had not only to be intimately acquainted with every foot of his river but constantly alert for the first subtle signals of a channel's changing. Even so routine a maneuver as rounding one of the Cumberland's endless series of hairpin bends would have to be started a long way ahead, and was likely to call for split-second judgment by the pilot as well as prodigious labor at both steering sweeps. The job became no simpler, either, when a raft happened to be overtaken in some tight stretch by a packet bound downstream, or met one going up. Nowhere was the upper Cumberland a very wide river. Passing room could be scant, and many a steamboat pilot was inclined to be pretty grudging about giving way to the raftsmen who were taking cash from his pocket, so to speak, with every board foot of the logs they rode. There were river traditions implying that the feuds occasionally waxed more than warm.

Yet rafting had its interludes of lazy pleasure too: fine days when a man had no more to do than idle in the sun and perhaps trail a fishing line astern, watching the banks glide past while the river did all the work. Again, one can only regret the absence of a Sam Clemens.

In spite of the rivalry, the Cumberland accommodated both steamboatmen and raftsmen for some years. Even in steady decline, though, the steamboats had the greater staying power. By the early years of the twentieth century the Cumberland timberlands were virtually exhausted, and rafting came to its end. But the packets managed to hang on a good while longer.

Strangely, the only steamboat race ever run on the Cumberland in the classic *Robert E. Lee–Natchez* pattern took place in 1896, when the packets' most lustrous glory days were long past. The race pitted the *R. Dunbar*, Captain Tom Ryman, Jr., against the *Will Cummins*, Captain W. S. Bowman, over the full upstream course from Nashville to Burnside. The *Dunbar* won, and in splendid, old-time go-to-hell style at that. Captain Ryman hung a keg of nails on his safety valve, so it was said, and forced his fires with pitch pine and slabs of fat bacon till the smokestacks glowed redhot. It was somewhat late in the day for that sort of thing, to be sure. Such dangerous capers had long been outlawed, and the statutes had teeth in them, what was more. But young Tom Ryman was the scion of an old, well-respected Cumberland steamboat family. The authorities suspended his master's license, though only briefly, and never took him into court at all.

The spirit of old days on the river was slow to die, apparently.

20

Another
Cumberland

YEARS of emphasis on the Cumberland as an artery of commerce had tended to make many people forget that above Burnside there was another river altogether. Effectively blocked to all rivercraft, first by Smith's Shoals and then by the falls, it was the *upper* upper Cumberland in fact if not by actual name.

Very little of importance had happened on that river since the slacking off of settlers bound up the Wilderness Road for Kentucky's bluegrass early in the nineteenth century. Not many of the homeseekers had stopped to put down roots. The few towns they founded along the river had not grown very notably, and families on the farms back in the hills lived very much as their forebears had. They scratched a bare living out of the thin soil around their squared-log cabins, raised meager crops of corn, potatoes, beans, and flax, still got much of their meat by hunting as men had since the time of Daniel Boone, and laid up scant stores of the world's goods. Such people were not the kind to alter the face of the land much. The valley of Yellow Creek—the same Dr. Walker had called Flat Creek so many years before—was no longer choked by the marshy canebrakes through which the little doctor and his companions had had to struggle. A few families had farms there now, and a man by the name of Jones ran a small wayside tavern up near the saddle of Cumberland Gap. Nature already was well along toward obliterating the remains of fortifications thrown up there during the late war, as well as the older ruins of a gristmill and a primitive iron smelter. Aside from these things, Dr. Walker would easily have recognized this country he had judged not worth his while as a land speculation.

The national enthusiasm for canal building that swept the nation around the 1830s had promised great things for the region, though only fleetingly. A visionary named Robert P. Baker, appointed chief engineer of Kentucky's Bureau of Internal Improvements in 1835, had presented the state legislature with a plan for a waterway so stupendous it merits telling in no other words than his own:

> . . . [it] would lead from the Ohio up the Kentucky River by locks and dams to the three forks of the Kentucky; then up the South Fork . . . by a canal into the Cumberland River at Cumberland Ford; thence four miles . . . to the mouth of Yellow Creek; thence by a canal in the bed of Yellow Creek to Cumberland Gap, thence through Cumberland Gap by tunnel, and by canal thence into Powell's River, five miles below; down that river successively into the Clinch and Tennessee, and up the Hiwassee by locks and dams; from the Hiwassee . . . by a canal to the navigable waters of the Savannah at the head of . . . navigation on that river. . . .

Thus, eventually, Mr. Baker would have had his waterway proceed down the Savannah to the Atlantic Ocean. Perhaps it was as well for the various rivers concerned that the legislators were somewhat stunned by the notion of canalboats floating through the bowels of Cumberland Mountain. It appears, anyway, that the tunnel beneath the Gap was the part of Baker's scheme at which they balked. His report was promptly tabled and soon forgotten, though its details may still be found in the archives of the *Kentucky House Journal*.

Some years passed. Canal fever died, was succeeded by railroad fever, and for a while it appeared likely that iron rails would blaze a trail roughly similar to the one proposed by Baker for his would-be waterway. The very eminent Henry Clay himself had been among the backers of the "great work" which would, as the *Kentucky Gazette* pontificated, not only strengthen the bonds of national unity but "make Kentucky what the God of Creation designed—the finest portion of the habitable globe!"

But the railroad never was built either, due to a variety of obstacles both financial and political. So the region between the Gap and the Falls of the Cumberland remained a land apart, the old Wilderness Road of Boone and Richard Henderson still its main connection with the nation outside. Over the years the road had gone through periods of sketchy improvement alternating with others of utter neglect; overall they added up to a steady deterioration. Parts of the route had been designated Kentucky's first toll road in 1797, and the first tollgate was erected at Cumberland Ford. The town of Pineville had grown up around it and still survived there, though the tolls had been abolished after several years. Collections never had provided sufficient money to keep the road in good repair, anyway, so the deterioration continued. Natives seldom used the name Wilderness Road anymore. Sometimes they spoke of it as the State Road, but most often it was the Kentucky Hog Road nowadays. For a long time its chief traffic had consisted of livestock being driven northward to the bluegrass for fattening or southward through Cumberland Gap for sale in Virginia or the Carolinas.

Not even the War Between the States had affected the region very seriously. Political differences had intensified old feuds, now and again, but most of the local folk had preferred to settle their differences among themselves, as was their way. The strategic Gap itself had changed hands a number of times before the Union finally established a lasting hold. Most of the fighting, though, had been done by comparatively small forces on both sides, for the problems of troop movements and logistics in that rugged back country posed greater difficulties than hostile armies. In 1864 General Ulysses S. Grant had inspected the Wilderness Road in person all the way from Cumberland Gap to Lexington, Kentucky. The general was thinking in terms of a supply line for a Union drive into East Tennessee, but found the road in such deplorable condition that he dropped the project out of hand.

The end of the war brought no improvement, though it did fetch a growing trickle of sightseers and journalists. It also fetched a clutch of learned geologists, belatedly awakening to the fact that the Cumberland Mountains offered, as one of them wrote, "a range through nearly the whole of the life-bearing rocks of the most ancient period of our world's history." Another observer who passed through the Gap in 1870 foresaw a day when progress would inevitably force the country to yield up "the treasures of mineralogical wealth now latent in its soil." He was dubious about the Hog Road, though, describing it as no more than "the enlarged war-trail of the ancient Cherokees."

Progress seemed in no hurry. Fifteen years later James Lane Allen, writing in *Harper's Magazine,* waxed ruefully eloquent over the road's "sloughs and sands, its mud and holes, and jutting ledges of rock and loose bowlders, and twists and turns, and general total depravity. . . ." He insisted with wry humor that companies of the more pious wayfarers, frequently overcome by despair, were wont to sit down, sing a hymn or two, and pray for strength to tackle that road once more. And he concluded, still in jest but half-seriously too: "Perhaps one of the provocations to homicide among the mountain people should be reckoned this road."

There Allen was putting his finger on a quality noted by others before and after him. The mountain folk did indeed appear to feel some extraordinary "provocation to homicide." They were a people stubbornly independent, impatient of restraint, cherishing a fierce, touchy pride. Generations of isolation had exposed them to very few softening influences and left ingrained in them the virtues and the faults—courage, self-reliance, suspicion of the outsider, a too-hasty bent toward violent solutions—native to their pioneer ancestors. Quick to resent an injury, slow to forgive, they made natural feudists. And once begun, perhaps over nothing of greater moment than an unwelcome flirtation between one man's son and another's daughter, or the disputed ownership of a stray hog, their feuds could go on year in and year out, dragging in even the most distant of both clans' relatives.

In spite of appearances, though, the people had their own kind of respect for law and order, and a hearty social life as well. Circuit Court days and election days would see the streets of little county seats like Barbourville, Williamsburg, and Pineville jammed to overflowing with men trooping into town to conduct their business, if any, and to meet their friends, talk, drink the fiery local whiskey —and trade. Trading was a compulsive be-all and end-all among these people, and a man could keep it up from daybreak till dusk if he was smart and had a little something to get him started. Fortunately, since nobody had much of it to spare, cash money was more or less superfluous. A likely-looking horse or dog made the best currency. Anything, however—a knife, gun, wagon, piece of harness—could be enough to put a man in business. An oft-told local story, possibly apocryphal, had for its hero a sharp young fellow who walked into town one court day leading a pair of coon dogs and rode home that evening on a lively two-year-old mare with saddlebags full of good things for the whole family.

Incidentally, town on court day or election day was not commonly regarded as any place for the womenfolk. Once in a great while some hangdog, work-worn wife might be permitted to tag along with her man if she had a few eggs to trade, or a bit of "fancy work," or something else. But this was a man's world, and a man's wife's place was in the home. She was not expected to forget it. And home, the cabin clinging to its steep-sided ridge above its rocky creek bed, was another world altogether from even the county seat—and still farther in time than in physical miles.

It was a world where simple fundamentalist religion had battled long ago to an uneasy truce with ancient superstition, so that even the God-fearing believed an enemy could put a curse on a man, or on his gun, his horse, his ax, his plow. It was a world of ancestral dialects, old folksongs scarcely altered from the Elizabethan English of the first colonists; of weather signs and portents and old adages believed as gospel; of crops planted according to the phases of the moon; of babies *birthed,* as folk said, by some favorite granny-woman in each neighborhood; of the ailing cured —or not cured, sometimes—by poultices and decoctions of dogwood, snakeroot, sassafras, black ash leaves, bark of the yellow poplar . . .

More than all that, it was a world set obstinately in its own ways, knowing next to nothing of how other people lived beyond the mountains, and uninterested in learning. Obviously, it was no kind of place to be conducive to the efforts of any bringers of commerce and industrial development. Yet surely those "treasures of mineralogical wealth" could not go begging forever.

21

When Midas Came to Yellow Creek

An earthquake shook the southeastern United States on the last night of August 1886. It was sufficiently violent near its epicenter to wreck much of Charleston, South Carolina, and as far away as Cumberland Gap the shivering of the earth tore huge chunks of rock from the roof of the cavern that had given the place its earliest name, and sent them crashing to the cavern floor. Aside from that, the quake left few marks on Cumberland country and was soon forgotten there. It was pure coincidence that placed another mover and shaker in the Gap that night. His name was Alexander Alan Arthur; he *would* leave his mark, and he would not soon be forgotten.

Cumberland Gap had seen no one like Alexander Arthur since the long-ago time when Judge Richard Henderson hurried through on Daniel Boone's heels. Nothing in all the years between had changed the pattern from which an ambitious man was cut. But where Judge Henderson had been a transient with his thoughts on a promised land ahead, Arthur already had fixed *his* ambition on the upper Cumberland. He meant to put down roots there.

Most new acquaintances were struck immediately by two things about Alexander Arthur. One was the pleasant Scottish burr in his voice, the other his marked resemblance to former U.S. President Chester A. Arthur. Both were legitimate. He had been born in

Glasgow forty-one years earlier, and he actually was distantly related to the President, himself a man of Scotch-Irish ancestry. For the rest, those new acquaintances usually found Alexander Arthur extremely personable: a large, sandy-haired, blue-eyed man with a jovial manner about him and a friendly self-assurance that put him at ease in any company. He came by that legitimately, too, having lived a roving life that took him to Canada at an early age, then back to Scotland for a while, then to Norway and Sweden for a while longer before he finally landed in the United States, at Boston. He had worked there as agent for a British steel firm, and later moved on to East Tennessee to manage a Scottish-owned lumber company. Active and gregarious by nature, he had soon made himself at home in the country around the Holston and the Watauga. Others before him had remarked on the region's similarity to the brakes and braes of old Scotland, and he was happy there. The people, largely of Scotch-Irish antecedents, too, quickly took to him. He had a knack for getting on. He had a keen eye for opportunity as well.

On the night of the earthquake Arthur was camped in the saddle of Cumberland Gap with a party of associates from Asheville, North Carolina. Most of them were sons of the wealthy eastern families that already had made Asheville a fashionable summer retreat. The quake shook everybody awake and afforded some pleasant titillations, but hurt no one. To the young gentleman, at that point, the trip to the upper Cumberland was probably as much a lark as a serious business exploration.

To them—but not to Alexander Arthur. He had been there the previous year, investigating the region for a projected railway line from East Tennessee. Nothing had come of that, but like Dr. Thomas Walker before him Arthur had seen the rich and apparently limitless seams of soft coal around Yellow Creek and the Cumberland's headwaters. He had admired the splendid stands of hardwood timber that clothed the land. And he had examined the deposits of iron ore east of the Cumberland Mountains, on the approaches to the Gap. All these things, of course, had been common knowledge for a long time. The coal had been mined in a small way and carried out through the Gap by wagon for nearly a century past. Even the iron ore had been worked, as was witnessed by the ruins of the old smelter still standing in the Gap. Too, Arthur no doubt had heard of the geologists who had poked about there in his own time. He himself was no geologist, or engineer either. He had all the makings of a first-rate promoter, though: the first to cast his eye over this country since the canal enthusiast Baker some fifty years before. And Baker had been far ahead of his time and nine-tenths dreamer besides.

Alexander Arthur could dream, too, and did. But he was also a realist, shrewd enough to sense the time was right, nervy enough to seize time by the forelock.

Within the next few days his friends saw everything that he had seen. He made sure of that. What was more, they saw it all in terms of the potential profit there. He made sure of that, too. When the party headed back to Asheville they already were agreed on the formation of an organization to be called the Gap Associates. In addition they held options on several thousand acres of the most promising land in the valley of Yellow Creek, picked up for next to nothing from mountain folk too guileless to suspect they might be throwing away their birthrights. This was but the bare beginning. Arthur, no small thinker, realized the need from now on would be capital: more capital, undoubtedly, than the Associates alone could swing. He was ready with a proposition and put it to them. He still had important connections among British steel men and others familiar with Britain's money marts. Send him to London, he suggested, and he would undertake to return with the necessary financial backing. The other associates thought it over and agreed. The investment involved in steamer ticket, lodging, and incidentals would, after all, be trifling.

Perhaps Arthur spoke with more assurance than he really felt. Nonetheless, he was not bluffing. England in the 1880s stood at the zenith of Victorian power and prosperity. It was no idle boast that Britannia ruled an empire on which the sun never set. The sun quite literally never did, and London was not only the political but the financial capital of that empire. Throughout the known world it would have been difficult to say whether the royal navy or the pound sterling commanded the greater respect. Even the United States continued to yield profits to investment-minded Englishmen, despite the events of 1776 and afterward. British money was helping to open up western cattle ranges, build American railroads, develop American mining properties. Extensive British investments in the south had done much to speed Reconstruction following the War Between the States. As an example there was Birmingham, Alabama, already growing to be a southern steel colossus and paying off richly to astute British financiers. Knowing all that, the personable Scotsman could scarcely have picked a more favorable climate in which to make his pitch for a new Birmingham on the Cumberland.

He made it well. When next he rode through Cumberland Gap, in the spring of 1887, a committee of very eminent British geologists and engineers rode with him. They were there to examine the prospects and report back to their principals across the Atlantic.

These men were experts, and theirs was no hasty survey. They rode farther than the Gap Associates had—all the way to Barbourville and beyond—and they looked with eyes far sharper and more skeptical. In the end, though, the cable they shot off to London was quite un-British in its enthusiasm. Their recommendations were explicit: buy out the Gap Associates and exercise their options; buy or option as much additional land as possible; above all, proceed at once to organize a new American development company. Their praise for Alexander Arthur was equally explicit. They recommended him unanimously for general manager of the new company.

The seeds of boom times had been planted. They sprouted rapidly.

Happily the Gap Associates traded off their land options for shares in American Association, Limited, at substantial paper profits. Good news came from London. Banking houses there were interested in the new firm's securities, and stock sales were going well. Arthur moved down to Knoxville, opened an office there, and soon had survey crews moving out to stake a right of way for the spanking new Knoxville, Cumberland Gap, and Louisville Railroad. Most of the money back of it was British, but East Tennessee men came in to the tune of a quarter of a million dollars, thanks to Arthur's local popularity and his inspired promotion. At the same time work began on a tunnel nearly a mile long, to pierce the mountain under Cumberland Gap. (Somehow, one sees old Robert Baker spinning in his grave as armies of workmen dug and blasted at headings both north and south!) The unemployed, the adventurous and the merely ne'er-do-well came drifting in from every neighboring state. They all found work if they wanted it. A town of tents and shanties grew up in the Gap itself, complete with forges and blacksmith shops, stores, sawmills, everything that went with the advance of civilization, including whore-houses and saloons. No one had time to sit down and think of a name for the community. Cumberland Gap, everyone called it, the same as the pass in which it stood, and let it go at that. It still is Cumberland Gap today: smaller, more modest but more permanent, too, and very much tamed.

From the beginning, Alexander Arthur's most ambitious plans had centered about the pretty bottomland where Yellow Creek wound its way down the north slope of the mountain. It went without saying that the industrial empire he envisioned would need its capital city, and there was the spot. By the summer of 1888 he had surveyors busy on the site of Middlesborough, Kentucky. The name was suggested by some of Arthur's British colleagues in honor of another Middlesborough, the one in Yorkshire: a thriving iron center well worth emulating. But irreverent Americans soon shortened it to Middlesboro, and so it would remain. Some five thousand acres were set aside for the city, and its projected population of 250,000 struck no one as unduly optimistic. Characteristically, Arthur brought in the most prominent engineers and architects available and ordered them to do their unstinting best. The plat they laid out provided for spacious streets a hundred feet wide, with a main north-south thoroughfare four miles long. Fittingly, it was named Cumberland Avenue. The names of parallel streets on both sides carried out the English motif: Ilchester, Exeter, Winchester, and so on. More prosaically, the east-west avenues were only numbered. Ample tracts on the low ground near the creek were laid out as potential industrial areas. Land farther out, sloping gently up to attractive wooded heights, would become choice residential districts.

Ever practical, Arthur had selected the Yellow Creek location partly because it was convenient to the surrounding mountainsides where some of the richest coal seams ran. Railroad spur lines thus could easily connect the mines with the smelters, blast furnaces, and forges along the creek. He had work started on them, and on a separate belt railroad that would circle the city for fast, efficient interchange. He had work started on a hotel. He had another spur line laid right down Cumberland Avenue to accommodate the eager entrepreneurs now flocking in to preempt good business sites, and build, and cash in on the boom. Middlesboro burgeoned, for the time being, as a plank-and-canvas city to match the one up in the Gap. New sawmills sprang up along nearly any creek large enough to float a log, feeding the insatiable appetite for lumber. The first coal tipples began to rise above the city: the vanguard of a future host.

Deerstalker hats, tweeds, gaiters, and regimental mustaches grew almost commonplace as more and more Englishmen made themselves at home in this rough countryside where Thomas Walker had once sought Kentakee. Among Arthur's top executives was the younger son of a baronet. Some others were retired majors and colonels of the British army. A pair of brothers by the names of Edgar and Frank Watts, representing England's prestigious Watts Steel and Iron Company, turned up to supervise the construction of two blast furnaces. A partner in a distinguished firm of London solicitors arrived and set up shop as a watcher over the legal interests of client-stockholders back home.

There was nothing small about these Britishers. Living accommodations were both scarce and primitive, what with the sudden jump in population. The Brothers Watts solved the problem handily by building a fifty-room hotel of their own on a Cumberland Mountain spur just south of the Gap. Apparently it still fell short of their notion of the style to which they were accustomed, however, for they purchased an extensive acreage nearby, put up a fine large house for themselves, and had the land adjoining landscaped to make a hunt club on the English model.

A hundred-and-some-odd years after the signing of the Declaration of Independence, England seemed well on her way to establishing a whole new colony in the Cumberlands!

What the natives thought of all this was not recorded. But some shook their heads and warned that Yellow Creek could be fractious. Past rainy seasons had been known to bring sudden tides that flooded the whole valley. Undaunted, Alexander Arthur put that problem to his engineers too. They pondered it, studied the topography, and proposed a canal to bypass the creek's meandering curves with a deep, straight channel that would carry the runoff from the mountain slopes safely down toward the Cumberland River and away. The cost should be no obstacle, they submitted, since the old streambed would become highly salable real estate once it was filled in. So a fresh army of laborers was recruited—many of them said to have been strong-backed Irishmen and Italians from New York City slums—and turned loose with pick and shovel to make sure Yellow Creek would never be the same again; and it never was. For good measure the engineers threw a dam across the tributary known as Little Yellow Creek, thus creating Fern Lake as a reservoir of the pure, fresh water a growing city would need.

Picking up steam, the boom rolled on.

In August of 1889 the two headings of the tunnel through Cumberland Mountain met, five hundred feet beneath the Gap. The crews joined in an impromptu, uninhibited celebration that soon spilled down the mountainside into Middlesboro, went on all night, and produced the predictable crop of wrecked saloons, broken heads, hangovers, and fines. Two weeks later tracklayers of the Knoxville, Cumberland Gap, and Louisville Railroad toiled through the tunnel from the south, and on September first the Louisville and Nashville pushed *its* tracks up Yellow Creek for a ceremonial meeting of the rails and another nightlong celebration. By the year's end, money invested in and around Middlesboro totaled a good round ten million dollars: no Herculean sum by today's reckoning, certainly, but impressive by the standards of the 1890s—and still only the beginning. Coal was being dug from a number of the mines now. Arthur's spur lines and his belt railroad had started operations. The finishing touches were being put to the hundred and fifty rooms of the Middlesborough Hotel, a posh establishment that insisted proudly on the ancestral English spelling. The Watts brothers had their blast furnaces well along toward completion. A large electric light and power plant was under construction. Announcements of the first public sale of city lots had brought buyers from as far away as Chicago and New York, and an auctioneer standing in a wagon bed at the corner of Cumberland Avenue and Twentieth Street had knocked down over a hundred thousand dollars' worth on the first day.

These mammoth strides were not accomplished without a few setbacks. A succession of bad fires wiped out whole sections of the rising city, delaying overall progress. The maiden trip over the K., C.G., & L. Railroad, planned as still another gala occasion, came to grief when Alexander Arthur's private palace car went off a trestle and plunged bottom-up into a ravine. Arthur suffered internal injuries, several invited dignitaries were also hurt, and there were some fatalities. Still, it stood to reason that mishaps were unavoidable in so headlong a rush to greatness as was taking place on Yellow Creek.

By early 1890 Arthur was sufficiently recovered to visit London for a personal report to American Association's board of directors. Again he acquitted himself nobly. He returned to a triumphal Middlesboro welcome, after cabling the glad tidings ahead that still more millions in development money would be forthcoming. Sales of stocks and bonds in England continued at a gratifying pace. Now, too, American investors were clamoring to get in on the bonanza. Alexander Arthur was not the man to disappoint them. He had a string of railroad coaches fitted out as rolling exposition halls stocked with maps, plats, prospectuses, samples of Cumberland coal, iron ore, timber, flora and fauna. Manned by salesmen and heralded by press agents, the train steamed off to carry the message of opportunity a-knocking all across the midwest.

Long before this, Middlesboro had taken to calling Arthur the "Duke of Cumberland." It was a nickname bestowed in genuine affection, and it fitted him. He went about these days in true baronial splendor, driving his rakish light runabout and high-stepping team of matched carriage horses, cutting a figure equally dashing whether he paused to egg on a gang of laborers with genial exhortations, or turned up at the depot to greet the distinguished personages who came more and more frequently to tour the miracle city on Yellow Creek. Pretty, Boston-born Mrs. Arthur made a highly acceptable duchess, too: likely to be seen riding almost anywhere on her spirited black mare.

Developments grew steadily more grandiose. Ground was broken for an exclusive residential community on the southern approach to Cumberland Gap, close enough to Middlesboro to be convenient for the executive and the plant owner, yet comfortably removed from the smoke, noise, and noxious gases of industry running full blast. Harrogate, the place was named, and Arthur himself was the first to order a palatial home there. New ideas kept occurring to him. Inspired by the wealth of salt licks and mineral springs noted by every traveler through the region from Dr. Walker on, he began to envision a medicinal spa and watering place that would be a climactic attraction for the world's elite. By this time—and no wonder, surely—the name of Alexander A. Arthur had a certain magic in it. He mentioned his idea to financier friends in New York City and at once things began to happen. The result, inside of two years, was a rambling, rococo pile of gabled and turreted and overopulent Victorian bad taste called the Four Seasons Hotel. Seven hundred rooms it had; every one was furnished with the ultimate in luxury, and most offered the prospective guest a breathtaking mountain view besides. The management boasted that thirty-five thousand dollars' worth of sterling silver graced the tables in the plush-and-gingerbread-and-crystal dining room. An adjoining sanitarium with two hundred beds promised to soothe the aches and pains of ailing millionaires with every variety of bath and healing water known to Vichy or Baden-Baden, plus a few American innovations the Old World had never heard of. All this stood in the midst of spacious, faultlessly manicured grounds just south of Cumberland Gap. It might have been the final, clinching testimonial to civilization's taming of the wilderness with the gift of gracious living. . . .

Then, incredibly, the Midas touch turned to a brutal backhand slap.

The first warning of trouble had come late in 1890, when the great British banking house of Baring Brothers and Company closed its doors. The bank had underwritten large amounts in American Association securities, among others, and its fall sent shock waves through every Commonwealth stock exchange. Conservative Englishmen began to shy away from an investment that all of a sudden looked more than slightly speculative. For a while it appeared that American capital might fill the breach. To most outward appearances Middlesboro remained a raw and lusty, striving, thriving boomtown. But the caution signals were flying now, and knowledgeable financiers heeded them. Relentlessly the flow of money dwindled. Bad luck spawned more bad luck. When the first blast furnaces got into operation, ironmasters discovered to their chagrin that the ore from the Cumberlands' southward slopes was of far lower quality than everyone had supposed. Then in March of 1893 Wall Street was shaken by an epidemic of spectacular corporation failures. They touched off an American financial panic, and time abruptly ran out on Alexander Arthur's empire.

Within the year, American Association, Limited, was floundering through a painful liquidation. A sheriff's sale disposed of the company's vast land holdings in the Yellow Creek Valley. Track and rolling stock of the railroad spurs and the belt line went to the Louisville and Nashville at less than three cents on the dollar. Middlesboro's four banks failed, one after another. A few depressed property owners hung on, mostly because they were too hard up to move elsewhere. Out on the other side of Cumberland Gap the opulent Four Seasons Hotel was torn down in 1895. After one gala opening week the place never had made money. A Chicago salvage company paid nine thousand dollars for the right to cart away the remains.

The first shock of British disenchantment had made a ruined man of Alexander Arthur. Amid charges of poor business judgment, mismanagement, even outright dishonesty, he was dismissed as the Association's general manager early in 1891. Later an official board of inquiry found him innocent of all charges, but the dismissal stood. His personal fortune, estimated at a cool million at least, vanished overnight. It had, of course, been only a paper fortune anyway. His home at Harrogate was sold to pay his debts. Refusing to give up, pinning his hopes on the Knoxville, Cumberland Gap, and Louisville Railroad he had sired, he endeavored to found a new boomtown down the line in East Tennessee. With nothing to feed on, it speedily languished and died. He moved back to his old stamping ground in the Watauga country and opened a land office, but that failed too. In 1896 the gold rush lured him to Alaska's Klondike. He joined a British trading company there, and for a while, perhaps, revived the same old dream of carving a business empire out of a raw new land. *Perhaps*. In 1897 he was back in New York City, though, so down and out— some said—he had to borrow rent and eating money from old friends there.

Eventually he drifted back to Middlesboro, no longer a mover and shaker with the Midas touch but just a tired man getting along in years and seeking rest. The town had made a modest comeback, based on the coal that first had excited his ambition, and he lived quietly there with his memories till 1912.

It appeared the prophet was not without honor in his own country after all. Middlesboro gave him a very nice funeral, with honors befitting a founding father.

22

Up to Now

THE twentieth century arrived on the Cumberland with no great fanfare. That was deceptive, for shortly afterward it began to put an end to some things and to change some others irrevocably— even, here and there, for the better. Yet through it all the river serenely went her way as always. One gets that feeling about the Cumberland. She has not so much yielded to change as absorbed it, while still clinging to some mystic rapport with times past.

But as to this twentieth century . . .

Though the records are somewhat vague, the last steam packet on the upper Cumberland probably was the *Rowena*, a Burnside-built stern-wheeler sunk at the mouth of Greasy Creek in 1933 or 1934. She had been laid up for several years before that, however, and was being towed downstream when she sank. In fact, the very early 1920s had seen the practical end of steamboating on the Cumberland. By that time the gasoline-powered towboat had appeared: a squat and unlovely giant wholly lacking in charisma but immensely more muscular than any steamboat ever launched. It first took over the lower river, but soon was shoving its bargeloads of slow bulk freight farther and farther upstream, and in its wake came the still more muscular, more practical diesel towboat. These were not the interlopers that finally ran the packets out of business, however. They never did, anymore than the railroads did, though given time enough they might have. But by the 1920s, also, the automobile and the paved road had come along to revolutionize transportation in America. Between them they put almost any place within easy reach of almost anyplace else—and of anybody and his brother to boot. What this meant on the Cumberland, among other things, was that the merchant in his country store was no longer dependent on the nearby river landing for his stock in trade. A truck could deliver the goods to his very door, and presently was doing so, and in no time at all customers were rattling up to his door too, in their own Tin Lizzies. A very few years more and *tourists* were rattling past as well, even poking up beyond the old barriers of Smith's Shoals and the Falls of the Cumberland, and coming in the opposite direction too, by way of Cumberland Gap, to mark the beginning of the end of the upper river's isolation.

Allowing for the great American penchant for high-speed mechanized mayhem—not so readily discernible in the early days —the revolution was comparatively bloodless. Unfortunately, that was more than could be said of some developments up around the Cumberland's headwaters.

The American Association debacle on Yellow Creek had only delayed the inevitable, not stopped it. The bituminous coal at the root of all the boom and bust was still there; it was so bountifully distributed throughout the region, moreover, that not even a reviving Middlesboro could claim to be eastern Kentucky's coal capital. That honor fell to little Harlan, up at the three forks where the Cumberland began. Till 1911 the place was a drowsing backwoods mountain hamlet. Then the Louisville and Nashville Railroad went snaking up the river and transformed it into a hardworking mining town.

Quite unpredictably, one would think, independent mountaineers whose sires—and the sires' sires for generations back—had fought Indians, the British, and each other with equal truculence, discovered in themselves an affinity for coal mining. Men who had lived all their lives in the clean mountain air and sunshine, beholden to no one, cheerfully crouched hunchbacked through long shifts in mole-tunnels far underground. Unprotesting, they risked being mashed in cave-ins or blown to bits in black damp explosions, or dying more lingeringly of the ailment they called miner's asthma. One day a week they saw the sun; the other six a man descended to the coal face before daylight and stayed till after dark. Having sold their land for a few dollars an acre to absentee owners who wantonly despoiled it, they came down into town with their families to live in company houses and go in debt to company stores. And for coming to terms with this new life, a good man could earn as much as two dollars a day. *Could,* that is, but frequently did not, for the companies paid by the ton and most would dock a man if even a little slate turned up in the coal he dug. There was a rueful saying that claimed a mine mule got better treatment than a man. The company could always hire another man, but buying a new mule took money.

World War I, with its heavy demands for coal and labor, boosted wages for a time. Then the war's end sent them down to starvation levels again. Things grew worse, if anything. Goaded beyond endurance, men went on strike, and lost, and got their jobs back only if they signed the infamous "yellow-dog" contracts that bound them never to join a union. It took nearly two decades of strike after strike, each one fought as bloodily as any old-time mountain feud—embattled miners on one side, imported company detectives on the other—before the union finally won a grudging foothold. Meantime the suffering and heartbreak were aggravated by the grim Depression of the thirties. It was that same Depression, though, that gave the nation Franklin D. Roosevelt and his New Deal, forced a hard, searching look at some of the industrial shibboleths of the past—and, ultimately, set off an age of social change that has yet to run its course. In 1938 an epochal contract was signed between the Harlan County Coal Operators Association and the United Mine Workers. It brought a measure of peace and better times, if not prosperity, to the devastated coalfields.

That was the least of it, really, on the Cumberland. The depressed 1930s were years of mighty public works, among the mightiest of them the Tennessee Valley Authority by which the Cumberland's big sister was broken to harness and made to serve man on a vast new scale. Inevitably, once that sort of thing was proved workable, it was extended to the little sister too. Before the U.S. Corps of Engineers ceased its labors, no less than twelve dams, in being or projected, were conjured up for the mainstreams of the Cumberland and some of her major tributaries.

Which poses a somewhat prickly problem. As a lover of rivers in the unspoiled, natural state one disapproves of dams on principle: all dams, anywhere. Yet one is also a user of electric

power—often a shamefully wasteful user too, like everyone. One disapproves, again on principle, of floods that ruin people's homes and businesses. One concedes that men must have the jobs industry provides. . . . And if in the process of reconciling all these things the river ends up less free than it used to be, it may be pertinent to reflect that today's man, himself, has lost a good many of the freedoms a Daniel Boone once had, or a Kaspar Mansker had. Today, at least, we are fortunate enough to live in a time of growing awareness that man and his natural environment *must* be reconciled, or we lose everything.

So far it appears that has been accomplished on the Cumberland more readily than on many another of the nation's heartland rivers. One of her great blessings is that Nashville is her only large city, thus reducing not only the volume of commerce she is asked to bear but the sources of pollution. That is not to say the pollution is lacking. Even far back up tiny creeks that flow into others that eventually reach the upper Cumberland, the traveler finds that poisons leached from mining wastes have all too frequently left the water lethal to any plant- and wildlife it touches. Yet the mountain country, much of it still impassable even to the all-conquering automobile, has clung stubbornly to some of its old-time ways and mores. Men still plow tilted ridgeside fields with horse and bull-tongue plow. Here is one of the few regions anywhere on the continent where one finds folk still practicing such skills as weaving baskets out of white oak strips, or splitting oaken shakes and shingles with that ancient, obsolete instrument known as a froe. There are not many such folk left, true, and they are a dying breed. These days, in this depressed country on the fringe of Appalachia, the young people are prone to pull out for the city, the old ones to give up farming and subsist on food stamps.

On downstream, though, and the twelve dams to the contrary, this river still is remarkably unspoiled by the works of man. This despite some early doubters, as for example one Christian Schultz, a visitor to America in 1807. Floating down the Ohio River, Mr. Schultz stopped awhile "at the mouth of Cumberland, known by its more ancient name of Shawanese . . ." where he found "the small settlement called Smith Town, consisting of only five houses." Later, in a book titled *Travels on an Inland Voyage*, he was pretty gloomy about its prospects:

> . . . it appears to be a kind of inland port where run-away boys, idle young men, and unemployed boatmen assemble to engage as hands on board of any boats that may happen to call. An amusement has already been introduced at this place, which although excusable in large towns and cities, yet in a new country, and especially an infant settlement like this, cannot be too much condemned . . . you will scarcely believe, that in a place just emerging from the woods, which although advantageously situated, can prosper only by dint of industry and care. . . . You will scarcely believe, I say, that a billiard table has been established . . . surrounded by common boatmen, just arrived from the Salt Works, St. Louis, or St. Genevieve, who in one hour lost all the hard-earned wages of a two-months' voyage. . . .

Plainly, the Cumberland was able to survive the evils of the poolroom. A river that did that is hard to down; she should be around for a good long time yet, and in reasonable purity too.

Bibliography

Books

Abernethy, Thomas Perkins. *From Frontier to Plantation in Tennessee.* University, Alabama: 1967.

Allison, John. *Dropped Stitches in Tennessee History.* Nashville: 1897.

Alvord, Clarence M., and Bidgood, Lee. *The First Explorations of the Trans-Allegheny Region by the Virginians, 1650–1674.* Cleveland, Ohio: 1912.

Arnow, Harriette Simpson. *Seedtime on the Cumberland.* New York: 1960.

Bogart, William Henry. *Daniel Boone and the Hunters of Kentucky.* New York: 1856.

Bond, Octavia Zollicoffer. *Old Tales Retold.* Nashville: 1905.

Bruce, H. Addington. *Daniel Boone and the Wilderness Road.* New York: 1910.

Bryant, William Cullen, ed. *Picturesque America.* New York: 1872.

Clayton, W. W. *History of Davidson County.* Philadelphia: 1880.

Crabb, Alfred Leland. *Nashville, Personality of a City.* Indianapolis: 1966.

Cramer, Zadok. *The Pittsburgh Navigator and Almanac.* Pittsburgh: 1814.

Douglas, Byrd. *Steamboatin' on the Cumberland.* Nashville: 1961.

Dunbar, Seymour. *A History of Travel and Transportation in America.* Indianapolis: 1915.

Eisenschiml, Otto, and Newman, Ralph. *The American Iliad.* Indianapolis: 1947.

Federal Writers' Project. *Kentucky, A Guide to the Bluegrass State.* New York: 1937.

Fite, Emerson D., and Freeman, Archibald, eds. *A Book of Old Maps Delineating American History.* New York: 1969.

211

Foote Shelby. *The Civil War, A Narrative.* New York: 1958.

Gosnell, H. Allen. *Guns on the Western Waters.* Baton Rouge: 1949.

Green, Thomas Marshall. *The Spanish Conspiracy.* Cincinnati: 1891.

Guild, Jo C. *Old Times in Tennessee.* Nashville: 1878.

Hamilton, James. *The Battle of Fort Donelson.* New York: 1968.

Hanna, C. A. *The Wilderness Trail.* New York: 1911.

Haywood, Judge John. *The Civil and Political History of the State of Tennessee.* Nashville: 1891.

Heiskell, S. G. *Andrew Jackson and Early Tennessee History.* Nashville: 1920.

Horn, Stanley F. *The Army of Tennessee.* Indianapolis: 1941.

James, Marquis. *Andrew Jackson: The Border Captain.* New York: 1933.

Johnson, Col. J. Stoddard. *First Explorations of Kentucky.* Louisville: 1898.

Killebrew, J. B. *Resources of Tennessee.* Nashville: 1874.

Kincaid, Robert L. *The Wilderness Road.* Indianapolis: 1947.

Matthews, Judge Thomas. *General James Robertson, Father of Nashville.* Nashville: 1929.

Myer, William E. *Indian Trails of the Southeast,* 42nd Annual Report of the Bureau of American Ethnology. Washington, D.C.: 1928.

Parton, James. *Life of Andrew Jackson.* Boston: 1887.

Putnam, A. W. *History of Middle Tennessee.* Nashville: 1859.

Ramsey, J. G. M. *The Annals of Tennessee to the End of the Eighteenth Century.* Charleston, Tenn.: 1853.

Roosevelt, Theodore. *The Winning of the West.* New York: 1889.

Skinner, Constance Lindsay. *Pioneers of the Old Southwest.* New Haven: 1919.

Thwaites, R. G. *Daniel Boone.* New York: 1903.

Turner, F. M. *The Life of General John Sevier.* New York: 1910.

Whitaker, A. P. *The Spanish-American Frontier, 1783–1795.* Boston: 1927.

Williams, Samuel Cole. *Early Travels in the Tennessee Country.* Johnson City, Tenn.: 1928.

Winsor, Justin. *The Mississippi Basin; the Struggle in America Between England and France.* Cambridge, Mass.: 1895.

———. *The Westward Movement.* Cambridge, Mass.: 1897.

Wooldridge, J., ed. *The History of Nashville, Tennessee.* Nashville: 1890.

Pamphlets, Magazine Articles, Manuscripts

Allen, James Lane. "Through Cumberland Gap on Horseback." *Harper's New Monthly Magazine* LXXIII.

"Correspondence of General James Robertson." *American Historical Magazine* I–V.

Goodpasture, A. V. "The Watauga Association." *American Historical Magazine* III.

Henderson, Archibald. "Richard Henderson, the Authorship of the Cumberland Compact, and the Founding of Nashville." *Tennessee Historical Magazine* II.

———. "The Spanish Conspiracy in Tennessee." *Tennessee Historical Magazine* III.

Kilpatrick, Lewis H., ed. "The Journal of William Calk, Kentucky Pioneer."
Mississippi Valley Historical Review III.

Luckett, William W. "Cumberland Gap National Historical Park." *Tennessee
Historical Quarterly* XXIII.

McMurry, D. L. "The Indian Policy of the Federal Government and the
Economic Development of the Southwest." *Tennessee Historical Magazine* I.

Roberts, Charles B. "The Building of Middlesborough." *The Filson Club
History Quarterly*. Louisville: 1933.

Sioussat, St. George L. "Some Phases of Tennessee Politics in the Jackson
Period." *American Historical Review* XIV.

"Valuable Letters of Andrew Jackson." *American Historical Magazine* IV.

Williams, S. C. "Henderson and Company's Purchase Within the Limits of
Tennessee." *Tennessee Historical Magazine* VII.

Newspapers

The Daily Gazette. Nashville: 1850–.

The Impartial Review and Cumberland Repository. Nashville: 1806–8.

The Knoxville Gazette. Knoxville: 1803.

The Nashville Whig and Tennessee Advertiser. Nashville: 1819–.

The Republican Banner. Nashville: 1858–61.

Index